THE ORDINARY
IS EXTRAORDINARY

◆

How Children Under
Three Learn

◆

Amy Laura Dombro
Leah Wallach

Simon and Schuster

New York   London   Toronto   Sydney   Tokyo

Published by Simon and Schuster
A Division of Simon & Schuster Inc.
Simon & Schuster Building
Rockefeller Center
1230 Avenue of the Americas
New York, NY 10020

SIMON AND SCHUSTER and colophon are registered trademarks
of Simon & Schuster Inc.

Designed by Beth Tondreau Design
Manufactured in the United States of America

10 9 8 7 6 5 4 3 2 1

Library of Congress Cataloging-in-Publication Data
Dombro, Amy Laura, date.
The ordinary is extraordinary.
Includes index.
1. Learning, Psychology of.   2. Infant psychology.
3. Child psychology.   4. Parent and child—Case studies.
I. Wallach, Leah, date.   II. Title.
BF318.D64 1988   155.4'22   88-4602
ISBN 0-617-63174-8

To my parents,
Bob and Peg Dombro,
With love
ALD

In loving appreciation of Ira Wallach
and
in Loving Memory of Devera Sievers
LW

ACKNOWLEDGMENTS

Many people have helped make this book possible.

We'd like to thank all the children, parents, and caregivers who shared their everyday lives with us.

The thoughtful comments of colleagues who reviewed our manuscript were invaluable and greatly appreciated. We'd like to particularly thank Susan Abrahams; Nancy Balaban, Ed.D.; Cheryl Davis, M.D.; Laura Guarino; Judith Leipzig; Joan Lombardi, Ph.D.; and Sally Volkert.

To Gene Spieler and Meme Black, who brought us together with our agent Joe Spieler and with each other, we offer our gratitude.

And last, a special thanks to Ed Silverman, Amy's husband, for his encouragement, hours spent proofreading, and the best chocolate chip cookies we have ever tasted.

CONTENTS

———————◆———————

PART FIVE: OTHER ADULTS   235

THE WONDER OF THE ORDINARY   323

INDEX   329

Part One

---◆---

THE ASTONISHING COMMONPLACE

1

HOW CHILDREN LEARN

Living and Learning

When a child is born she doesn't know she has hands. It's an amazing thing to watch her discover them and learn their use. She begins by aimlessly moving her arms. Her eyes track their motion through the air. She comes to realize that these things which keep sailing by are part of her body. Though she can't move much of herself, she is figuring out where she begins and where she ends. With this fundamental discovery, she has started the process of defining herself, the ongoing task of her emotional life.

Eight to twelve weeks after she is born, the baby will have learned to control her hands well enough to bat and swipe at things. If there is a mobile hanging over her crib, she stares intently at it and tries to hit it. When she succeeds, it moves. She is thrilled: she has had an impact on the world. She keeps practicing, consolidating her new powers.

The baby's fingers, which have remained curled, are opening now, and a new part of her body is becoming available to her: she sucks on her fingers to soothe herself. She practices bringing both hands together over her tummy where they touch and explore each other.

She begins using her new skills to collect more information about the world. She starts reaching for objects and grasping them with both hands. She brings anything within reach to her mouth and examines it with her lips, gums, tongue. She distinguishes objects by texture and taste: the stuffed bear feels soft and gets wet as she sucks; the plastic rattle is hard and cool.

As she acquires more control, the baby begins purposely studying the effect of her actions on objects. One of her favorite experiments is to drop a spoon or cup from her high chair. This game, which seems simple to her parents, is complicated and absorbing for her. Each time she drops her cup on the floor, she is demonstrating her growing and satisfying power over her environment. She is learning that people will respond to her behavior in predictable ways: her mother usually picks the cup up. And the game helps her gather information about the physical world: What happens if you drop a cup of milk? An empty cup? What sound does a metal cup make? A plastic cup? A spoon? A piece of potato?

The child learns to use her hands by herself, practicing on her own while she lies in her playpen or crib, playing with her toys, handling utensils and objects that are part of her daily toilet, feeding, and housekeeping routines. Her parents encourage her manual adventures by making her world safe for her, by praising her, and by surrounding her with interesting things to touch. They help her by paying attention to her work—for example, by noticing when she is learning to extend her arm and offering her a soft cloth toy to reach for instead of placing it next to her.

But the baby is the one who does the work. Her parents can't show her how to focus her eyes. She doesn't need to be urged to practice batting and holding. She doesn't need instruction to learn the difference between herself, her environment, and other people. She was born with the impulse to learn these things in her own way and on her own schedule. She learns them simply by living every day. For infants and toddlers learning and living are the same thing. If they feel secure, treasured, loved, their own energy and curiosity will bring them new understanding and new skills.

Discovering the Ordinary

This book is about the tremendous education you give your child simply by loving her and living with her. Recent child-rearing literature often stresses the importance of "quality time"—time parents dedicate wholly to their children. Many of the books suggest games and exercises and props that parents can use to make "quality time" a structured learning period. Some promise that if they acquire the right "parenting skills," mothers and fathers can give their children a head start at developing intellectual and academic skills like counting and reading.

The hour you set aside just to teach your child is exciting and valuable for both of you, but it is only a small part of the time you spend with her, and it is not the most important part. Most of your time together is inevitably spent on personal and household routines: changing, dressing, and bathing her, cleaning the house, preparing dinner, paying the bills, doing the laundry, reading the paper.

These everyday activities are not just necessities that keep you from serious child rearing; they are the best opportunities for learning you can give your child and the most important time you can spend with her, because her chief task in her first three years is precisely to gain command of the day-to-day life you take for granted.

Ordinary time is "quality time" too.

Everyday activities aren't very interesting to us precisely because we do them every day, over and over. We walk to the bus stop, do the laundry, make coffee, for the most part without paying much attention, our minds elsewhere.

But to a small child, our chores are intriguing performances: fresh, complex, and absorbing. For children, the mundane is new, unclassified territory, and it's magical. They set about exploring every day by collecting, organizing, and reorganizing information about their bodies and their environment, about people and how people behave and communicate with one another.

To learn, they need practice. Routines give them the opportunity to observe the same sights, sounds, smells, and behaviors until they make sense of them; to make the same movements until they can coordinate confidently; to hear and use the same words until they can take possession of them.

Learning by Doing

Children learn to participate in everyday activities by stages. As they become more mature, the same, familiar activities reveal new meanings and offer new challenges. At first, children collect information primarily through their senses. A trip to the post office, for example, is predominantly a sensual experience for a six-month-old. The changes in temperature and light when her mother takes her inside, the sound of voices, the face of a stranger standing in line are what the experience means to her.

Older children learn about the physical world as they learn about their bodies through active play. For an eighteen-month-old interested in how objects and spaces fit together and in what grown-ups do, the post office is a playground. If the line is designated by cords strung between posts, she wants to move the posts or climb under and over the cords or make them swing. She can show her independence by carrying a letter and helping her mother drop it in a slot. The different tones of voice of the people she hears on the line intrigue her, but strangers are strange; she's disturbed if someone reaches out to pat her, and may retreat even from a friendly "Hi."

The two-and-a-half-year-old, fully mobile and determinedly self-reliant, understands the purpose of a trip to the post office. She is learning about the world through language and is interested in rules and regulations. She sees that here people stand in lines the way they do in the supermarket and at the bank. They give money to the person behind the counter. She sees the picture of a stamp and says "stamp." She is delighted when her mother lets her help her lick a stamp and press it on an envelope. She listens carefully when her mother tells her where the letter is going.

At each stage of a child's development, daily chores are a source of different kinds of learning. If you've been reading child-rearing books you may be familiar with categories of learning like sensory development, gross motor skills, fine motor skills, emotional or psychological development, cognitive development, social development, and language acquisition. Dividing learning into these different components makes the complex process of growing up more understandable. Though we won't use the same categories employed by developmental psychologists, we will also analyze children's experience to show the many different kinds of skills, ideas, and feelings involved in even the simplest household task.

Breaking down the learning process into elements shows what children learn, but it doesn't really describe how they learn. Children learn by doing things, and their activities integrate all different kinds of learning at once. When a child is asked if she wants "milk" or "juice," for example, she is not only learning words, she is learning about choices. When a child learns to dress herself, she is learning about how her body is put together, developing fine motor coordination, improving her ability to perceive and match shapes and developing a notion of planning (putting shoes on before socks doesn't work; putting socks on first does). The child is also learning social conventions (you can't go naked even when it's hot, there are occasions when you dress up), about the weather, and about the difference between indoors and outdoors. Whenever a child practices any new skill and perfects it, she is learning persistence, developing confidence, and confirming her sense of independence—that is, she is growing emotionally. Ordinary, everyday activities teach the whole child.

Learning with Your Child

The following chapters take a close and affectionate look at ordinary family life and discuss some of the ways you can make habitual chores more stimulating for your child and more satisfying for you. Growing up is your child's business; she's going to do the work. But you can help, and you don't have to be a perfect parent to do it.

If you're like most parents, you don't always have enough time to give your children all the attention they need, or enough patience to keep everything under control without snapping. You make mistakes. But that's part of everyday life, too. Even when you are tired, angry, discouraged, or confused, you are still teaching your child just by being with her.

By being a little more aware of how much you already help your child, you can help her even more. You can involve her in everyday tasks, and in the ways she finds most interesting and absorbing. You can help her feel proud of her accomplishments and unashamed of her failures. You can let her know that her efforts to explore the world are important to you. You can step back when it is best for her to work things out on her own, and guide her when guidance is what she needs.

The next chapter talks specifically about how you can sharpen your powers of observation to make daily life more enjoyable for both you and your child. It also discusses the importance of family members' making a special effort to show their respect for one another and explains why respect is just as important to children as love.

The remainder of the book follows three individual families as they engage in simple activities like setting the table, walking through the park, and getting dressed. It does not tell you how to turn these activities into educational exercises; some may not even be part of your routine. But reading about these families may make you more observant of your own. Understanding the ways their children experience the small events of ordinary life can help you to see the world through your own child's eyes and to appreciate the extraordinary opportunities to learn that you give her every day.

2

PARENTS AND CHILDREN LEARNING TOGETHER

A newborn baby doesn't seem to do much. She eats. She sleeps a large part of her days, busily: flexing, making fists, making noises, seeming to dream, though it's difficult to imagine what could fill her dreams. Awake, she sometimes stares at a face or listens to a sound with a curious intentness, but often she seems unfocused, disconnected from the world and the people around her. Newborns, even some love-struck parents find, are a bit boring. New parents sometimes feel as though the birth process isn't quite over, as though they're still waiting for the person they brought into the world to emerge.

In a way a parent's job is to wait. You help your baby by giving her love, encouragement, and security—and you watch while she does the work of becoming herself. It's her business, and at birth she's equipped to begin. Though your tiny baby can't even roll over without help, she's not passive: there's tremendous activity going on inside her. From the moment she's born, she's busy making sense of the world: looking for patterns in her sensations, finding them, putting them together, creating herself, the things and people around her, in her own mind. Her world doesn't happen to her. From the beginning it is *her* world, something she makes for herself, something she experiences aggressively. You can best support your child by paying attention to the small and amazing ways she's learning each minute and by helping her learn her way.

Watching Your Child Think and Feel

You can learn a great deal about how your child is experiencing the world by looking closely at what she does, because children think and feel physically, with their bodies.

When your baby grabs your thumb or pulls at your shirt, she's not just practicing reaching and holding. She's also learning to feel her own hand better, to distinguish the sensations of moving her fingers from the particular sensations she experiences touching different materials. She's thinking in her way about who she is. When she smiles and you smile back, and she works her face like a piece of rubber until she finds her own smile again, she's learning about communication. When she makes and breaks eye contact, she is exploring separation, appearance and disappearance. She continues to think about these things with her whole body later on, when she begins playing peek-a-boo.

When she begins to crawl, your baby uses her new mobility to learn about all the objects she can get her hands on. When she pulls a pail of toys off the shelf, dumps them out, and begins chewing on one, she is learning about relationships like up and down, inside and outside, rough and smooth. Learning to walk frees her hands to investigate objects in new ways. When she drags a stool to the bureau and tries to stand on it to reach something on top, she is thinking about space and size. When she turns on the faucet, flushes the toilet, switches the light switch, she is learning about cause and effect. Her mobility helps her think about herself too; now that she can move through the world on her own, she can get to know herself as someone who is separate and who is always herself wherever she goes. She also begins learning, with her body, about relationships between people. When she goes off exploring into the next room, she is learning about how it feels to be on her own, away from you. When she comes back looking for you, she's had all the independence she wants for the moment—she's feeling alone. Hide-and-seek becomes one of her favorite games.

By the end of the period we're writing about here, children are beginning to speak and to use ideas as adults do, to think and feel about things that aren't physically there. But even thought, speech, and imagination are linked to physical activities for children in the beginning. A child first uses words as a kind of gesture. When she looks at the sparrow on the fence and says "bird," she is using language to point and touch. Physical objects help her build her interior world. The picture of a dog she sees in a storybook at day care helps her imagine her dog at home.

Because your child does things you can see to explore, think, and feel, observing her can help you understand what she is trying to learn and how you can enhance her learning.

Parents naturally observe their child closely to figure out what she wants or needs. You'll probably learn rather quickly, for example, to read the different sounds of restlessness, hunger, pain, discomfort, and indignation in your infant's cries. When you are doing chores with your child around, a part of your mind will always be on alert, ready to sound an alarm when the baby is about to lean backward and fall off the couch or tries to take the cover off an electric outlet. You'll pay attention to your child too because you want to, because you love looking at her. She'll look at you for the same reason. When you watch your infant's face and try to imagine how life must feel to her, you are giving her the chance to look back at you. The human face —and your face above all—engages her intensely. At the same time as you learn to read her cries and respond to her gestures, she'll be learning to make the sounds and gestures that win a response from you. Watching you, responding to you, imitating you are things she needs to do to grow up. She'll observe you at the same time and for the same reason you observe her, because it's part of building a relationship.

Though observing is something you'll do naturally and can learn to do better, it's not something you can do all the time. Energy is a badly strained resource in the lives of parents of babies and toddlers. Paying attention to all the small emotional shifts and hundreds of little discoveries that fill up your child's day is impossible. If you're making breakfast while deciding how to deal with a problem at work and discussing weekend plans with your spouse and keeping an eye on your daughter to make sure she doesn't get into the garbage, you may understandably feel that paying attention to what she's learning by examining garbage is not a practical goal. When you've been with your child eight hours without a break, you may find yourself hoping she'll stop learning and just sit still for a while. After spending your workday giving your attention to your boss, your colleagues, your clients, and the task at hand, even if you're not in the mood to do any of those things, you need to be able to relax at home with your family and just feel what you are feeling. If what you're feeling is tired, irritable, or worried, you're not going to have the emotional energy to observe every nuance of your child's behavior.

You don't need to observe every nuance of your child's behavior all the time. Your main job as a parent is being with her, doing things with her, not observing her. You're not cheating her by being tired or grumpy or short-tempered or preoccupied or generally human either. Trying to mask your feelings at home the way you do at work would be a hopeless task and wouldn't make sense. Your child needs your genuineness. She is learning a great deal about feelings by living with an adult who is sometimes tired or grumpy or short-tempered and loves her anyway. But observing doesn't have to add to your work as a parent; it can make it easier. When you're in a rotten mood, pausing for a second to look at what your child is doing can help you figure out how to keep her reasonably amused and out of your way. If you're in a good mood, it can help you enjoy her more. Attentiveness needn't be a job you work at; it can simply be an attitude that becomes part of the way you and your child live together.

Your Very Individual Child

Observing your child will help you get to know her. You may welcome your baby with a name and a room filled with things you think she will like, but she comes into your life as a stranger. She'll be discovering herself as you get to know her, gradually and over time. She already has a unique personality to discover. From the moment they are born, babies are distinct individuals.

You can begin getting to know your child by watching to see how she responds to changes in the environment. Does she approach a new food or toy cautiously? Refuse it? Grab for it right away? If a light goes on or you pull out a bright blanket, does she stop what she's doing to look? Is her attention caught right away when you turn on a music box or a radio? When you take her someplace new or there's a change in your household routine, does she get excited or upset or seem not to notice? Does she seem bothered by commotion, or is she the kind of baby who would respond to a major earthquake without a blink? Is she even-tempered or moody? Some children seem to respond to everything with sharp intensity and to feel whatever they feel deeply, while other children take the world more lightly.

Children have characteristic ways of responding to people too. Some babies, even in their clingier periods, can be readily persuaded to introduce themselves to the world, while others are always reserved with people they don't know. Does your child crawl over to strangers to check them out—or stay close by your side and retreat behind your legs when an unknown adult or child approaches?

As your child grows, you'll gradually learn more about her learning style. Though all babies learn by doing, they learn in different ways. One child, for example, may learn to speak a word at a time, slowly building up a small vocabulary before she begins to make sentences. Another may never say a single word at all. She listens to you talk, chats with herself, and then one day comes out with a complete—if short—sentence.

One of the most difficult things to learn about your child is how she expresses anxiety. Some children let their parents know they're troubled in unmistakable ways: they fight, hit, and cry a lot more than usual. But small children, like adults, can express anxiety more subtly. Sometimes children are quiet when they're unsure of a situation or of themselves, as if they were trying to hide until they feel safer. Sometimes anxiety shows itself indirectly: a child who seems chirpy and cheerful has trouble sleeping or can't shake off a cold. As you get to know your child, you'll learn what she's like when she's happy and become more sensitive to small signs that she isn't feeling as good about life as you would like.

Getting to know your child will help you make her life pleasanter. If you realize your child is anxious, for example, you could make sure to give her some extra cuddling. If you find your child gets upset when she's surrounded by loud noises or when strange people come up to her, you might decide not to take her with you to your annual office picnic even though you are eager to show her off. If you do take her to a party, you could ask the people there to say hello one at a time. If your child makes no visible efforts to creep, then suddenly crawls straight forward at a fast clip, you'll be less likely to worry, or pressure her, if she doesn't seem to be practicing walking.

Your Child's Individual Development

Your child's interests and needs, of course, have to do with her age as well as her personality. As we hope this book will illustrate, at different stages of her life your child will learn different things about herself, about the world around her, and about being with you, from the same activities.

The best way to figure out what your child knows about the world and what she's trying to learn at each period in her life is to watch her. Reading books, including this one, is no substitute for observing your child. The books may say that nine-month-olds crawl, say their first words, and are afraid of strangers. But the books are talking about abstract and average children. Your exuberantly concrete and special nine-month-old hasn't read them. She may be walking already, not saying a word and smiling gleefully at every stranger she sees. She's following her own timetable, and her timetable is the important one. You can support her best by helping her learn what she's trying to learn, not what the books say a typical child ought to be learning.

What the books can do is to give you a good sense of the whole process of development during a child's first years. Children learn different things at different times in different ways, but they all manage to cover the same ground within a few months of each other. If your child doesn't seem to be learning the way she should, even if you can't pinpoint exactly what seems wrong, discuss your concerns with your pediatrician. He or she will probably reassure you. Most of the time when a child is a little behind in a certain area of development, there's nothing wrong: she'll catch up when she's ready. Sometimes, of course, there is something wrong. If your doctor says not to worry, but you continue to feel concerned about your child, trust your feeling and pursue it. Consult another doctor until the problem is diagnosed or you are truly confident there really is nothing to worry about. Experts may know more about child development and children in general than you do, but you know your particular child better than anyone else in the world.

Deciding What to Do

Getting to know your child and becoming attuned to the ways she's growing and learning are ongoing processes. But observing can also help you understand what your child is doing from moment to moment. It can help you decide how to respond to the multitude of minor parental dilemmas you confront every day.

One tricky problem for many parents is deciding when and how actively to intervene in their children's play. Suppose, for example, your child is struggling to free the string of a pull toy stuck under the chair. Should you untangle it for her or let her solve the problem herself, even if she seems to be going about it in an excruciatingly inefficient way? Children don't solve problems abstractly, they learn by trial and error. They need the opportunity to experiment and play with things in different ways to figure out how the world works. When you stand aside and give your child the time and space she needs to learn her own way, you aren't ignoring her. You're supporting her in a different way than if you joined in. You're also showing her your respect for her play. On the other hand, your child simply can't do many of the things she wants and needs to do without help. Sometimes she will just get upset when she can't complete a task.

A quick look may be enough to tell you what to do. If your child seems absorbed in untangling the string, for example, you might decide to continue reading your newspaper. If she begins to whimper and clench her teeth the way she does when she gets frustrated, the problem might be too much for her to handle and it might make sense to put down the paper and help. But what if your child is trying to climb up the couch and each attempt ends in a fall? If she keeps picking herself up to try again, the bumps evidently aren't bothering her: she wants to practice couch climbing. Should you stop her anyway? How dangerous is dangerous? What if your child is obviously frustrated because she can't open a box of crackers, but becomes furious when you try to help her?

Deciding what to do when something upsets their child can also be a problem for parents. When she is a baby, you'll probably ask yourself hundreds of questions to figure out what your crying child needs: Does she need a bottle, a fresh diaper, some company? Can you let her cry for a few minutes while you finish putting the fast-melting frozen foods away, or is it important that you go to her right away? Sometimes it's fairly obvious what your baby wants. If she hasn't eaten for a couple of hours, she's probably hungry. If her cries are the whiny, restless kind, it's likely she's bored or lonely. In either case you can unpack the ice cream and frozen juice while assuring her verbally you'll be there soon. But when your child gets a little older, it won't always be clear that going to her is the best thing to do. Suppose your child's toy breaks and she starts to cry. Does she need you to comfort her or does she just want to cry? She might feel suffocated if you coo, stroke her, and offer her a new toy when all she wants to do is feel bad for a while—but then again, she might want you to take her in your arms and make her feel better.

Observing your child's behavior doesn't guarantee you'll always respond to her in the best ways. One day you may nervously go over and guide your child up the slide ladder just as she is mastering it herself. Another afternoon, you may let her try to open the drawer herself until she gets so discouraged she starts kicking the cabinet. There will be times when you won't be able to figure out anything you can do to get your baby to stop crying. You'll just have to wait until she stops on her own. But observing can help you do the best you can.

Respecting Your Child

The more you observe how quickly your child learns, how hard and creatively she works at growing up, the more you will respect her. And by observing her, by trying to understand what she is experiencing, you are showing her respect.

Respect is something you can always give your child—even if there are times when you're not sure you like her. Adults, especially women, are supposed to like children, all children, and their own most of all. No doubt most adults do, in principle; in practice they may find it more difficult. Because children are individuals, some of them are pleasanter to live with and easier to like than others. Parents too are individuals with their own personalities, habits, likes and dislikes. They may feel more rapport with one child than another.

If you find your child difficult, you're entitled to feel that way. Maybe she is difficult. If she isn't now, chances are that sometime or other she will be. (Perfect children are as rare as perfect parents.) Observing her won't necessarily make it easier for you two to get along, though it will probably help. It will surely help you appreciate her individuality.

Your appreciation and respect for her individuality are the most important things you can offer your child. Though she'll be pleased if you create a stimulating environment or play learning games with her, she doesn't really need those things. She will find stimulation for her eyes and hands and mind just in living with you. She can learn a great deal by herself. But without your active help, she'll have a difficult time developing confidence in herself, a sense of her own dignity, a feeling that being alive, on the whole, is a fine thing. Faith in herself and in the world are what fuel her natural drive to grow up. Your respect for her, for both her strengths and limitations, is what gives her that faith. She will learn naturally, but she will learn best within a relationship where she is honored.

Respecting your child isn't something you have to try to do. You're already doing it when you pay attention to her and do your best to take care of her. Respect is worth thinking about, however, because it's so very important to children.

Even babies can suffer from wounded dignity. You can show your baby that you regard her as a person, not a toy or problem, by talking with her when you carry her or feed her or change her. She may not understand the words, but she'll know you are addressing her. When she's old enough to respond to her name, it's time to stop talking about her in her presence. Sensing that she's being discussed without knowing what's going on might worry her.

Anyone who has lived with a toddler realizes that toddlers feel something like pride and satisfaction about their accomplishments and that their feelings can be hurt. Toddlers are impressed by their own skills. They like to follow their favorite adults around and in their own, often counterproductive ways, help the adults do whatever they are doing. You can show your respect for your toddler's growing competence by figuring out ways she really can help you: you might ask her to wipe up a spill, for example, or to carry your bag to the car. Shooing a toddler away too often can make her feel you don't value all the things she's learned.

Twos, like toddlers, are sensitive to exclusion. It's respectful to acknowledge their feelings when you can. If you and your husband get into a serious discussion at the dinner table, for example, you might want to explain to your two-year-old that you need to talk about work or her grandmother or the plumbing or whatever it is. She may still fret, but telling her that you're having an adult conversation now at least lets her know you haven't forgotten her existence. When your two starts showing off in front of company, it's a sign that she's becoming more self-conscious and more responsive to social situations. You might want to avoid embarrassing her by not reprimanding her in public.

Twos often like to feel in charge of themselves (and maybe everyone else). Other times they like to be babied, but they don't like being treated like babies when they're feeling grown up. You can show respect for your two-year-old by organizing her world so she can manage it successfully herself. If it's a rainy day, for example, and you ask your antsy child whether she'd like to draw or read a story or make a tent or play with clay, she may feel confused. She can't think about four different things at the same time. If you ask her if she'd like to draw or make a tent, she can have the satisfaction of making a decision. By limiting her world a little for her, you're giving her freedom of choice.

You have to set other kinds of limits to your child's behavior, of course: you have to discipline her. When you set up rules, you probably won't be thinking about respecting your child or helping her learn. You'll just be concerned with making sure she doesn't hurt herself or someone else or make life intolerable for everyone around her. You can show respect for your child, however, by controlling her behavior in a way that's appropriate for her age.

It's not appropriate to punish children under three, because they really can't evaluate or control their own actions very well. You can stop them from doing whatever they shouldn't be doing and suggest something they can do instead. You should tell them why, so they understand there is a reason. But most of the time they won't understand what the reason is. For example, you can stop your twelve-month-old when she pulls the dog's ears. You can tell her pulling its ears hurts the dog. (The dog may try to get this idea across too.) You can show her how to pat the dog the way he likes it. Stop her enough times, and your daughter will realize you don't like dog ear pulling. She'll stop—and might begin patting instead—because she wants to please you. But she won't understand that the dog can be hurt. She won't realize that if you shouldn't pull the dog's ears, you shouldn't pull its tail either. Punishing her for bothering the dog isn't fair, because she really doesn't know what she's doing.

To be able to follow rules, to discipline herself, a child has to understand not only the rule, but the ideas behind it. She has to be able to recognize similar but not identical situations where the same rule applies. She has to have enough self-control to stop herself from acting on impulses (a separate problem from knowing she shouldn't do something). Children are just beginning to acquire the understanding and control they need to set limits for themselves at the end of the three-year period we're considering here.

Even though they're still too young to take responsibility for their behavior, rules and limits make some kind of sense to older toddlers and twos. Unlike babies, they know they can hurt themselves. They realize they can't do all the things adults do. When they feel certain you won't let them do anything dangerous, they feel safer.

Twos, who can feel overwhelmed by the intensity of their impulses and feelings—including the impulse to rebel—are often relieved when their parents assert their authority. Your two may refuse to put on her hat, for example. Ten minutes later, when you try again, she may find herself shouting no even though her ears are turning blue and beginning to hurt. She'll be grateful to have the struggle ended for her and her ears properly covered. If she trusts you to keep her from going too far, your child will feel more confident about asserting herself.

Your child will only be able to trust you if you're reasonably consistent about limit setting. Being consistent is a way of showing respect for your child's ability to learn. Children are able to learn about the world, including the social world, precisely because it is fairly consistent. If you tell your child to stop every time she throws toys, she will realize that the consequence of toy throwing is your displeasure. But if one night you laugh when your child flings her toys around the living room and the next night you lose your temper and yell at her, she'll be confused and unsure of herself. She won't be able to predict the consequences of her own actions.

You can't and needn't be perfectly consistent, of course. You're going to have days when you're in a bad mood and can't tolerate behavior you'd normally allow, and days when you're feeling especially tolerant. It's helpful to your child simply to let her know the exceptions are exceptions. Tell her you'll let her stay up a little later tonight because it's been a "special day." Or tell her, "I don't want you to paint today. I'm too tired to clean up the mess." She probably won't understand everything you're saying, but she will realize there is a reason why things are different this time. You'll be showing her that rules aren't arbitrary but that a little inconsistency is one of the predictable things about the world.

Respecting your child means doing your best to see her for who she is, not for who you would like her to be or who you are afraid she will become. That can take a bit of work. People's values, hopes, and fears naturally affect what they observe about their children and how they interpret what they see. A father who is worried that his daughter will be self-effacing, for example, will probably notice right away when she behaves aggressively or timidly, but he may not be particularly attentive to her response to music. A father who loves music and wants his child to share its pleasures may be attuned to signs of musical talent but less observant of his child's social development. Many parents are particularly anxious to avoid repeating what they perceive as their own parents' mistakes. Our children remind us of ourselves: we try with them to right the wrongs all of us felt we suffered long ago. A woman who believes she was overprotected as a child, for example, and senses an overly protective streak in herself, may make a point of encouraging her toddler to take risks. A woman who felt she was neglected may try to respond to every shift in her child's moods. A man who was frightened by violent family arguments when he was young may discourage his child from showing anger, while someone who came from a family where expressions of anger were forbidden may want his child to feel free to throw show-stopping tantrums.

You can't discard your values and your history. You shouldn't try. Your values and your history are part of what you have to offer your child—but it's best, of course, to offer them as gifts, not to impose them as demands. Observing yourself, trying to get to know your particular hopes and fears for your child, will help you see her better for the unique and separate person she is.

Your Child and Your Family

Your child will be very observant of your moods because you are so important to her well-being. But she won't understand them. She won't realize that you have a life apart from her, feelings and needs of your own. Small children are completely self-centered. They want you to be there for them in whatever way they need you, whenever they need you. And babies need their parents all the time.

Because your child is so totally dependent, you and your family will have to reorganize your lives to accommodate the huge task of taking care of her. But your child, from the moment she's born, is part of a family. For her own welfare, her needs have to be balanced with the needs of other members of the family and the needs of the family as a whole. Some of those needs are practical. You have to earn your living on the days when the baby wants you with her. You have to clean the house even if your child thinks it's a good time to finger paint. Some of your needs have nothing to do with practical matters; they're just part of being human. Observing your child, yourself, and your family can help you decide how to balance your life together to make it satisfying for everyone.

Your baby isn't going to make an effort to amuse herself because you want some time to rest, or your older child is sick and needs extra attention for herself, or your spouse is worried about a problem at work. She can't be considerate yet, which means most of the time you should try to adjust your behavior to make yourself available to her. But you can't do that all the time. Becoming a parent probably isn't going to turn you into a saint. And there may be times when your child evokes such strong feelings in you that you really do have trouble responding to her sensibly. If your child is crying in a whiny, low-key way, for example, you might normally finish up what you're doing before you go to her. But if you've been feeling painfully sorry for yourself that day, something about her cries might revive the fearful child in you and you'll find yourself rushing over to her in a frenzy of smothering solicitude. On the other hand, if you've had a bad day, that whiny cry might suddenly make you feel so put upon that you want to start screaming and kicking too. When you're in an irritable mood, even though you know better, your child's demanding behavior can seem like a deliberate, intolerable attack.

Observing yourself, just recognizing how your mood is affecting your response to your child, will sometimes be enough to give you back your perspective. A sense of humor helps too. If you really feel you just can't deal with her, try to find some way out of the situation. If your spouse can't take over, see if you can park your child at a relative's or friend's. Or take her out for a late-night walk till you both get sleepy. Remind yourself that you only have to get through a bad couple of hours. Remind yourself too that in just a few weeks your child will be over one set of annoying habits and on to the next, and in just a few years this period of total dependency on you will have passed: she won't be a baby anymore, she'll be a young girl.

Those few years of your child's baby- and toddlerhood should, of course, be a time in your own life to enjoy, not just struggle through. Inevitably, there will be times when you feel overburdened—but if you find yourself feeling overburdened all the time, you might try to figure out what you need to preserve some peace of mind and then try to organize your household to see that you get those things. For example, you may have decided that you don't want your child to watch television. You prefer her to learn by playing in more active ways. But if there's no one else in your family you can ask to watch her, and you really need a half hour of quiet at the end of the workday to avoid a psychotic breakdown, and TV is the only thing that keeps your child quiet, it's probably best to do what you didn't want to do and use it as a pacifier for a short period of time. A half hour of television is not going to hurt your child as much as a berserk parent. The point is, you're not being a selfish parent when you consider your needs along with your child's. Your child's happiness is bound up with yours.

Observing yourself and your baby to balance your needs is more than enough emotional work for anyone, which is one of the reasons why young children are not good for marriage. A couple's sex life frequently goes into suspended animation for a while after a child is born because of exhaustion, lack of privacy, lack of time, and the normal hormonal changes associated with childbirth and nursing. Sometimes parents even stop talking when their child is small. Children are good at interrupting attempts at adult conversation. Often the only time parents have alone together is late at night, after the child is asleep, when they're both tired and still have a few chores left to do. If you're on a tight budget, you may find months have gone by without you and your spouse taking a single evening off to go out for dinner and talk. And you probably need to talk: the responsibility of having a child is putting new pressures on your relationship. The divorce rate among parents of children under three is distressingly high.

There's not a lot you can do about this. But if you can muster the energy, it's a good idea to pay some attention to your marriage. If you feel real strains developing, make an effort to find some way you and your spouse can be alone once in a while. You need to remember from time to time that you're friends and lovers as well as colleagues in child care. If you're raising your child by yourself, it's important to try to find some way to date or see friends on your own now and then so you don't feel your relationship with your baby is the only relationship in your life.

Your baby might appreciate your total and exclusive devotion now. It may be hard to bring yourself to leave her with someone else even for an occasional evening or weekend afternoon when nights and weekends are the only time you have with her. It's hard to find good affordable baby-sitters. But your child's life as a whole will be richer if your adult life is a reasonably full one.

Learning with Your Child

As we've implied, taking care of a small child is hard work. It can be very tedious work. There's an immense satisfaction in guiding a new person toward adulthood, but you will not always feel that satisfaction deeply when you're changing diapers, racing to prevent a fall, or trying to manage a stroller and two bags of groceries at the same time. Happily, children give back some of the energy they take away. They share with us their freshness of vision. Your child can help you rediscover the shimmer of a raindrop on a screen, the delectable squooshing sounds of a boot stomping mud, the clever design of a screw-top jar. She will give you opportunities to reexamine your values from a different perspective. She confronts in the most primitive forms problems that adults too must struggle to resolve. (What should she do when another child hits her? Hit back? Ignore it? Call you or the caregiver? It's not an easy question.) Your child can help you feel more vividly too. Watching her grow will make you more aware of your own need for love and love of independence, of your fears of helplessness and abandonment, of the delights of discovery and communication. Observing your child won't guarantee you'll always do the best thing for her, but it will make life richer for both of you. It will also help you collect information and make conscious choices about what you do and why. It will give you the sense of purpose and order that most adults need and that can be sorely lacking in life with a young child.

The scenes that follow will illustrate most of the ideas we've suggested in this first section. We hope to show that observing how your child perceives and explores all the routines of daily life is something you are already doing naturally—and can perhaps learn to do a little more skillfully.

3

THREE CHILDREN, THREE FAMILIES

The remainder of this book will present scenes from the everyday life of three fictional children and their families. The three families aren't meant to be typical or representative. We observed many children while doing our research, and if there are typical children, we never saw any. There's nothing especially unusual about our families, however, except that all the parents have strong marriages and they have all found very fine day care.

Our first family lives in a large apartment in a big city. Jennifer is six months old. She's a sensitive baby, very responsive to sounds, color, and light. She's clever with her hands, but only now beginning to figure out how to move her whole body.

Jennifer is Carol's first child. Carol, thirty-eight, is a lawyer. Her husband, Sam, fifty, is an insurance company executive. He has two grown children from a previous marriage—a daughter who lives in another part of the country and a twenty-year-old son who is attending college in a neighboring state.

Sam left the care of his first two children to his former wife. He wants to be more closely involved in raising Jennifer, but it is Carol who has cut back her work hours from a lawyer's normal overtime to an ordinary forty-hour week—effectively ending any possibility of career advancement for the time being.

During the day, Jennifer is cared for by Mrs. Semple, an experienced nanny and housekeeper in her fifties.

The second family lives in an attached house in an outlying neighborhood of a medium-sized city. Alex, fifteen months, is a good-natured, easygoing boy and a determined explorer. Alex's five-year-old brother, Mike, is in kindergarten. Alex's father, Robert, thirty, owns a small air-conditioner repair shop. His mother, Rita, twenty-seven, works mornings as a word processor.

In the morning when Rita is at work and Michael is in kindergarten, Alex stays with his neighbor, Mrs. Weiss.

The third family lives in a small town that is the county seat of the surrounding rural area. Katie is a bright, strong-willed girl of twenty-eight months. Her parents, Sarah and Joe, really do share the work of raising her. Joe, thirty-five, is a former high school teacher who now works for the regional department of education. Sarah, thirty, is a social worker. Sarah has just found out she is seven weeks pregnant with their second child. She and Joe haven't told Katie or anyone else yet. Sarah has a bad back.

Katie spends weekdays at a day-care center run by a local university. Karen, Paul, and Linda, all in their early twenties, are the caregivers there.

We'll be showing these three families engaging in ordinary activities like shopping, preparing dinner, and getting ready in the morning. Each scene will be followed by a section called "Observations," where we'll look at what the children did in the scene and what they were learning. We've tried to limit our comments to behavior the reader can observe too, though we've made free use of our ideas about development in interpreting Jennifer's, Alex's, and Katie's actions.

We've used four categories to analyze what the children are learning: The World of Things, The World of People, Ideas and Words, and Sense of Self. This division is somewhat artificial. Children learn about ideas and words by playing with things. They learn about things and people through ideas and words. They learn about themselves through all their activities. But dividing the children's experience this way makes it easier to see what they are learning at different ages and how their interests change as they grow.

The three children's growing understanding of their physical environment and their acquisition of physical skills are discussed together under "The World of Things." The two topics fit together because a child learns to control her body by physically exploring the world, and she learns about space, objects, and materials by moving, touching, and manipulating.

"The World of People" considers all the things the children are learning about sharing daily life with others. That's a great deal. In her first three years a child learns to distinguish herself from others, parents from strangers, males from females; she forms her first attachments and experiences her first separations; she realizes that there are rules governing what people are and are not allowed to do; she begins to experiment with different strategies for getting others to do what she wants.

"Ideas and Words" examines the children's astonishing efforts to visualize, organize, and talk about their experience. A six-week-old lives very much in the immediate, but she is already thinking when she looks, listens, and moves. By three, she will have entered the world of language and concepts, metaphors and make-believe.

"Sense of Self" looks at how the children are developing their sense of identity, competence, and dignity. A child acquires a sense of herself as she learns to govern her body, her behavior, her feelings, as she begins to communicate with others and to influence the things and people around her.

Part Two

---◆---

PERSONAL CARE

4

GETTING DRESSED

Small children can go through more changes of clothes in a day than their parents do in three. They are dressed and undressed in the morning, before nap, after nap, after spitting up, after an apple juice spill, before bath, after bath, before bed, in the middle of the night when urine soaks through diapers. Taking a child outside means adding shoes, a bonnet, a sweater, the dreaded snowsuit in wintertime. Coming home means taking pants and sweaters and jackets off. Apartment-dwelling parents build up their triceps carrying baskets of clothes back and forth to the laundry room. Washing-machine owners get used to life with a low background rumble.

Many of the times a parent dresses his child, both of them are in a hurry to get the chore done and neither is in the mood to pay much attention to what is going on. But once or twice or a few times in the course of the day, dressing a child can become a small opportunity for play and closeness, a few seconds to touch each other's faces, to touch a toe or tickle a tummy, to examine and discuss the pattern of green, yellow, and red boats on a tee shirt or enjoy the pert sound of a snap.

Though dressing is something adults in large part do for children, even very small babies involve themselves mentally and physically in the process in active and important ways.

During their first six months, infants set to work on three important tasks: figuring out where their bodies begin and end, perceiving some kind of orderliness and predictability in the world, and enjoying being alive. Getting dressed gives them hundreds of occasions for all these kinds of learning.

Having their arms, legs, toes, and tummies touched by an adult's hands and by articles of clothing, feeling the differences in sensation when skin is covered and when it's bare, listening to their parents saying the names of different body parts as they pull on shirts and slip feet through pants holes, all help babies identify the boundaries of their bodies. Because they are dressed several times a day every day from the moment they are born, and because their parents tell them what they are doing and about to do when they change them, dressing also helps babies learn to anticipate. By four or five months, your baby will begin closing her eyes and squinching up her face when you pull a shirt over her head, preparing herself for the feel of cloth on her cheeks and nose. These early experiences of expectation are her first steps toward an understanding of time and order.

Though babies don't speak and can't understand what specific words mean, they are acutely sensitive to the tone and expression of their parents' voices, the temperature of their skin, the quality of their touch, the tension in their muscles. You are saying "I want you to be comfortable" when you smooth out a sleeve along your baby's arm. When you tell your child, to avoid startling her, that you are going to take off her shirt, you are showing tenderness and respect for her feelings. When you hold her securely and confidently while you pull her pants on, you are telling her "You can trust me." These demonstrations of your love and reliability help your baby establish the safe base she needs before she can feel confident about reaching out into an unfamiliar world.

For a child just beginning to walk, getting dressed is equivalent to being restrained. At twelve to sixteen months, she's rejoicing in the new-found sense of independence that comes from being able to move herself. When you change her shirt or pants, you not only stop her from climbing on the couch, banging on pots in the kitchen, or crawling under the bed, you actually move *her* arms through a sleeve or *her* legs into overalls. It's understandable, then, if your toddler gears up for battle when you tell her, "Let's change that wet shirt." She has an important cause—her selfhood—to defend. Even though the ensuing struggle can be a considerable inconvenience to you, it's valuable and important for her. Learning that she can struggle against you is something she needs to do at this time (and one way or another for a wearyingly long time to come) to consolidate her sense that she is her own person.

Fortunately your toddler won't want to fight every time you want to dress her. Sometimes she will want to help. Getting dressed gives toddlers the chance to use a wide variety of new physical and mental skills. They are interested in learning to use their hands better; pulling off socks, opening and closing Velcro fasteners on sneakers, and putting dirty clothes in the hamper give them nice opportunities to practice manipulation. They are beginning to learn words, and they like hearing the names of different parts of their bodies. And when you ask your toddler if she wants to wear the green shirt or the shirt with the blue stripes, you're giving her the chance to practice a new mental skill, making decisions.

Many two-year-olds find the opportunity to make choices one of the most appealing aspects of dressing. If you have a two-year-old, however, you should be thoughtful about when you give her choices and what kind of decisions you let her make. Avoid questions like "Do you want to get dressed now?" unless you are prepared to take no for an answer. Given a choice of yes or no, chances are she will go for the no. For two-year-olds, as for toddlers, saying no is an irresistible way of declaring independence.

It's also wise to avoid offering a two-year-old wide-open choices like "What do you want to wear today?" They can leave her feeling overwhelmed. (Even after thirty years of making decisions, adults facing their closets often feel overwhelmed by the same question.) To help your child practice decision making and to keep the dressing procedure running smoothly, try providing her with two clear-cut alternatives. For example, ask her, "Do you want to wear your blue pants or your red pants?" or, "Would you like to get dressed in your room or in the bathroom?"

If it's important to you that your child always wear matching clothes, it's probably not a good idea to let her choose her outfits at all. It's not fair to ask her if she wants the red shirt or the polka-dot one and then to try to persuade her to change her mind when she says polka-dot. She'll either feel that you don't value her decision or that you are being insincere when you offer her a choice. Instead, preselect matching tops and bottoms before you offer her a choice, or pick out her clothes yourself and give her opportunities to practice decision making in some other area, where you can genuinely respect her choices. There are many other aspects of getting dressed that you and your two-year-old can enjoy together.

Clothes, in and of themselves, are interesting to two-year-olds. Great observers of details, they are quick to notice pockets, belt loops, collars, buttons, buckles, and snaps. They want to figure out what each of these devices is for and how they work. They are learning colors and enjoy observing and identifying the colors in their clothes. Some two-year-olds like simple dress-up games and will parade around proudly in a big hat or a string of beads. They feel grown up when they wear grown-up clothes.

Two-year-olds want to use their new abilities and knowledge to help dress themselves, and they can help to some degree. Many of them can take off pants and socks, and some can wiggle part way into their clothes. Sometimes they will insist on doing more all by themselves, crying in frustration when they can't get their shoes or dress on but still refusing help. Other times they appreciate help and will follow simple directions.

Jennifer, as you will see, has learned to pay attention to dressing in a way she couldn't just a few weeks before. Alex sometimes helps Rita get him dressed, but today in the doctor's office he is letting her do most of the work. Katie likes dressing as a kind of game; making fashion decisions is part of the play.

JENNIFER
(Six Months)

Jen, in Carol's arms, is sucking on a bottle, drooling a little milk. After a while she opens heavy-lidded eyes, looks up at her mother, and squirms. Carol repositions the bottle, but Jen pushes it away and whines. A bubble of milk forms in the corner of her mouth.

"Had enough breakfast?" Carol puts the bottle down on the kitchen table and stands up. She wipes Jen's chin with a napkin. "Okay, it's time to get dressed."

Carol carries a wiggly Jen into Jen's room. "I'm going to put you down now." Carol lays her on the changing table. Jen grabs a piece of Carol's hair and hangs on, twisting her body and making a fussy sound.

"Let go, darling." Carol unwinds the small fingers. "You're soaking wet. I bet you were getting cold." Jen touches between her legs as the wet diaper is peeled away. Carol reaches for a wipe. Jen squeals, startled by the touch of the cool, wet material. "Shhh, there." Carol rubs cream on Jen's thighs. She slips the new diaper under Jen. "Now," she pats the second tape closed and brings her face a little closer to Jen's, "what do you want to wear today?"

Jen crinkles her nose and smiles. One hand on Jen's tummy, Carol reaches into the dresser. Jen stretches and twists her body to watch her mother. As she does, she catches sight of the bell mobile above the changing table. She arches back and reaches up to hit one of the bells. The mobile tinkles and turns. Jen gurgles.

"What about the stretch pants and shirt Grandma sent you from Hawaii?" Carol takes a package wrapped in tissue paper from the shelf. The red wrapping ribbon is still on top.

"Look, Jen." Carol holds up the ribbon. "It's a pretty red ribbon." Carol ties the ribbon to one of the mobile bells. Jen grabs for it at once with both hands.

"Careful, you'll pull the mobile down." Jen looks at her mother. The ribbon slips out of her hand. The mobile starts spinning and clanking. The red ribbon swings like a horse's tail. Jen laughs.

Carol unwraps the outfit and looks at the little Hawaiian shirt. "Very fifties, Jen." She tries to slip Jen's arm into the sleeve. Jen is trying to get the red ribbon as it passes by.

"Hey," Carol says, touching Jen's stomach. Jen whines, still tracking the ribbon. "We've got to cover this belly," Carol says. She kisses Jen's belly button. Jen grabs her hair.

Carol undoes her fingers. "Let's get this little arm through." Jen stops moving as she feels her hand going into the shirt. "Now the other arm." Jen looks at the arm Carol is touching and blinks. "Now we're getting somewhere." Jen stares at her wide-eyed and gurgles. Carol buttons the shirt, wipes a bit of spittle from Jen's cheek and then brushes the cheek with her finger. "This is your soft cheek, Jen." The soft cheek expands as Jen smiles.

"Ready for the foxy stretch pants? First your right leg." Carol lifts Jen's right leg and puts it through the pants. The leg kicks. "Now your left." Carol touches the left foot. Jen kicks it too. "That's right." Jen arches as Carol starts to pull the pants up, but before Carol gets them up to her waist Jen starts twisting and fussing again. "Okay, okay, we're almost through."

Carol flicks a bit of dried baby oatmeal off the sleeve of her robe. She looks at her watch. She still has five minutes before she has to get dressed. She puts her hand in front of Jen's face and wiggles the fingers. "Jen." Jen stops wriggling and looks. Carol slips one arm under Jen and raises her to a sitting position so Jen can see. Then she wiggles her fingers again and slowly brings her hand toward Jen's feet, a guess-what-is-going-to-happen-next expression on her face. Jen opens her eyes wide. Carol's fingers get closer. Jen shrieks with anticipation and wiggles her toes. "This little piggy went to market," Carol says, touching Jen's big toe. "And this little piggy. . ."

◆

OBSERVATIONS

The World of Things

Jennifer is learning to observe details and to distinguish small differences (skills she will be using in a few years to distinguish between letters of the alphabet). She is quick to notice anything new and bright in her familiar environment. Carol has observed this and knew Jen would enjoy playing with the red ribbon. When Carol hung the red ribbon on the mobile, the mobile looked different to Jen and it caught her attention immediately.

Jen can now focus her eyes on something interesting and move her hand toward it. She can hit and grasp. These are relatively new skills for Jen and very exciting to her. With them she can begin to satisfy her powerful curiosity by grabbing hold of a piece of her world. Today she reached out to grab Carol's hair and to get hold of the red ribbon.

The World of People

Jen develops relationships with other people as they take care of her. She feels close to her mother because they are physically close, because her mother feeds her and dresses her and touches her and talks to her the way she did today. When Carol dresses Jen, Jen feels her mother's hands on her body, hears her voice, smells her smell, and touches her hair. Jen is learning about Carol the same way she is learning about herself, through her senses.

Ideas and Words

Jen kicked each of her legs after Carol put them in the pants as though she wanted to feel them more. She blinked her eyes before Carol put her arm in her shirt, as though she were concentrating on what was going to happen next. Carol was helping Jen feel what is herself and what isn't by touching her legs, arms, stomach, and cheek and sometimes by naming them. Jen is too young to understand the words, but by saying "your cheek" as she touched it or "your left foot," Carol was helping Jen pay attention to different parts of her body.

After Carol took off the wet diaper, she put a fresh one on. After she put one of Jen's arms in the tee shirt, she put the other one in. She does these same things in the same order every morning. Experiencing this procedure again and again is helping Jen develop a sense of predictability. She can already anticipate many events with which she is familiar. She knows "This Little Piggy" well enough to sense when Carol is going to touch her feet. As soon as Carol signals the beginning of the game, Jen's toes start wiggling.

Sense of Self

When Carol dressed Jen, she was very attentive to all Jen's expressions. When Jen was fussy or whiny, Carol responded with a gentle touch or by saying something soothing, the way she said "Shhh, there..." when Jen was startled by the wet wipe. When Jen was delighted by something, like the red ribbon or "This Little Piggy," Carol was pleased too. Carol's responsiveness is assuring Jen that her feelings are important and that she is safe.

ALEX
(Fifteen Months)

"Eeaaaaah!" Alex protests. He is sitting, dressed in a diaper, on Rita's lap and doesn't want to be there. Rita has to use all her strength to keep him in place. "Just a few more minutes, honey . . . please."

Alex stops struggling for a second. He has caught sight of the small reflex hammer in the doctor's hand.

"I'm going to hit your knees now, Alex," the doctor says. Alex makes a grab for the hammer. "Okay." The doctor hands it to him.

"It's a hammer, Alex," Rita tells him mechanically. He turns it over in his hands, carefully feels the handle and then the rubber head. He tastes it with his tongue and smells it. "Maybe I'll just do this with my hand," the doctor says. Alex is so absorbed in the hammer he scarcely notices when the doctor hits his knee.

"His reflexes are fine," the doctor says to Rita. "We're almost done."

Rita, wan, takes advantage of Alex's interest in the hammer to relax her shoulders, which ache from wrestling with Alex and from tension. For as long as she can remember, she has been terrified of doctors' offices. Though she is very pleased with this pediatrician, walking into the office still makes her sweat.

Alex twists to the side and hits the white cabinet next to the chair with the hammer. He laughs at the sound. He looks at Rita. She attempts an appreciative smile.

The doctor has gotten her otoscope from the drawer. "I'm going to look in your ears now, Alex." She puts her hands gently on Alex's head to steady it. He pulls away. "This will only take a second. See the light?" She turns the otoscope light on. "I'm going to look in your ear with this." Alex quiets down to watch the light. "Now let me look in your ear." Alex touches his ear. She moves closer. Alex pushes her hand away.

"Alex, you have to let Dr. Adams look in your ear." Rita holds his head against her chest with one arm and wraps the other arm around him to hold him tight. The doctor looks in the right ear. Alex cries angrily, kicking his legs to get down. He manages to free an arm long enough to fling the hammer across the room. He yells. The hammer bangs against the examining table. "Alex, please, it's almost over. We've got to let the doctor look at your other ear." Rita holds him forcibly while the doctor completes the exam.

"Okay." The doctor steps back, smiling at Rita. "Everything is fine. I just have to vaccinate him and that's it." She goes to the cabinet and quickly prepares the measles/rubella/mumps vaccine.

Rita relaxes her grip. Alex stays still for a second, sniffling, then squirms his way down before Rita can stop him. "Alex." Alex squats down and picks up the hammer. He hits the floor with it. "Room room!" he says. He stumbles, slightly pigeon-toed, around the room, hitting things. "Room! Room! Room!"

The doctor looks at him. "Alex, you've got to sit down one more time."

"Alex," Rita says. Alex cocks his head and looks at her.

"Come here, honey." Alex walks over to her. "Give Mommy the hammer. Please. I'm just going to put it here on the cabinet, okay?" Alex lets her take it. "Up you go," Rita picks him up and sits down again.

"This will sting a little, Alex," the doctor says.

Rita holds Alex tightly, pressing one arm around his arms so he can't slap either the needle or the doctor.

"Ow!" Alex shrieks when the needle pricks him, more in surprise than pain.

"There," the doctor says, ruffling his hair. "It's all over."

Alex burrows his face against Rita and clings. He cries a little, not protesting but telling the story of all he has just been through. He sucks his fingers.

"You can get him dressed now. Then come into my office." The doctor leaves the room.

"There." Rita rubs Alex's back. "You're all right. We're going to get dressed now. Then we can get out of this place." She puts Alex down and steps over to the examining table, where she deposited Alex's clothes and the baby bag. Alex stands still, staring hard at nothing, sucking his fingers. After a few seconds he reanimates, walks over to the white cabinet, and pulls to open the door.

"Alex!" Rita snaps. "I want you to behave!" She grabs his hand and pulls him away. "There are medicines in there. You can't touch medicines. Now come here." Alex tries to pull away. He screeches.

"Enough!" Rita screeches back. Alex stares at her, startled. "Come here."

Alex takes a worried step forward. Rita bends down and puts a diaper through his legs. He leans on her shoulder, sniffling. "I'm very tired, Alex," she explains. "And I don't like being here. Please don't make a fuss." She holds out his tee shirt. "Put your arms in." Alex automatically sticks his arms out for Rita to guide through the holes. Rita lifts the shirt over his head. Alex closes his eyes and wiggles to help pull it down.

While Rita is untwisting his overalls, Alex walks around the room, running his hand along the cabinets until he comes to the door. He puts both hands on the doorknob and tries to turn it. "Aww aww," he says.

"Alex, let's put on your overalls. Come on," Rita says.

"Aww aww," Alex continues.

Rita looks around for help. She sees a tongue depressor on top of one of the cabinets, breaks open the paper wrapper, and offers it to Alex. "Do you want to finish unwrapping this?" Alex smiles, takes the depressor, and busily starts to tear the paper off. He is too absorbed in this project to offer Rita any more help. She manages to get one of his feet into the pants leg while keeping him upright. "Now the other foot." Alex is running the tongue depressor along his lips. Rita wiggles the overalls up. "Let me get this arm through." She guides his arms through the straps one at a time.

"Okay, honey, I'm going to put your socks on. Do you think I can get you to sit down?"

◆

OBSERVATIONS

The World of Things

Alex is always busy, and for him being busy means moving. When he isn't learning by walking or crawling, he's exploring with his hands. He can't look at something and think about what it is the way an adult would. He studies things—the reflex hammer, the tongue depressor, the light on the otoscope, and the cabinets in the doctor's office—by touching, tasting, smelling, and playing with them. He is a small scientist intent on learning about his new environment by manipulating everything he can get his hands on.

The World of People

The doctor treated Alex considerately and with respect. She warned him before she touched him and was sympathetic when he struggled. The visit would have been harder for Alex if the doctor had been brusque.

Today Rita wouldn't let Alex do what he wanted. She restricted and guided his behavior so his checkup could be completed and so she could get him dressed. She held him forcibly still for the ear exam and the vaccination. She called him to come to her when he started hammering things. When he tried to open the cabinet door, she yelled at him. She got him to stand still to be dressed by offering him the tongue depressor to play with. The doctor also succeeded in distracting Alex by giving him the reflex hammer and showing him her light.

Rita and the doctor had no choice but to frustrate Alex's need to move and actively explore. But a bit of frustration didn't hurt Alex. As soon as Rita put him down on the floor so she could get his clothes, he began examining the cabinet with his usual cheerful enthusiasm. Even after Rita got cross with him, he held out his arms to help her put on his shirt.

It was Rita, who dislikes doctors' offices and was tired, who felt her frustration building. She finally lost her temper and yelled at Alex when he went for the medicine cabinet. While she dressed him, Rita explained that she didn't like the place and wanted to leave. Alex couldn't have understood her words, but he probably felt as Rita talked that things were all right and that the sharp tone of Rita's voice a moment before wasn't anything to worry about.

Ideas and Words

Alex is beginning to learn the names of his body parts and already knows *head, eyes, ears, nose,* and *tummy.* When the doctor said "ear," Alex touched his ear. When Rita said "Put your arms in," he put his arms in the armholes of his shirt. Every time Rita dresses him, she helps him learn about himself.

Alex knows the routine of dressing well enough to participate even when he has just been poked, prodded, and pricked in a relatively unfamiliar place like the doctor's office.

Sense of Self

Alex gets upset very quickly when he is restrained. He didn't like being held down and examined. He didn't even like standing still to be dressed. He has a strong drive to be up and moving, so it is natural and healthy for him to protest when he is held still—and protest he did. Today he wrestled with Rita, pushed the doctor, and flung the hammer.

Alex feels what he feels very intensely, but he can leave one feeling behind and go on to another with very little transition time. His need to be physically active seems to push him, almost literally, from one experience to the next. He cried awhile after the vaccination, for example, but when Rita put him down he sucked his fingers quietly for a few seconds, then blithely went over to the cabinet. He's a resilient little boy.

◆

KATIE
(Twenty-eight Months)

Sarah looks at her daughter for a few seconds before waking her. Katie's face, so busy when she is awake, is as still and soft as the early-morning light. Sarah strokes the small back. "Katie. Oh, Katie," she half sings. Katie begins stirring. "It's time to wake up, darling."

Katie rubs her eyes and reaches toward her mother. Sarah picks her up, kissing her head. Her hair and neck are wet. "You must have been hot last night," Sarah says. "Do you want to sit on the potty?"

"No," Katie says fuzzily. She rubs her eyes again.

"Okay. I'm going to change your diaper and then I'll help you get dressed."

Katie yawns deeply and then seems to wake up. "Mommy change diaper," she repeats.

If only she'd stay sleepy, Sarah thinks, I could get her dressed in half the time.

Sarah changes Katie in the bathroom, carries her back to her room, and puts her down. Katie, now awake and bouncy, pulls her stuffed dog, Franklin, out of her crib. She carries Franklin over to Sarah, who is taking a pair of red-striped cotton shorts out of the top bureau drawer. "Pants!" Katie says. "Red pants." Katie puts Franklin down, opens the lowest drawer, and starts taking out socks. "Socks," she says, tossing them on the floor.

"*Katie, we only need one pair. You've only got two feet.*" *Sarah starts putting them back.* "*I'm in a hurry this morning, darling. I have a meeting with my boss.*"

Katie notices her felt pen on the floor by the bureau. She opens the top and smells it. Forgetting about the socks she goes over to the desk and draws a purple line across the cover of one of her books. She continues the line off the book onto the desk.

"*Katie,*" *Sarah says.* "*Don't draw on books. When you draw on books you can't see the words and the pictures.*" *Katie draws a line on her arm. She holds it up for Sarah to admire.* "*Come on, Katie, let's get your pants on. You can't go to school dressed in ink.*"

Sarah hears the toilet flushing; Joe must be up. "*Joe,*" *she calls,* "*could you take over?*"

"*All right, just a minute,*" *he calls back.*

Katie is adding to her tattoo.

"*Katie, let me have that marker,*" *Sarah says firmly. Katie hesitates. Sarah takes it, puts the top on, and sticks it in the pocket of her robe. Joe comes in.*

"*Daddy!*" *Katie trots over and hugs his legs. He bends down and kisses her.* "*Good morning, Nutmeg.*"

"*I overslept,*" *Sarah says, handing him the pants,* "*and I can't cope.*"

"*Okay,*" *Joe says,* "*I've got time today.*"

Sarah kisses Katie's head. "*Daddy's going to help you get dressed. I'll see you downstairs, okay?*"

"*Okay,*" *Katie says.* "*Bye,*" *she adds, as Sarah leaves the room.*

"*Are those what you want to wear today?*" *Joe asks, holding up the pants and looking at them quizzically.* "*Do I put these on over my head?*" *He tries them on as a hat.*

"*No,*" *Katie says, laughing and snatching them.* "*Legs.*" *She tries to step into the pants, which are wound up. She realizes something is wrong, but she keeps trying to get her leg through the half inside-out waistband anyway.*

"*Let me help you,*" *Joe says.*

"*No!*" *Katie tells him. Joe reaches out his hand to take the pants. Katie clutches them.* "*My do.*"

"*Katie, we don't have time. I'll hold them out for you.*"

Katie relinquishes the pants with a grin. Joe shakes them out on the floor so Katie can see the two legs, then holds the right leg out. "Your right foot here." *He indicates Katie's right. Katie carefully puts her foot in.* "Now the left." *Katie puts her left in and pulls the pants part way up. Joe helps her get them over her rear. Katie sticks her fingers under the waist to feel the pull of the elastic.*

"Now we need a shirt." *Joe pulls out two tee shirts, a blue one and one with orange and black flowers.* "What'll it be?" *he asks Katie.*

"All right," *he says with enthusiasm when Katie points to the floral number.* "They'll see you coming today. First your right arm." *Joe touches it. Katie puts it in the armhole.* "Then your left." *He touches it.* "Now"— *Joe brushes her nose with his fingertip*—"your head." *Giggling, Katie raises her arms. Joe lifts the neck hole up and puts it over her head.*

"Now we're cooking. Let's put on these socks." *Joe picks up one of the pairs Katie dumped on the floor. He sticks them on his ears.* "Do I put my socks on my ears?"

"No!" *Katie shouts, laughing.* "Feet!"

"Oh," *Joe says, taking them off and looking at them.* "That sounds like a good idea. Come over here and sit down." *He pats her small chair. Katie giggles and backs away.* "Katie, we don't have time."

Katie runs to the window and hides behind the curtain. Joe looks at his watch and decides to play one round. "Let's see . . . Is Katie in the closet?" *He looks.* "Nooo . . . Is she under the desk?" *He peeks.* "Nooo . . ." *He walks over to the curtain. Katie giggles.* "What's this?" *Joe asks. He pulls the curtain open and grabs his giggling daughter.* "Now," *Joe says, picking her up and carrying her over to the chair so she can't try to hide again,* "it's sock time."

Katie laughs and begins struggling.

"Katie's going to put on her socks," *Joe says. He puts her down on the chair and kneels in front of her. Katie, giggling, wiggles both feet and tries to move them out of reach. Joe catches the right foot and puts a sock on.* "You try putting this left sock on while I look for your shoes, okay?"

"Okay," *Katie says. Joe turns to get Katie's sneakers out of the closet. Katie jumps out of the chair.*

Her motion catches Joe's eye. "Katie," *he says firmly,* "sit down and get to work on that sock. It's getting late."

The sneakers aren't in her closet. Joe looks for them in the same places he looked for Katie: under the desk, behind the curtain, then in the pile of clothes in the corner and under the crib. Katie struggles with the sock. She holds it up and looks at it. She finds the top part with the hole and manages to put it over her big toe, but with the heel facing up.

"Sarah!" Joe calls from the door. "Do you know where Katie's sneakers are?"

"In the living room," Sarah calls from the kitchen.

Katie tries to pull the sock up. It's caught between her big toe and her second toe.

"No," Katie says when Joe comes over to help. But it's not a serious protest: she sticks her foot toward him.

"Let's start from scratch here. You turn it around so the heel is in back," he explains, illustrating. "Then you put your toes in. And you pull it up." He pulls the sock over Katie's heel. "Now you pull it up the rest of the way." Katie carefully pulls the top of the sock over her ankle. "Good girl. Now how about some breakfast?"

◆

OBSERVATIONS

The World of Things

Katie is learning how to dress herself. She is familiar with all the different articles of clothing and how they work. She wiggled her toes when Joe mentioned her shoes because she knows they go on her feet. She knows her legs go through her pants and her shirt covers her torso. She is practicing pulling her pants all the way up and putting her socks on.

Joe let Katie try putting on her pants herself a few times before he intervened. Katie might have learned more if she had had the chance to play by herself a bit longer, but Joe couldn't experiment very long. If he had let Katie take as long as she liked, she would never have gotten to day care—and his patience would have been strained. Watching a child try to do something the wrong way over and over again, the way Katie stubbornly tried to get into the twisted pants, can be maddening. Joe ended up working with Katie on the pants as a partner: he did part of the job for her, explaining as he went along, then let her do the part she could do herself.

The World of People

Katie's growing sense of competence makes the business of getting dressed even slower than it used to be. Her parents can't just dress her anymore: she insists on doing as much of the dressing as she can the way she did this morning. Sarah, who gets up earlier than Joe and usually gets Katie ready, was in a hurry today. She wisely asked Joe for help as soon as she felt herself becoming seriously impatient. Dressing Katie wasn't a familiar chore to Joe and he didn't feel as pressured about time as Sarah did. He gave Katie plenty of time to help dress herself and to play. Both parent and child were actively involved in getting the chore done.

Ideas and Words

Sarah and Joe had a clear morning objective: getting Katie and themselves dressed, fed, and out of the house. Katie wanted to help get herself dressed too, but she kept getting distracted by more immediate goals, such as hiding behind the curtains and drawing with her marker. Sarah and Joe had to keep calling her attention back to the chore at hand.

Katie knows the names of all her articles of clothing. She is beginning to distinguish and name colors. (For a while, according to Katie everything was blue.)

Joe touches Katie's right and left arms when he asks her to lift them. This is one of many daily experiences that will help Katie learn her right from her left. Dressing is also helping her learn about shapes. She didn't know how to look at her pants and socks and position them properly. When Joe did it for her, however, she recognized the shapes and knew what to do next.

Katie finds the ideas of socks on ears and pants on heads funny because she knows where things belong. It takes quite a bit of sophistication to distinguish between the right and wrong way of doing something and to laugh at the difference.

Sense of Self

This morning Joe gave Katie a real though beginner-level decision to make: the choice between two shirts. Katie wasn't shy about picking, though she probably just took the first one that caught her eye.

Katie shouted "No!" when Joe tried to help her with her pants, but her protest was good-natured—almost obligatory. She yelled "No!" very loudly to let Joe know he was wrong about where you wear socks. She enjoys shouting and making noise. It makes her feel strong. It is a way of saying "I'm here."

Katie is very aware—and wants her parents to be aware—that she can do more things for herself every day. She is no longer a baby but a capable child. On the other hand, she likes to be a baby when she feels like it. Today she wanted Sarah to carry her to the bathroom and change her diaper.

5

TAKING A BATH

Children like bathing for the same reasons adults do, because the warmth soothes them, the feel of water on the skin is delicious, and the way water catches the light and makes it tremble enchants the eye. They also like bathing because, for them, water is something remarkable.

They are fascinated by the liquidity of water. Water doesn't have a body, but you can pick it up. It moves like something living. It responds when you touch it. When you splash, it makes drops and waves and arcs. It comes out of faucets in firm streams or sprays, but slips through your hands if you rub it. It fits into containers of any shape and streams out of holes in long ribbons. Still water feels soft when you touch it softly, hard if you slap it. Drops cling to your skin and the side of the tub and the sides of cups, and they move toward each other. Water can be hot or cold, and it changes temperature all the time.

A baby enjoys the power she has in water. When she kicks or flails her arms in the crib, nothing much happens to the air, but water responds in amazing ways. Her limited repertoire of movements has great effects in the bath. She can push objects that float in the water long before she can push objects on land.

Baths are laboratories for older children and also stage sets with a wealth of special effects built in. Toddlers and twos study properties of water—how it flows, wets, fills spaces, and the way various objects behave in water—more deliberately than infants, though they don't structure experiments the way adults would. They play game after game and through play discover how water moves and how they can move in water. An investigative seventeen-month-old, for example, might press a plastic container on the water, open side facing down, and feel the pressure of the air inside. Then he might reverse the container and watch it float, and then repeat the whole sequence ten times with no signs of flagging curiosity.

Probably the least interesting part of taking a bath for a child is the part her parents regard as most essential: washing. If you put your child in the tub hoping to give her a quick scrub and take her right out, she may give you a hard time. It's not the washing itself she will object to so much as being rushed. To avoid this problem, extend bath time to include the play she enjoys whenever you can. At least a few times a week try to bathe her when you are not in a hurry, so you can let her do the things with water she likes to do. If you work, for example, you might bathe your child in the evening, rather than trying to fit bath time into the morning rush hour.

When your child has plenty of time to pour and splash, slide and slither, and send her toys on watery adventures, she will probably be willing to be washed too. In fact, you can make washing into another game. Toddlers enjoy identifying different parts of their bodies when you touch them with the washcloth. Twos like to make soap lather voluminously. Babies just like being touched.

The one aspect of personal hygiene few children enjoy is having their hair washed. They particularly dislike having their heads bent back. You can't avoid washing your child's hair; the most considerate way is to do it as quickly as possible.

Bath time can be pleasant for you too. Your child will of course splash water everywhere. After a few minutes of peaceful water play, the floor of the bathroom will be a puddle (you'll want to keep a good supply of cleanup materials on hand). But you won't have to do something to amuse your child every thirty seconds. Small children can keep themselves amused in the bath much longer than they can on dry ground. Infants, for example, usually need adult help to play because their ability to move and make things change on their own is so limited. In the bathtub, however, your baby can make lots of things happen without your help. An older child can amuse herself—watching soap float, pouring water in and out of strainers and cups, and making splashes—for quite a long time without driving you crazy, which she can probably do in two minutes of turning light switches on and off or building up block houses and knocking them down.

You do need to keep an eye on your child when she's in the tub; tubs are hard and slippery and children can drown in them. You should be on hand to guard against accidents, but you won't need to interrupt the play very often. A quarter hour of watching your child play joyfully without having to intervene can be very relaxing for you—and for your child too. Children have an enviable capacity to be totally absorbed by play problems they set themselves. They like to investigate the things that interest them thoroughly. It's important to find times when you can give your child the chance to carry on her explorations undisturbed.

Though most children in their first year of life love playing in the bath, some go through a brief period toward the end of their second year when the bathtub scares them. Psychologists usually attribute this particular fear to anxiety about drains and the way they suck the water away, but this may not always be the reason. If a child cannot explain her fears verbally or in some other way, adults can only guess at what's behind them. But whether it's the drain or the tall sides of the tub or the slipperiness or the fact that things sink that scares her, a child's fear of the bathtub is a sign that she understands what a bathtub is in a way she didn't before. A six-month-old couldn't conceive that water disappearing down a hole might mean she's next, for example.

If your child becomes afraid in the tub, her fears deserve respect: being afraid of something that might hurt you is sensible, and trying to protect yourself is grown up. You might consider giving her sponge baths for a while. When you want or need to bathe her in the tub, be as gentle and reassuring as you can. If you're not modest about nudity, encourage her to come into the bathroom while you bathe to remind her that baths are a regular part of your life. Most children overcome their fears of the bathtub pretty quickly on their own.

Katie, like many twos, enjoys the tub so much she doesn't want to get out. Alex seems unable to sit still for more than four minutes lately but will happily stay in the tub with his brother Mike a half hour, making water do things. Jennifer coos and gurgles the minute she feels the warm water.

◆

JENNIFER
(Six Months)

"What's this? Carrots on your tummy?"

Jen, who has an orange-streaked stomach, has just woken up from her Sunday afternoon nap. Carol is bending over her, smiling. Jen reaches up to touch Carol's face.

"I'm going to get that hand," Carol says, kissing Jen's fingers. Jen giggles and reaches for Carol's mouth again. "Umm," Carol says, "tastes like carrots on your fingers too."

Carol reaches into the crib and sits Jen up. "How about a bath? Would you like that?" Carol pulls the yellow tub out from under the changing table. "Arahhbahhbah," Jen says.

"I'll be back in a minute," Carol says.

"Aah," Jen whines. She twists to watch Carol leave, falling forward on her hands for balance.

Carol reappears a few seconds later carrying the tub, now filled with water. She sets it down on Jen's changing table. She takes squeeze bottles of baby shampoo and soap and a small plastic cup from the top of Jen's bureau and puts them by the tub. Jen stares at the tub intently, then looks up at her mother's face. "Ah rah" she comments, kicking her legs.

Carol lifts Jen out of her crib, sets her down on the changing table in a standing position and, holding her around the waist, removes her diaper. Then she puts her hands under Jen's arms and lifts her down toward the tub, feet first. Jen kicks as her feet hit the water. Carol tries to lower Jen in, but Jen holds her knees stiff. Jen smiles, standing and kicking.

"Come on, Jen," Carol says. "We can't wash your tummy if you are standing." She tries to lower Jen into the tub. The plump knees, locked, refuse to give. Jen puffs her cheeks out into an even bigger grin and kicks some more. On the third try, Carol succeeds in lowering Jen to a sitting position, placing her back against the back of the tub.

Jen's eyes open wide as the water covers her legs. "Ahh bahh." She grips the edge of the tub with one hand.

"Hold on," Carol says, placing Jen's other hand on the side too.

Jen lets go, shifts her weight forward, and reaches over to touch a picture of cows on the wall. "You're going to get your picture all wet," Carol warns. Jen pats the picture with her hands. Water drips down the wall. "Jennifer," Carol calls. Jen looks at her. "Here, play with this duck." Carol reaches for a plastic duck on the bureau and floats it toward Jen. Jen sees it. She bats at the water, then kicks her feet, splashing more water on the wall and over the front of her mother's shirt. She picks the duck up and begins chewing on it. "Ah rah," Jen says.

"That's better," Carol says, brushing some water off her own cheek. "I'm going to wash your hair while you play with the duck." Using her free hand as a cup, she wets Jen's head. She takes the shampoo bottle, opens it, puts one arm behind Jen's back to support her, and squeezes a dab of shampoo on Jen's head. Jen spots the bottle. "Ehhh!" she shrieks, dropping the duck and reaching for it. Carol snaps it shut and hands it to her. Jen brings the shampoo bottle up to her mouth and she feels with her lips for a good place to mouth.

Carol rubs the shampoo over Jen's head, scoops the small cup full of water, leans Jen back against her arm and pours the water over Jen's head to rinse the soap away. Jen stiffens. Her arms tense. "Ahhbah." Jen coughs and sputters. She blinks rapidly as water runs down her face. She tries to shift position, can't, stiffens again, and whines shrilly.

"Let's try this sitting up," Carol says. She straightens Jen up. Jen stops whining. Her body relaxes a little. Carol pours the rest of the water over her head. A good bit of water flows over Jen's face. Jen blinks hard and makes a squeaky sound. Carol wipes her face with a cloth. Jen tosses her head to the side. "Eeeeh," she says.

"That's it," Carol assures her. "You are all right."

Jen reaches for the cup still in Carol's hand. "You want this cup?" Jen takes it and slaps the cup on the water. She blinks in surprise at the sharp sound and splash. Carol licks her lips as water hits her face. "Jen, what are we going to do with you?" she says, glancing at the dripping wall.

Carol pours some baby soap on a washcloth and begins washing Jen. "I'm going to wash your legs," she says. She touches each in turn, then giggles. "Jen, you've got old lady's knees." She strokes her fingers under the folds of fat around Jen's knees. "Adorable old lady's knees. Now let's wash that carrot off your tummy. There you go." Carol splashes water over Jen to rinse her well. Jen smiles at her mother and kicks her feet under the water.

"That's it," Carol says. She lifts Jen from the tub. Jen's eyes open wide to take in the changing view. She kicks her feet in the air. Carol sits her on the edge of the table, puts the hood of a blue baby towel over Jen's wet head and wraps her up. "That's my big girl." Jen begins squirming. "Hey, wiggle worm," Carol says, "we'll get you dressed in a second."

OBSERVATIONS

The World of Things

Jen visibly enjoys being bathed. She likes the feel of the warm water on her skin and the sensation of kicking her bare legs through the water and feeling the water move.

Jen dropped the plastic duck to reach for the shampoo bottle. Later she reached for the rinsing cup. The bottle and cup may have interested her more than the duck because she saw them in Carol's hand and she saw Carol use them.

Jen can't crawl yet, but something in her already wants to stand and walk. She likes the sensation of being upright. She smiled and kicked with relish when Carol held her upright over the tub. It took Carol three tries to get Jen to sit down.

Jen's body tensed in protest when Carol leaned her backwards. She preferred to sit up straight while her hair was being rinsed, even though more water fell on her face that way. Perhaps Jen doesn't like being laid back because she is so eager to sit and stand, or perhaps, despite Carol's supporting arm, the reclining position makes her feel unsteady and insecure.

The World of People

Jen was able to relax in the bath and become absorbed in playing with the water because Carol was there. When Carol is with her, Jen feels safe. Carol made Jen feel safe by literally supporting her. She seated Jen so her back touched the tub. When Jen moved forward, Carol kept an arm behind her to make sure she couldn't fall.

As Carol noted, Jen is becoming a "wiggle worm." She twisted and turned in her bath and reached all the way over to the wall to touch the picture of the cows. Jen's new capacity for movement is changing her relationship with her mother and making her bath a different kind of experience for both of them. Carol is still getting accustomed to handling a splashier and more mobile baby. (Soon she will probably start putting Jen's plastic yellow tub in the regular bathtub to better contain the water.)

Ideas and Words

Jen watched intently as Carol got the yellow tub ready for her bath. She has had many baths in that tub and seemed to recognize it. She cooed and kicked her feet with excitement. She seems to be able now to distinguish between familiar and unfamiliar events, which means she is beginning to develop memory.

When Carol called "Jennifer" to get Jen to turn away from the cow picture, Jen responded. After hearing her name thousands of times over the past six months, Jen is figuring out that the sound *Jen* means her.

Sense of Self

Carol always makes a point of talking with Jen about the parts of her body when she washes her. Today she told her the names of her tummy and legs. Jennifer is too young to distinguish parts of her body, but the naming games are helping her get a sense of her body as a whole. The "I'll get those fingers" game that Carol and Jen play helps Jen distinguish between herself and her mother. The game focuses attention on how her hand feels when she touches her mother's mouth and how it feels when she pulls it away.

When Jen put one hand on the side of the tub, Carol put Jen's other hand on the other side. She was showing Jen how to support herself. Jen didn't get it—she let go. But Carol's encouragement will make it easier for her to figure out different ways to keep herself safe—without her mother's help—as she grows stronger.

◆

ALEX
(Fifteen Months)

"Robert!" Rita calls.

Alex, who has just gotten into the tub, drops a sponge on the water and watches it float. Mike, naked, is squatting by the tub rummaging through a plastic grocery carton filled with bath toys. "Mike, don't throw everything out on the floor, just take the ones you want."

Alex puts his hands on the edge of the tub and pulls himself upright to see Mike better.

"Careful, honey." Rita steps closer. "It's slippery. Robert!"

"Look out, Alex!" Mike puts two boats and a small pink rubber ball into the bath.

Rita bends over and lowers Alex. "Sit down, honey." Rita reaches into the carton. "Here's your container strainer," she says, offering Alex a margarine container with holes punched in the bottom.

"Caina staina," Alex says, looking up at her. "Caina staina caina." He dips it in the water, lifts it up, watches the water fall through the holes, and babbles to himself.

"I can't find the good submarine," Mike says, going through the toys again.

"Alex, try to keep the water in the tub. Robert!"

Robert appears at the door. "What?"

"You said you'd watch the kids while they take their bath, that's what."

"Oh God, Rita. I'm tired. Why can't you watch them?"

"Because I'm tired too."

"You know I had a long day."

"What do you think I did all day, sleep? And I've still got to sort the laundry, put away the dishes, make up a shopping list, and iron your goddamn shirt. What were you going to do, drink beer?"

Robert glares. Mike concentrates very hard on the toys. Alex sits quietly in the corner of the tub, holding the strainer in one hand and staring at the place where the ceiling light is making the water sparkle. Robert sighs. "All right."

"Get in, Mike," Rita says.

"I can't find the other boat."

"Get in anyway."

"Move over, Alex." Mike deliberately plops down, creating a wave that just manages to climb over the front edge of the tub and slosh onto the floor.

"The mop is over there," Rita points it out to Robert. "I just squeeze it into the toilet. It's easier if you try to clean up as you go along. I'll be in the kitchen if you need me."

"Bye, Mom," Mike says.

"Bye, sweetie."

"Bye-bye," Alex says. He raises his right hand and waves good-bye, making a fist, then opening it. When he opens his hands drops of water fly off his fingers. He gurgles to himself and tries it again. Nothing happens; his hand is dry now. The container strainer, abandoned, is sinking.

Mike slides down in the water, pushing Alex toward the corner. Alex picks up his cup and hits the water with the open side. It makes a slapping sound. Alex hits the water again. "Yee, yee, yee," he says, slapping down hard and making little waves push out. Mike straightens up, reaches over the edge of the tub and, dripping on the floor, feels around in the carton for another cup. Alex is staring at the ripples. He puts the cup down and tries to pick the ripples up with his hand. Mike fills his cup and pours water on Alex's back. Alex looks up at Mike, startled. He slowly smiles. He fills his cup and tries to pour water over Mike's chest; his aim is not too good. Mike pours more water over Alex, and Alex, giggling, tries pouring more water over Mike. He splashes Mike in the face. Mike retaliates. Alex lets out a cry when the water hits him. He starts whining.

"Can you do this, Alex?" Mike asks. He drops his cup, sticks his face in the water, and blows bubbles. Alex stops crying and watches. He reaches out to touch the bubbles.

Mike comes up for air. "You try it." Mike does it again.

Alex bends over and just touches his face to the water. He lifts it up and smiles. A drop of water rolls off his eyelash down his cheek and into his mouth. He touches his face.

"Rrrrr." Mike blows bubbles again, moving through the tub like a lame motor boat. Alex sticks his face in again. Robert, who is sitting on the toilet, shifts restlessly.

One of the boats has drifted behind Alex, nudging him in the back. Alex can't locate the sensation. He squirms around. The boat floats out. He grabs it, picks it up, and starts sucking water out of the deck.

"Hey," Mike says. "You'll get tooth marks on it." He tries to take the boat from Alex. Alex grunts and clutches it to his chest defensively. "Alex!" Mike tries to pull the boat away. The tug of war is making big waves.

"Hey," Robert says. "Cut it out!"

He gets up and walks to the tub. "Alex, give Mike the boat." Alex presses it more tightly to his chest. "Here." Robert rolls up his sleeve and fishes under the water for the strainer. "See, Alex." He dips the strainer in and then lifts it very high in the air so the streams of water fall down from above Alex's head. Alex is charmed. Robert takes the boat from him and hands him the strainer.

Alex dips the strainer in the water and lifts it up high the way Robert did. He giggles as the water falls through.

Robert is examining the boat he has rescued. "It's a submarine," he says.

"Yeah," Mike says, "but I can't make it stay under."

Robert examines it. "It's not made right," he says.

"I have a better one but I can't find it."

Robert hands the boat to Mike, who pushes it off on a reconnaissance mission, treating Alex as an island.

"Where's the good sub?" Robert asks.

"I don't know. It's not in the box."

Alex puts the strainer down and reaches for the rubber ball, which is floating past. It shoots away when he touches it. He reaches for it again, capsizing the boat.

"Dad! Alex is hogging all the water," Mike complains.

"Well, give him the ball." Robert, bored, begins looking through the toys.

Mike grabs the ball. "Here." He holds it in front of Alex, but before Alex can take it, Mike suddenly pushes the ball down. It pops right up, making an impressive splash.

Alex is delighted. He goes after the ball, pulling himself along the floor of the tub with his hands and indeed hogging the water. A huge wave sloshes over the side.

"Move over, Alex," Mike yells.

"Take it easy," Robert growls.

Alex, oblivious, continues crawling around the tub. He puts his chin in the water and lets it flow into his mouth.

"Rrrr," Mike says, pushing one of the boats toward the ball. He misses.

Robert has found the good submarine. He is looking at it with real interest.

"Rrrrr," Mike says, aiming the boat at the ball again. This time it hits. The ball shoots toward the side of the tub and bounces back.

Alex reaches for the ball with both hands and slips, falling face forward in the water. He starts splashing, trying to right himself. Mike, pushed into the corner of the tub, is quiet for a second, frightened. Then he reaches out to help Alex. Robert reaches over at the same time and lifts Alex upright. Alex cries.

"Shhhh," Robert says, patting his head. "You're all right."

While Alex cries, his right hand gropes along the bottom of the tub and pulls out the container strainer. He clutches it and rocks himself, whimpering.

"I found it," Robert says to Mike. He puts the good submarine in the water and takes aim at the ball himself. "Pow," he goes.

"Da," Alex says, looking at Robert. Robert turns back to Alex and rubs his back. "How are you doing? Are you feeling better?"

OBSERVATIONS

The World of Things

Alex relishes water and all the things it can do. Today he tried to pick up waves with his hands. He hit the water to make it splash. He picked it up in a cup. He made it fall through the holes in the strainer. He watched a sponge float and get wet. He saw that some things stayed on top of the water, like the boat, while other things, like the container strainer, sank.

Mike is helping Alex learn about water. Alex might not have thought of putting his face in the water on his own at fifteen months if Mike hadn't shown him.

Alex had trouble getting hold of the ball. He hasn't yet learned how to grasp something that's floating or rolling. When he tried to grab the ball, he pushed it away instead.

The World of People

Having an older brother influences Alex's life in many ways. Almost everything Alex does he does with Mike nearby. Alex is alone with Mrs. Weiss in the mornings and alone with Rita in the early afternoon, but the rest of the day he spends with Mike. They share a room, take baths together, go to the park together, and play together. Alex is interested in everything Mike does. Today, for example, when Mike was looking through the carton of toys, Alex stood up to see what was going on. Alex learns many things simply from being around his more capable brother.

Mike, because he is so much older, dominates the relationship.

Today his behavior toward Alex was very changeable. In the short time they were together in the tub, Mike went back and forth between being a patient, generous big brother and being bossy and a little mean. He was obviously enjoying being a teacher when he showed Alex how to put his face in the water. But he also ordered Alex around and teased him by pushing the ball underwater so it popped out of Alex's reach.

At Mike's initiative, Mike and Alex played the water-pouring game and the face-in-the-water game together. More often, they played separately. While Mike was conducting naval battles, for example, Alex was absorbed with his strainer. Sometimes they got in each other's way by hogging the water.

Though Alex is certainly not aware of it, taking baths with his brother this way every day will help him learn that people can enjoy being together even when they do things separately and even though they don't always get along. Since Mike can be very provocative and combative, he is also teaching Alex to protect himself and his activities. Today Alex held onto the boat, firmly, despite Mike's efforts to take it away.

The boys' play might have been a bit more rambunctious than usual tonight because Robert was there. Robert rarely spends bath time with the boys and his presence may have excited them.

Robert loves Alex but he doesn't like taking care of him. He's uncomfortable when Alex is upset, and he really doesn't know how to play with a toddler. For example, while Robert became genuinely interested in Mike's boat, he only played with the strainer to distract Alex. (Many parents find they respond more easily to their children at one age than at another.)

After Alex slipped, Robert comforted him, but he didn't give Alex as much attention as Alex wanted. Alex called for more. When he did, Robert responded.

Rita and Robert squabbled tonight, as they have many times before and no doubt will many times again. His parents' arguments, like his own fights with Mike, are part of Alex's social world. He is learning that people who love each other sometimes fight.

Ideas and Words

Alex babbles to himself in the tub, combining nonsense sounds with a real word from time to time. He is practicing the rhythms of speech. He likes words like *container strainer* that rhyme or have a special rhythm.

Alex didn't understand most of the words his parents were saying to each other, but he sensed they were fighting from their tone of voice, expression, and posture.

Alex put his face in the water after Mike showed him how. Later he put his chin in when he was crawling after the ball. He lifted the strainer high the way Robert did. He learns by imitating people as well as by conducting his own trial-and-error experiments.

Sense of Self

Whatever Alex did in the bathtub, he produced a grand effect: he made the water splash, he made it hit the side of the tub with a slosh, he made it fall from a cup or through holes in a strainer. Alex feels pleased with himself when he makes things happen, and he felt pleased with himself in the bathtub.

When Rita and Robert were arguing, neither Mike nor Alex became visibly upset but both became a little more quiet than usual. Being quiet seems to be one way Alex deals with a situation that makes him uneasy.

When Alex needed more attention from Robert after his fall, he asked for it. He called "Da." He has learned to ask for the reassurance he needs, and he trusts his father to provide it.

KATIE
(Twenty-eight Months)

Sarah is sitting on her knees at one end of the bathtub. "All right, little fish. Swim over here so I can wash your hair now."

"No," Katie says. For the past five minutes she has been going up and down the length of the bathtub, walking her hands on the tub bottom and pulling her legs, floating like a fishtail, after her.

"Katie," Sarah says firmly. "Come on now. Fish swim over to the end. I told you I've got to wash your hair." Katie inches reluctantly toward Sarah. "That's my girl—or are you still a fish?"

"My Katie," Katie says with a grin. She turns to sit on her rear so her knees poke up through the water.

"I thought so," Sarah said. "I thought I saw Katie's clean elbows and knees."

Katie looks at her elbows and knees. Then she bends her head down and studies her left knee carefully. "Look, Mommy," she says urgently. She sticks the knee out of the water and holds it up for inspection. "My boo-boo."

Sarah looks carefully. "Where?" Katie points and looks up at her mother, deeply concerned. "Shall I kiss it for you?" Sarah asks, though she still doesn't see anything. Katie nods. Sarah kisses her knee.

"Okay, Katie," Sarah says. "Let's get back to business. Close your eyes." Sarah fills a plastic cup with water and wets Katie's hair. Katie blinks as water trickles over her face.

"My do," she says, grabbing for the cup. She lifts the cup as high as she can but positions her arms a little too far back. The water misses her head and hits the back of her neck.

"Now for the shampoo," Sarah says. "Close your eyes."

Katie squinches her eyes shut so tightly her nose almost meets her forehead. Sarah pours a drop of shampoo on Katie's head and lathers it. Katie squirms.

"Just a second more," Sarah says. "I have to get that peanut butter out of your hair."

"No more," Katie says. She pushes Sarah's hands away.

"I know you don't like this," Sarah says, rinsing her hands. "Let's rinse the soap off and then you can swim a few more minutes. Ready?" Sarah puts one arm behind Katie and begins leaning her back.

"Noooo," Katie protests. Her body tenses as Sarah lowers her. She begins kicking, splashing water all over Sarah.

"Katie! This will just take a second if you cooperate," Sarah says. She fills the cup with water. "We'll be finished by ten." She begins reciting "One, two, buckle my shoe." She pours the water over Katie's head and runs her fingers through the hair behind Katie's ears. "Three, four, shut the door." She refills the cup. "Five, six, pick up sticks." She pours water over Katie's head again. "Seven, eight"—she pours yet another cup full of water over a particularly soapy section of Katie's hair; some water streams over Katie's face; Katie sputters and kicks—"lay them straight."

"Nine, ten, a big fat hen!" Katie joins in as Sarah helps her sit up.

"Good girl," Sarah says. "See, we got there by ten." She wrings out a washcloth and hands it to Katie.

"My wipe." Katie grabs the washcloth and dabs it on her cheeks, drops it, pushes away from Sarah and fish swims to the end of the tub, kicking water out of the tub as she goes.

Sarah straightens up, rubs the small of her back, and glances at her watch. It's almost eight-thirty. If she can get Katie to bed by nine, she'll still have the energy to enjoy a bath herself.

"Katie-fish," she says, "you can swim for two more minutes, and then it is time to get out of the tub and put your pj's on."

Katie looks at her mother. Then she reaches for the washcloth and swishes it at arm's length across the water. "My play," she says. She begins flicking the cloth, splashing water out of the tub.

"Katie, keep the water in the tub," Sarah says. "You are getting the floor all wet and Mommy too."

"Mommy's shirt wet," Katie says, looking up at Sarah.

"Guess who had something to do with it?" Sarah says. Katie giggles and flicks the cloth again.

"I'm serious about splashing, Katie. I've got your towel ready. One more minute and it's time to come out of the bath."

Katie catches Sarah's eye. "Look, Mommy," she says, dipping her face into the water. She lifts her head, shaking it from side to side. Sarah smiles dutifully.

Katie slides back and forth across the tub. She takes the cup Sarah used to rinse her hair, fills it with water, gives Sarah a very brash look, and takes a sip.

Sarah shakes her head no. "I don't want you to drink bathwater," she says. Katie peeks up from the cup and takes another sip. "All right, time's up."

"No, my play." She drops the cup and scoots on her bottom away from Sarah.

"Katie," Sarah says.

"Nooooo," Katie says, sliding from one end of the tub to the other.

"Katie, you've got to get out." Katie giggles and slides back and forth faster. "I mean it," Sarah says in her low, I-mean-it voice. She stretches out her hand to help Katie out. Katie laughs loudly, and slaps a spray of water at her mother.

Sarah gets up, remembering to bend her knees to minimize the strain to her back, and takes a deep breath. "Katie, you're getting out now." She reaches over, takes Katie under the armpits and lifts her up.

Katie kicks, splashing water over Sarah and the sides of the tub. "No!" she shrieks, kicking furiously as Sarah lifts her through the air. "My swim!"

She is so big and slippery that Sarah barely manages to get her out and stand her down on the bath mat. Katie, trembling with fury, hits her mother in the stomach. "My swim!" she cries, "My swim!"

She turns to the bathtub and starts to step in again. Sarah puts her hands on Katie's shoulders and turns her away. "No, Katie, I said no."

Katie reaches for the shampoo on the edge of the tub and throws it across the room. Then she turns to the sink, crying so hard she has to gasp for breath, and grabs the toothpaste. "No, Katie." Sarah takes Katie's hand and pulls the toothpaste away.

Katie screams, "No!" apparently not sure what she is screaming about anymore. Sarah wraps a towel around her. "No!" Katie pushes the towel away, not very vigorously. She is worn out and caught up in sobbing now, not struggling.

Sarah wraps the towel around her again. "Katie," she says. "That's enough. It's over." Katie glares at her. But when Sarah starts rubbing her back through the towel, Katie leans against her. "There you go." Sarah rubs Katie's wet hair softly with the towel. Katie sniffles and wipes a tear from her eye. "My brush teeth," she says, reaching up for her toothbrush.

◆

OBSERVATIONS

The World of Things

Katie can wipe her face with a washcloth and pour water (almost) over her head. She wants to brush her own teeth. She is beginning to develop the skills she needs to take care of herself. By letting Katie help clean herself during her bath, Sarah is helping her develop these skills.

Katie is figuring out different ways she can move in the water. She has discovered that her legs float.

The World of People

Tonight's bath gave Katie and Sarah time to be alone together and to be physically close. Katie no longer needs her mother to move her and feed her, but she still depends on Sarah's touch to help her feel safe and loved. Sarah's kiss made Katie's knee feel better, because to Katie, Sarah's touch heals and protects. At the end of the tantrum, Sarah helped Katie quiet down by rubbing her back. When Katie felt Sarah's hand, she leaned closer.

Though Katie still needs to be physically close to Sarah, she also needs to feel physically and emotionally separate. Tonight she declared her independence by testing the limits Sarah established about splashing and drinking bathwater and getting out of the tub. Sarah gave Katie some time to play and then let Katie know that she, Sarah, was in charge and that it was time to get out. Sarah's assertion of authority probably made Katie feel safe and loved too. Katie can be as rebellious as she likes because she knows Sarah will always be there. She can count on Sarah to order their life.

Ideas and Words

Katie plays with imagination now. Tonight she enjoyed pretending she was a fish in water. She remembered that fish like water, thought of fish when she got in the water, and used the image of a fish to discover another way to move in water.

Katie uses personal pronouns (*I, my, me*), though not always correctly. She uses two or three words in most of her sentences.

Katie has memorized the words of "One, two, buckle my shoe." She joined in to recite "Nine, ten" with Sarah in celebration of the end of the awful hair rinse.

Sarah and Katie used the rhyme to get through an unpleasant chore. The game put hair rinsing into a structure Katie understands. She could anticipate that the rinsing would be over when the rhyme neared its end. She is learning that language and ritual can help her control and get through difficult situations. The rhyme worked well for Sarah too. She could pause or slow up her recitation to give herself as much time as she needed.

Sense of Self

For Katie, becoming more aware of herself as a person means becoming more aware of her body. She likes to examine herself. She can identify many parts of her body now, including her knees and elbows. Cuts and bruises concern her in a way they didn't before; the idea of a hole in her valuable self disturbs her. Sarah's kiss was enough to assure her that all was well tonight. Other times it might take a Band-Aid to convince Katie she is intact.

Katie asserted herself forcefully tonight, insisting on doing things herself and having her own way. She is proud of her accomplishments and likes to test her strength by opposing her mother. But Katie hasn't learned how to control her own feelings yet and has little sense of proportion. Tonight she got carried away by her own protests. Her first playful noes when her mother asked her to get out escalated into kicking and screaming. Katie didn't plan this. It just happened. Her emotion and the rhythm of refusing intensified until they dominated her. She needed something to do with all that feeling and began throwing things. But after a few minutes, she stopped throwing and just cried. Her tantrum seemed to tire her out and maybe frighten her a little as well. She was relieved when Sarah finally got her into a towel and told her it was all over.

In a few seconds, Katie had recovered and was ready to move on to toothbrushing. (Sarah is probably not so resilient.)

6

CHANGING DIAPERS/ TOILET TRAINING

Changing diapers is one aspect of infant care that does not invite sentimentality. Parents' pride in their children's accomplishments is sometimes mingled with a touch of sorrow at how quickly they grow —but hardly anyone speaks of taking off diapers with tender nostalgia. The bigger the baby, the more disagreeable it is to change her. An infant produces a comparatively small amount of waste, but an eighteen-month-old toddler can soak through paper diapers to make a puddle on the floor or release a smelly bowel movement that seems almost as big as she is. Then she may want to play with it. Children's lack of bowel and bladder control also contributes mightily to the difficulties of going anywhere with them: diapers and wipes have to be carried along too. As you may have learned, changing a diaper in a public bathroom is a singularly unpleasant experience.

Because we dislike changing so, we tend to rush through it, without paying attention to how the activity is perceived by our child. Slowing down is worth the effort from time to time. If a child has her diaper changed six times a day until she's thirty months old, she will have had more than 5,400 changes in her first two and a half years. Anything a child experiences 5,400 times is an important part of her life.

During the first few months of her life, a baby doesn't understand why she is being changed or why she feels more comfortable afterwards, but she still learns from being changed and enjoys it. She enjoys being shifted to a new place—the changing table or bathroom—that gives her another view of the world. She enjoys the special feelings and smells. She enjoys the physical intimacy and emotional interaction with her adults. Being changed, along with being fed, bathed, and put to bed, is one of several events of the day when adults regularly touch her in predictable ways, talk to her, and focus all their attention on being with her.

To a small baby, urinating and defecating are things that happen, not things she does. She isn't clear about the differences between the inside and outside of her body. She doesn't understand that the sensations of internal movement, external warmth and wetness, cold and itchiness are related to the same event. But as she gets older, a child gradually begins to associate the pleasant sensation of warmth and release and the unpleasant sensation of wet diapers. She understands that waste products are related to her body. She realizes the purpose of changing. She has also acquired enough skills to become more actively involved in the changing process. She may indicate that she needs to be changed by crying in a particular way and later on by pointing at her diaper. Some toddlers even fetch a diaper and bring it to their parents when it is needed.

Some time in her second year, a child begins to feel herself urinating and defecating, usually before she is aware of the pressure indicating she has to go. She realizes that she herself is making something when she has a bowel movement or wets her diaper. The process of elimination, like everything that concerns herself and her ability to make and do things, becomes extremely interesting to her. She may take off her pants to study what she's produced. She may announce when she has had a bowel movement or even when she is going to (though too late to get her to the bathroom in time). Her parents, of course, are pleased by such signs that diaperless days will come. Their encouragement nourishes a child's fascination with her own waste.

A child's interest in elimination develops around the same time she is putting together a more sophisticated mental picture of her body in general. She is beginning to distinguish different parts of herself and how they fit together. She is touching her genitals for pleasure as part of these explorations. And she is busy learning some of the social activities that relate to her body, how to eat and dress in ways adults approve of, for example. She is naturally very curious about how adults relieve themselves. She likes to follow her grown-ups into the bathroom to watch what they do and listen to the sounds they make. She picks up and studies all the objects in the bathroom and is fascinated in particular by toilet paper. She may flush the toilet over and over again. When she realizes one day that it sucks things in until they disappear, she may suddenly refuse to go near it—or flush even more to try to overcome her fear. Not all children become afraid of toilets, but such fears are fairly common. The sound of flushing, formidable in itself (stop and listen next time), becomes terrifying when it is associated with things, particularly things which are also part of the body, going away. And the toilet is as big as a small child. To the toddler looking down into a bowl half her size and just six inches below her nose, the idea of being flushed away does not seem far-fetched.

Though it will be many months before she actually uses the potty regularly, the process of toilet training really begins here, when a child first becomes curious about elimination and bathrooms. Because it's such a trying process in so many families, we thought it would be helpful to discuss it at some length.

If you've been reading about toilet training and find the dire warnings or the disagreements between psychologists worrisome, it may help to remember that toilet-training customs are quite different in different countries and children everywhere get toilet trained and grow up. Applied with common sense and a sense of humor, no toilet-training method is going to make or break your child's psyche, and no method is the "right" one. It's up to you to decide what approach will be most comfortable for you and your child and to keep the whole issue in perspective.

Children do learn to relieve themselves the way adults in their society do—but not magically, or necessarily conveniently. Before a child can learn to use the toilet, she has to have the requisite neurological and muscular control, she has to understand what she's expected to do, and she has to want to do it.

As you probably know, small infants literally can't hold back their urine or bowel movements. They acquire the capacity to control elimination in stages. First they become aware of the feelings that accompany urination or bowel movement, then they become aware of the feelings that precede elimination. Finally, they develop the internal muscles they need to postpone the process and learn to use them. There's no point in starting toilet training before a child can feel she is wetting herself and no point in expecting her to use the potty before she can control urination and defecation.

Most children begin to acquire the skills needed for toilet training sometime between eighteen and twenty-four months. There's no exact age, any more than there's an exact age when all children learn to walk or talk or throw balls. The age when your child starts noticing her eliminations and becomes interested in bathrooms is the age when she's ready to begin toilet training.

Parents who are concerned about pressuring their child unduly sometimes just wait for her to begin on her own. Believe it or not, there are children who begin using the potty one day on their own and that's it—but there aren't very many of them. Toilet training involves social learning as well as physical skill. Children acquire the physical skills on their own, but they need guidance from their parents to learn how to use them appropriately. If their parents don't instruct them, children won't necessarily figure out that they're supposed to use the toilet for quite some time.

From their point of view, it's not at all obvious why they should use the toilet. Their parents' behavior in this area may confuse them. When a toddler first realizes that bowel movements come out of her body, she's excited by them. When she tells her parents she's made one, they are excited too. She assumes they are interested, as she is, in the object itself. But then they take it, often with a noticeable lack of relish, and throw it down the toilet and flush it away. The attitude of the adult world in general to bathrooms and elimination is also puzzling. What does dirty mean? How can something that comes from her be dirty? Why are some adults secretive about what goes on in the bathroom?

When a child begins to notice her bowel movements and urine, she needs to have clear information about what she's supposed to do. She needs to understand that adults think feces and urine belong in the toilet and don't enjoy seeing them elsewhere.

She also has to want to learn to use the toilet. Using the toilet is a different kind of skill from crawling or picking up blocks. The rewards are more complex and less immediate. Learning to use the muscles in her arms and legs gives a child more power to move out into the world. That means she can gratify her own needs when she feels like it. But why should a child decide to make herself uncomfortable by waiting until she gets to the toilet when she can have a bowel movement whenever and wherever she wants—and get attention from an adult when she does? Since children do not like having a wet wad of material between their legs, being free of diapers is one motivation. But it is not the primary motivation for most children. Most children learn to use the toilet not to gratify their own desires but because they want to be like the adults they care about.

Being more like an adult means learning self-control. The feelings —physical and emotional—of letting go, giving in, holding back, pressure and relief and the act of deliberately choosing are central to learning how to use the toilet. When a child learns to use the toilet, she learns to enjoy denying herself immediate gratification—a very sophisticated pleasure. (They do learn to enjoy it: older children sometimes make a game of seeing how long they can hold their urine in.)

Toilet training, in short, is the first context in which a child is expected to take responsibility for how she expresses internal sensations. Meeting those expectations is a very big step toward growing up.

It's a scary step for many children because children sensibly feel some ambivalence about becoming "big." Taking a step forward means leaving something behind. There are definite advantages to running faster, climbing higher, wearing comfortable underpants with fire trucks on them, and doing it yourself. On the other hand, you have to give up the bottle, follow more rules, and deal with the fact that you are a separate, fragile person and your parents aren't always there to help you out. Most two-year-olds, if they had the words, would probably say they wanted to be big, but only when they felt like it. They have to decide they feel like it before they will use the toilet consistently.

All children do decide to use the toilet a little sooner or a little later. The point is that in order to make that decision, they begin working on a rather emotionally complicated batch of problems. Since by the time a child is nearing two, her parents usually have pretty strong feelings about diapers themselves, toilet training is an emotional business for everyone.

Three aspects of toilet training can be particularly troublesome for parents: telling their child about her body functions, deciding how firmly to make demands on her, and managing to keep reasonably even-tempered themselves.

Many parents let their children come into the bathroom with them. This is probably the simplest way to let a child know about bodies and about what she will be expected to do when she gets older. Children naturally imitate adults, even when they don't understand why the adults behave as they do, because becoming like grown-ups is their job.

But demonstrations are not a good idea unless parents feel relaxed about being naked with their children. Some people prefer privacy when they use the toilet. Others don't mind having a child of the same sex watch them but are uncomfortable exposing themselves in front of a child of a different gender. Women raising sons alone, for example, sometimes feel uneasy about being naked in front of them. And even if they don't, they obviously cannot provide as good a role model in this particular regard as a man. Fathers may get nervous when their daughters stare at their penises or try to touch them—which they do.

If you're uncomfortable having your child keep you company while you use the toilet, don't force yourself to do it; your child will feel uncomfortable too and may be confused by the feeling. You can find other ways to show as well as tell her what she will be doing one day. Picture books can help. A single mother can ask male friends or relatives to show her son what they do in the bathroom. Single fathers with daughters can get help from women friends.

Sexuality comes up in more direct ways during toilet training. The age when children acquire control of their bladder and bowel muscles is also the age when they begin studying the differences between men and women. Some parents tell their children about their genitals earlier, while they are bathing or dressing or changing them, but the subject naturally comes up again, or for the first time, in the course of toilet training. In fact, it would be difficult and confusing to tell your child about using the toilet and not tell her about her genitals. If you're uncomfortable talking about sexual parts with your child, talk the problem over with other adults. Tell your friends how you feel and ask them what they say to their children. Discuss different ways to talk about sexual organs with your spouse. And bear in mind that whatever adults tell them, children have a way of embroidering their own odd explanations of important and mysterious things like body orifices. They need repeated explanations to get the facts straight.

The trickiest question about toilet training, and the one which psychologists discuss most frequently, is how strict parents should be. Should parents set firm rules about what they want the child to do? Praise a child when she uses the potty and scold her when she doesn't? Or should parents just let the child know what they want and let her come around to doing it in her own way?

The right approach for you and your child is probably the approach that suits your particular personalities. By the time your child reaches toilet-training age, you'll probably know her style of learning. Is she a step-by-step learner, or does she play in a seemingly aimless way and then get up one morning and show off a new skill? Does she respond best and seem most relaxed when you are very firm about how you expect her to behave at bedtime and always stick to the same routine, or does she do better when you are more flexible? Is your family more comfortable when you stick to regular daily schedules, or are you more relaxed when you adjust routines to the mood of the day? There's little purpose in approaching toilet training abstractly. It makes more sense to go about it in the way that's easiest for your very individual child.

Whatever method you choose, your child's progress will probably involve lots of stops, steps backward, new starts, and sideways excursions. This is perfectly normal but can nonetheless make adults nutty, especially if all their friends' children seem to pick up using the potty in two weeks. It's easy to get impatient: if she was using the potty regularly last week, why is she using the carpet now? Her behavior can seem willful.

If your child is angry at you or feeling pressured, it's possible she is being willful. More likely her regression is just part of the usual uneven course of learning. Everyone learning a new skill, whether it's an improved tennis backhand, deep breathing, or the pronunciation of the French r, finds it easy one day and hard the next. It takes time to consolidate new abilities. Emotional learning is more roundabout still, and as we have suggested, toilet training involves emotional issues too. Children may sometimes backslide in their toilet training if they become too anxious about pleasing you and doing well (an experience many adults have had in the realm of sexuality). They may also go back to wetting themselves if they are upset or threatened by something else—an illness, a change in routine, the arrival of a sibling—and need to retreat into babyhood for a while. Knowing this is not going to keep you from becoming impatient. If you don't have a placid nature, you will get irritable and probably lose your temper in the course of toilet training. If you start screaming one day, apologize to your child and explain that you were busy or tired and weren't in the mood for changing her.

Adults can control children in many ways, but self-control is something people—with encouragement—have to learn themselves or it isn't self-control. If you feel you are getting too impatient too often, if there is an increase in accidents, if your child is sleeping badly, if you have the feeling your child is wetting or not wetting herself to send you messages, or if there are other signs that one or both of you is under stress, it's probably a good idea to step back for a while. For a few days or a week, let her relieve herself however she wants. By the time she's in kindergarten she will have traded in diapers for society's —and in the most immediate sense this means your—approval. It won't really matter whether it took her six months or eighteen to learn.

We've been looking ahead at some of the things your child will be learning as she moves into her third year of life. But even in her first twenty-four months she is learning a great deal from being changed and sitting on the potty. She is learning about her body and about adults' attitudes to bodies, and she is learning, as she always does, by being with you.

Jennifer isn't yet aware of eliminating, but she has gotten used to the changing ritual and participates in small ways. Alex is madly in love with himself and his own accomplishments, including the production of big bowel movements. Katie knows what toilets are for, but she isn't sure whether she wants to use the potty just now.

◆

J ENNIFER
(Six Months)

"We're home, Jen." Sam puts the bag of groceries on the hall table. Jen, sitting in her green backpack on Carol's back, smiles and raises her arms toward her father. Sam lifts her out of the backpack. Jen reaches up and hits his face. "Ow," Sam says. Jen smiles, her face rounding out like a full moon. "You like that, huh? You like making your dad say 'Ow.'" Sam carries her over to the sofa and props her up against the cushions. "You're getting very good at sitting," he tells her as he unbuttons her yellow sweater.

Carol watches, feeling motherly toward them both. Saturday afternoon has become Sam's time to be with Jennifer, and both her husband and her baby seem to enjoy it thoroughly. "I wouldn't mind taking a nap," Carol tells them, picking up the groceries to take to the kitchen. Jennifer turns her head toward her mother, falling a little forward from her sitting position and catching herself with her hands.

"Sure," says Sam, not looking up. "We'll be fine, won't we, Jennifer? Your mommy is going to take a nap while we play."

Jen is not listening. She is wiggling toward the edge of the couch. Sam puts his hand on her rear to support her. "Wait. You're soaked, aren't you? Let's change your diaper. Then we'll watch the baseball game."

Jen gives a token kick of protest when Sam picks her up, then relaxes in his arms. As Sam walks toward her room, Jen cocks her head to look at the wall sideways.

"There's Froggy," Sam tells her. He turns her so she can look down at a green stuffed animal with a vaguely amphibian shape sitting on the changing table. Jen stares, wiggling as though she needs her whole body to see.

"I'm going to lay you down right here. There you go." Jen reaches for Froggy and begins sucking on his right front leg. She is very still for a few seconds, absorbed in sucking.

Sam pulls off one sock. Jen kicks her leg and looks up at Sam. "Now for the other sock. Ready?" Sam pulls it off. Jen kicks her leg. "Now let's take these wet pants off." Sam pulls the elastic waistband down. Jen arches her back and wiggles. Sam taps the bell mobile above her. Jen turns her head a little to the side. Her eyes follow the slow motion of the bells.

Sam opens her diaper. "You made a B.M. too." Jen coos.

Placing one hand on Jen's tummy, Sam folds up the dirty diaper, steps on the release of the diaper pail, and drops the diaper in. Jen lets go of Froggy and squirms toward the edge of the table to see what is going on.

"Oh no you don't," Sam says. He moves her squarely back into the center of the changing mat and reaches for the box of wipes. Jen's mouth puckers as if she might cry. "Look, Jen," Sam says as he points to the picture of the baby on the box of wipes. "There is a baby just like you."

Jen flails an arm, pushing the box away. Sam wipes her bottom with one of the moistened tissues, puts it down on the table and reaches for another.

In the second he looks away, Jen has reached for the used wipe and is moving it toward her opening mouth.

"No!" says Sam. "That is ucky. Here, play with Froggy." He drops the wipe on the floor beside Jen's wet pants and socks.

Jen begins squirming as Sam finishes wiping her off. "Is it too cold?" he asks. "Be still a minute, it's almost over. Let me just get this new diaper on you and we'll be finished. Where's Froggy, Jen? Froggy says, 'Ribbit, ribbit, ribbit.' "

Jen looks directly into Sam's face and laughs.

Sam bends his head closer to Jen: "Ribbit, ribbit." He closes the diaper. "Okay now, that's better. Come on. I'll put your pants on in the living room."

"We forgot to buy garlic," says Carol, walking into the room. Jen turns to look at her. "How are you two doing?"

"Much better," Sam says, picking his daughter up. "Right, Jen? She was soaked and had a B.M. We just changed her diaper."

Carol walks over to Jen and strokes her face. "Do you feel better now, sweetheart?" Jen coos. She reaches out and grabs a piece of Carol's shirt.

Carol notices the dirty pants and wipes on the floor. When Sam takes care of Jen, he always leaves a trail of debris behind for Carol to pick up. Carol wonders whether she should pick the stuff up now or tell Sam to do it. He and Jen look so cute together and she is so looking forward to a peaceful nap that she decides to just let it go. She pries Jen's finger off her shirt and strokes her head. "Good-bye. I'll see you after my nap, Jen."

OBSERVATIONS

The World of Things

Jen can reach, push, and grasp and is constantly using these skills. When she gets hold of an object, she immediately puts it in her mouth. This is how she learns about things. The used wipe with streaks of excrement was something else to find out about, so Jen wanted to mouth that too. Sam and Carol must make a constant, rather tedious effort to check out everything within Jen's reach to make sure she doesn't mouth anything dangerous.

Jen's lower torso is covered by diapers most of the time. When Sam took her diaper off, she felt the heavy wet feeling go away; she felt the air on her buttocks and between her legs, her father's warm hand on her stomach, and the coolness of the wipe.

The World of People

Jen has learned to recognize voices. When she heard her mother's voice, she turned her head to see Carol walking into the room.

Jennifer knows her father is a different person from her mother. His voice is deeper. His hands are bigger and rougher and feel warmer than Carol's. He strokes her in a different way. He amuses her with funny noises like the frog noise.

Jennifer makes many expressions and noises now. Some of these, like smiling and crying, may be instinctive, but she has already learned that when she does these things, her parents respond in predictable ways. When she cries, they try to make her comfortable.

When she smiles, they smile back. She is discovering that she can communicate.

Ideas and Words

When Jen is in different positions, objects look different to her. She doesn't understand they are the same objects. For example, although Sam pointed down to Froggy when he was holding her over the table, she did not know Froggy would be next to her when he put her down. When Sam took her out of the pack, she saw the sofa from above. She watched it change as Sam lowered her, and then saw the familiar sofa on which she often sits. To Jen, these are different sofas.

Seeing things from different angles fascinates Jen. She likes to turn her head, the way she did when Sam carried her into the bedroom, simply to look at things from another perspective. Jen's experiments with looking will help her understand that objects are the same no matter how she sees them.

Looking and concentrating is hard work for Jen. Sometimes, as when she first started sucking on Froggy's leg, she stops attending to the world and takes a rest.

Jennifer is getting a lot of experience listening to her father's words and sounds. While he was changing her, Sam talked to Jennifer as if she could understand what he was saying. He told her Carol was going to take a nap. He explained what he was going to do next before he took off her wet pants. He called her toy by name. When she was squirming, he made frog noises to distract her. Jen laughed when he said "ribbit" over and over because she noticed that he was repeating the same sound and she anticipated hearing it again. Noticing repetitions and picking out the same words even though they aren't pronounced precisely alike are skills she will use later as she learns to understand and make words.

Sense of Self

Jen can sit, wiggle, turn her head, follow things with her eyes, reach, grasp, hold her bottle, bat things, smile and frown. She already has many resources which let her interact with the world and people around her.

For Jen, being changed was an opportunity to use her new skills to feel her body and examine the things around her. She felt the wipe, tried to wiggle to the end of the changing table, arched and squirmed as Sam touched her. She also used her communicative skills. When Sam made noises, she made noises back. When he reached to pick her up, she lifted her arms toward him. Sam encouraged Jen's participation. He explained what he was going to do. He warned her before he moved her. She didn't understand the words he was saying, but she realized he was addressing her and she paid attention. Jen is learning she can trust her parents to let her know when they are going to move or touch her.

♦

ALEX
(Fifteen Months)

"Mommy!" Mike calls. "Mommy!"

Rita is in the bathroom sorting laundry from the hamper. She puts the colored clothes on the changing table, the whites in a basket on the floor. "What is it, Mike?" she calls back. "I'm here in the bathroom."

"Alex has a stinky poop."

Rita sighs. "Can you bring him here to me? Alex, come with Mike down to the bathroom."

Mike comes into the bathroom holding his nose with one hand and leading Alex with the other. An ill-smelling cloud wafts from Alex, who looks up at Rita and smiles.

"Thanks, Mike," Rita says, taking a white shirt from the hamper and putting it in the basket. "You've got a good sniffer." She strokes Mike's cheek. "You're a big help. You know that?"

Alex tries to look in the open hamper. It is too high.

"He stinks," Mike says. "I'm getting out of here."

"Okay, honey, I'll see you later."

Alex squats down, reaches into the laundry basket and pulls out the white shirt. He drops the shirt in the hamper. "No, Alex," Rita fishes the shirt out again, puts it back in the basket, and quickly pushes the basket out into the hall.

When she turns back, Alex is taking apart the potty seat she brought into the bathroom the week before, wistfully thinking Alex might at least get used to seeing it around. Alex, sitting on the floor, has taken out the bowl and is turning the plastic seat upside down.

"I wish you knew what that was for," Rita says. She clears off the changing table and turns to Alex. "We're going to change your diaper." She soaps up a washcloth, then puts her hands under Alex's armpits and raises him to a standing position. He kicks. "I have to get at your diaper, honey." She peeks in. "I'm sorry, that's a big poop. You're going to have to lie down for this one."

Rita lifts Alex—he's getting pretty heavy—and lays him flat on the table. "Whew," she says. "Mike was right." Alex begins squirming and starts to sit up. Rita places her hand gently on Alex's belly. "Please," Rita tells him, "lie still and let Mommy change you. She doesn't like this either." He quiets down, watching Rita's face as she talks. "The day you start using your potty chair, we'll have a real party. I'm going to take off your shorts first and put them right here in the laundry."

Rita tears open the tape on Alex's diaper and reaches for a wipe. "Ar-aaahahah," Alex says, sitting up. He picks up a handful of excrement. "Pooh," he says, squishing it between his fingers and rubbing his hand on his thigh.

The tuna fish casserole she ate for dinner does a high jump in Rita's stomach. "Ick," she says with true disgust. Alex looks up at her. Rita swallows, looks away for a second, and breathes hard. "Relax," she tells herself. "Don't think about it."

"It's okay," Rita explains as her stomach settles. "It's just that you are such a mess." Alex reaches for her with the dirty hand. "No, Alex." Rita pulls back. "Lie down." Carefully avoiding his embrace, Rita pushes Alex gently back down and cleans his hand with the wipe. He starts squirming and trying to get up again. Rita holds him down with one arm while she wipes the excrement from his bottom and thighs with the clean edge of the diaper. She folds the diaper up, puts it on the edge of the sink, and takes a handful of wipes. Alex has sat up again and is turning to lower himself off the table. "No, Alex." Rita lifts him back on the table and wipes his hands again. "Now lie back again, that's right." She wipes off his rear. Alex giggles.

"Just another minute." Holding him down, Rita grabs the washcloth and scrubs Alex's bottom and thighs. "Okay. There you go." Rita drops the cloth in the sink and helps Alex down. "Now give me your hands." Rita gives them a final scrub in the sink.

"Bay, bay," says Alex, pointing to the picture of the baby on the box of diapers under the sink.

"That's right," says Rita. "There's a baby just like you. Now stand still."

Rita kneels down and puts the diaper on Alex, who for once stands obligingly still. "There you go. Now do you want to dump your poop in the toilet?"

He stares at her. "Pooh," he repeats.

Rita lifts the toilet seat up, then gingerly opens the used diaper. "Alex, do you want to dump your poop into the toilet?"

Alex makes a grab for the diaper. "No, honey." Rita lifts it out of reach. "Come here." She walks to the toilet. "We're going to turn it upside down and drop the poop in." She squats down and guides Alex's hand so he is holding one end of the diaper. She keeps her hand on top of his. "Ready? One, two, three." There is a splash. Alex looks down into the bowl and grins.

OBSERVATIONS

The World of Things

Alex learns about things by touching them. Textures interest him. Like many children, he wants to touch his excrement the way he wants to touch everything else. Since it is connected to him, he naturally wants to learn about it.

The World of People

Most parents of small children have frequent close encounters with excrement, vomit, and spittle, and many parents at some time or another feel disgusted, as Rita did today. Rita had to turn away to overcome her repulsion. Alex didn't notice: he was busy enjoying himself and Rita recovered quickly. If Rita had been unable to relax, Alex might have sensed from her way of moving and touching him that something was wrong.

Though Alex now anticipates the ritual of being changed and participates actively when he feels like it, he didn't particularly feel like it today.

Ideas and Words

Alex understands simple commands like "Come" and "Lie still." He points, gestures, babbles, and says a few words to communicate.

Alex is learning that when he has a bowel movement, he is changed, but it will be quite a while before he thinks to alert one of his parents when he needs a fresh diaper. And though he has logged a lot of bathroom time watching Mike and his parents sit on the toilet, he hasn't yet figured out what the potty seat is for. To him, it is just an object to be taken apart and examined.

Alex likes some textures and doesn't like others, but he has no concept of dirtiness. He doesn't classify things as dirty or clean, disgusting or not disgusting. He didn't realize Rita was disgusted by his excrement and that Mike hated the smell. Eventually, Alex will notice that everyone in his family thinks certain things are disgusting and he will probably begin to think these things are disgusting too.

Sense of Self

Rita knows Alex can't help having big bowel movements and doesn't understand that she doesn't like excrement. She did her best not to show her disgust and make him feel bad.

Being forced to lie still on the changing table made Alex very uncomfortable. He doesn't like being physically controlled by others. Rita knew Alex wouldn't like lying down. She explained to him why she had to put him on the changing table instead of changing him standing up. She didn't give Alex a choice about what he would do, but she acknowledged his desire to be up and exploring. Though Alex couldn't understand every word Rita said, by talking to him Rita made the changing something they were doing together, not something she was doing to him.

◆

KATIE
(Twenty-eight Months)

"Mommy! Mommy!" Katie calls, walking down the hallway dragging Franklin, the scruffy stuffed dog, on the floor behind her. She is wearing a tee shirt and diaper. "Mommeee!"

"I'm here, Katie. In the bathroom."

The bathroom door is open a crack. Katie pushes it open. Sarah is sitting on the toilet reading a magazine. Katie reaches up for the doorknob, pulls the door shut, then opens it again. She walks over to Sarah and rubs her hand across Sarah's bare thigh.

"What is it, sweetheart? I told you I was going to the bathroom."

"My too," says Katie. Whatever had been on her mind before has vanished.

"Why don't you go see what Daddy is doing?" Sarah halfheartedly suggests. She had been looking forward to sitting on the toilet as a chance for a few minutes alone.

"No, my too." Katie drops Franklin on the floor and reaches under the sink to pull out her white plastic potty seat.

"Watch out. Don't bump your head," says Sarah, spreading her hand out between Katie's head and the sink.

Katie, wearing her diaper, sits on her potty seat at Sarah's feet and smiles. "Magazine, please," she says. Sarah hands her one.

Katie turns the pages. She stops to look at one of the photographs. "House," she says.

Sarah puts her own magazine on the toilet tank and reaches over for some toilet paper. Katie drops her magazine on Franklin.

"My too," she says, standing up and beginning to pull toilet paper off the roll.

"Whoa. That's enough paper, Katie. I only need a little bit of paper to wipe myself." Sarah takes a piece of paper from Katie.

"Mommy wipe jina," comments Katie.

"No," says Sarah. "Mommy is wiping her B.M. hole in the back. She doesn't want B.M. in her vagina. Remember I told you. The hole where the B.M. comes from is in back of the vagina. The vagina is where babies come out of their mommy's bodies when they are born. You have to wipe the B.M. hole from the front to back so you don't get any B.M. in your vagina."

Katie is rolling a sheet of toilet paper into a ball.

Sarah stands up and begins pulling up her underpants.

Katie takes a long look into the toilet bowl. "Mommy make B.M.," she says.

"Yes."

"Big one," Katie observes.

Sarah sighs. She doesn't enjoy this close scrutiny.

"Katie flush," Katie says. She pulls down the toilet handle with both hands. *"Bye."* She waves to the swirling whoosh of flushing water. When it is gone, she flushes again.

"Do you have to go too?" Sarah asks without expecting much of a response. Last week Katie was using her potty regularly, but for the last two days she has strongly protested any suggestion that she sit on the potty seat without a diaper. *"I can help you take off your diaper so you can make a B.M. in your potty seat just like I did."*

"Okay," says Katie.

Sarah moves quickly to undo Katie's diaper before the opportunity passes. Katie sits down on the potty. Nothing happens for a few seconds. Sarah tries not to stare. Then Katie grunts. *"My make B.M.!"* Katie says. She looks up wide-eyed at Sarah.

Sarah claps. *"Good girl,"* she says. Katie claps too.

"Here," says Sarah, handing Katie a piece of toilet paper. *"Now you can wipe yourself. Remember, wipe from the front to the back just like Mommy does."* Katie wipes herself and looks at her mother for approval.

"That was good," Sarah says, giving Katie an extra wipe to be sure. *"Let's put a new diaper on you."* Katie stands while Sarah fastens the diaper around her. *"Now do you want to flush your B.M. down the toilet?"*

"Yes!" Katie bends down to take the pot out. She can't get a grip on the edge. Sarah shifts impatiently, fighting the impulse to take over.

Katie starts to tip the seat but realizes that will be a mistake. Finally she gets the pot out and, holding it carefully, walks to the toilet. Sarah bends over and takes hold of the pot too.

"No," Katie says, pulling away. *"My do."*

"It's too high for you to do alone," Sarah says. *"Let's do it together."* Katie hugs the pot tightly and steps away from Sarah. She raises the pot. Without saying anything, Sarah reaches over and helps Katie turn it upside down. Katie watches her bowel movement slide and splash with deep interest.

Using both hands, she reaches up and pulls the toilet handle down. "Bye," she says, waving at her bowel movement as it swooshes away. When the water stops moving, she flushes again.

◆

OBSERVATIONS

The World of Things

Katie practices making delicate movements when she plays with toilet paper: she has learned to roll and twist sections and to rip off individual sheets. She is also practicing using doorknobs.

Katie is fascinated by toilet paper and everything else that has to do with bathrooms and toilets. She especially likes flushing the toilet and rarely flushes it just once, unless her parents pull her away.

The World of People

Katie watches and imitates the way adults act. She knows what she is supposed to do with the potty. She likes pretending she is doing it. She has copied her parents' behavior down to turning the pages of the magazines she "reads" as she sits on her potty seat. She knows that it makes her parents happy when she makes a bowel movement on the potty instead of in her diaper. But she has mixed feelings about doing it.

Sarah and Joe are anxious to get Katie out of diapers before the new baby arrives, but they decided not to make an issue of her abrupt retreat from the potty. Sarah has found that insisting her daughter do something usually makes Katie refuse to do it more stubbornly. On the other hand, Sarah knows that Katie eventually comes around to doing whatever pleases her and Joe.

Ideas and Words

Katie can turn the pages of a magazine by herself and become absorbed looking at pictures. This is an early step toward reading.

Katie was practicing using the potty today even when she sat on it in her diaper. She realizes that sitting on the potty wearing a diaper is not the same thing as using it. But to her, sitting on the seat and opening a magazine are an important part of using the potty too. She is toilet training herself by imitating all her parents' bathroom behavior.

Katie says good-bye to everyone and everything including her excrement. It's her way of trying to understand separation. Saying good-bye gives Katie some control over what is happening.

Sarah has been teaching Katie to wipe from front to back in order to avoid bringing bacteria into contact with her vagina and urinary tract. She explained that girls and women wipe themselves this way to take good care of their bodies. She told Katie where bowel movements come from, and where babies come from. Sarah's explanation was a bit too detailed for Katie. Katie stopped trying to follow and began rolling toilet paper into a ball. But Sarah was at least letting Katie know that her body is something they can talk about together.

Sarah and Joe discussed what words to teach Katie for her body parts and products. They settled on using *pee* and *B.M.* and *vagina*. These are the words they feel comfortable with, so they are the right ones for them to use with Katie.

Sense of Self

Katie wants to be a baby and a big girl. Unfortunately, this is impossible. Wanting opposite things at the same time affects her attitude to the toilet and everything else she is learning now. She was being a big girl with Sarah in the bathroom and enjoying it, but during the previous two days she had preferred being changed like a baby.

Katie took her stuffed dog, Franklin, into the bathroom with her today. Since she was about a year old, Katie has been carrying Franklin with her everywhere. His presence reassures her. Her dependency on him isn't babyish, it's helping her become more grown-up. She has taken some of the feelings of warmth and security she gets from her relationship with Joe and Sarah and attached them to Franklin. She can comfort herself independently of her parents by keeping Franklin near her. Eventually, she will be able to carry the feeling of connection inside herself without the help of a special object. When that time comes Franklin will probably be exiled to the bureau.

Part Three

---◆---

HOUSEHOLD CHORES

7

PREPARING AND EATING DINNER

Dinner is family life's center of gravity: it pulls everyone in from the separate worlds of work and school and holds them together for an expansive hour of confidences and arguments, laughter and quarrels. Unless, of course, the household includes a child under three. A small child can effortlessly turn dinner into an exhausting struggle against the forces of chaos.

Parents of small children have different dinnertime strategies. Some feed their child separately, waiting until she's safely stashed away in the crib to prepare and savor a disaster-free meal for themselves. Some like to have their child with them at dinner as soon as she's old enough to sit up. If she's too small to actually eat with the adults, they feed her first and then let her watch from a high chair while they cook and eat themselves. Others improvise, figuring the main point is to get everyone fed, together or separately. One night they may prepare a big meal for the whole family; the next, dinner will be slapdash, one by one, out of the carton and onto the kitchen table.

The best way to deal with the evening meal depends on what's important to you. If you see dinner as an oasis of serenity in a busy day or look forward to having time alone with your spouse, you'll want to feed your child separately. If dinner is not a special family time in your household, you may choose to provide something nourishing in the most convenient way possible. If you relish having everyone you love together at the end of the day—even if the smallest person you love makes collages on the table with her vegetables, gets bored and starts squirming to get down before you're done, or won't let you talk without interrupting—you'll want to have your child eat with you.

Even if you prefer keeping dinner an adult affair, try to invite your child to join you at the dinner table once in a while: it will be a special occasion for her. When you give your child food, you're not only giving her physical nourishment: by taking care of her in this basic way you're giving her love she feels directly, with her body. You're giving her emotional nourishment too. Your physical presence, the joy of being with you, of receiving something needed and pleasurable from you, is part of what dinner is for her. When she eats not only with you but with your spouse and her siblings, the occasion is even richer. Sharing food with all of you together gives her direct experience of the social and emotional connections that make you a family. It also gives her an opportunity to listen to the patterns of sounds you make when you talk together and to begin to participate (even if her participation is disruptive) in the dinnertime news reports that keep your individual lives tied together.

Very small babies need help to eat. By nine months or so they begin to feed themselves, but they still need moment-by-moment supervision. They are learning to use a spoon or a cup but tend to treat them as toys. When they get serious, they use their hands. They like seeing all the different things they can do with their fingers and feeling different textures by mushing, squooshing, smearing, and flinging food around. If you're fainthearted, you may have to allow yourself some recovery time between feeding the baby and having your own dinner. When you do sit down to eat, let her join you in her chair. Older toddlers and twos can feed themselves well enough to eat along with you. Being with everyone they love all at once makes them happy (and they don't like being left out).

Your child will also enjoy being involved in the preparations that precede dinner. Most children like spending time with their parents in the kitchen. They are delighted by the procession of changing smells and temperatures that accompany cooking and by the drama of culinary creation.

Watching you cook can be your child's first encounter with skilled work and applied science: the systematic transformation of one thing into another. Cans, jars, boxes, bags are opened; their contents shaken, poured, scooped out into pots, pans, bowls, cups, food processors; then cut, heated, blended, mixed, and stirred. Different kinds of objects—cloths, mats, napkins, plates, forks, knives, spoons, glasses, cups, and bowls—are placed on top of each other or side by side on the table.

Though infants lack the physical and mental skills to actively participate in the dinner preparation, they enjoy looking, listening, and smelling. Toddlers can actively help with dinner preparation and they like to. They sometimes make their own work for themselves in the kitchen, deciding to put all the pots together in a pile, for example, or pulling out everything on the bottom shelf. But even though they don't intellectually understand the distinction between their games and necessary tasks, they sense when they are being given an opportunity to do genuine work. They will appreciate an assignment. Assuming you're in a patient mood and have time to be involved, you can ask your child to snap beans, stir, wipe up something that's spilled, carry a package. You'll have to finish up for her, of course, but she'll have a good time and feel proud she really helped.

Setting the table is a particularly good first job. A small child obviously shouldn't be allowed to carry sharp knives, but even a new walker can handle napkins without hurting himself or destroying a whole room. Toddlers have the basic skills for carrying and placing objects, and they like to practice them. The job gives twos an introduction to trickier skills they'll be interested in a little later on: for example, folding and placing things symmetrically. As they get older they will also explore ideas through table setting. The task involves concepts that children work with when they begin reading, such as right- and left-handedness, arrangement, and order. Finally, setting the table and eating with adults are among a child's first encounters with social conventions. There's no logical reason why we eat soup before meat, or why we place the fork on the left and not on the right—but with or without rhyme or reason, social activities are ordered by rules.

Your baby certainly isn't going to grasp all of this the first time you hand her a napkin to place on the table. The napkin may end up crumpled on the floor. Children's ways of helping often amount to getting in the way. They will bang pots and pans in your ears, reach for sharp knives just when a pot is boiling over, and get food all over the floor. There will be times when keeping your child out of the kitchen makes sense. If you're grumpy or in a hurry, see that she stays out of provoking range. Ask your spouse to cook or to keep the baby out of the kitchen while you do. If that's not possible, put the baby in her playpen or find a toy that will keep her attention for a while. But even if helping you prepare dinner is a once-in-a-while event, your child will learn from it and enjoy it. Cooking, setting the table, and eating are jobs with enough different components to provide her with learning material for many, many months, as Jennifer, Alex, and Katie will illustrate.

Jennifer is learning to hold a spoon and works hard smearing her carrots. Alex can carry things to the table. Katie is already an old hand at table setting, though her mother will not let her carry anything sharp or easily breakable.

JENNIFER
(Six Months)

A small bit of applesauce hits Carol on the cheek.

"I could get up," Carol thinks, "walk out of the door, change my name, and move to another city."

Jen, in her high chair, is still waving the spoon, flinging more applesauce around the room and gurgling happily. Her forehead and hair are covered with shiny streaks of applesauce.

Sam is coming home late again.

Carol had felt like staying late too—everyone was going out for drinks to celebrate a big new client—but of course she had to leave. The thought of seeing Jennifer sweetened her disappointment. Then she got home and Jennifer was crotchety, fussed when she held her, and cried when Mrs. Semple left as though Carol didn't matter at all. Now Jen was finally cheering up and getting peppy, tossing in her chair—and making an incredible mess. She had put both hands in the little dish of carrots and rubbed the orange stuff all over the tray. Then she'd snatched the applesauce spoon from Carol.

Jennifer reaches the spoon awkwardly toward the bowl of applesauce to do it again. Seized by a masochistic impulse, Carol moves the bowl close to her daughter. Jen digs in, holding the spoon at a 45-degree angle, and shovels applesauce onto the tray. She smooshes the applesauce on the tray with the back of the spoon. She sticks the fingers of her left hand in the smoosh and then takes them, more or less, to her mouth. She sucks her fingers happily. Applesauce overflows the corners of her lips.

The pale pink applesauce and orange carrots do look sort of pretty together, Carol notices. What the hell, she thinks, let Sam clean up for a change. Carol gets another spoon and makes three little piles of mashed carrots along the tray, smoothing the sides to make neat cones. Then she puts three small oval mounds of applesauce in between. Jen watches her, giggling and cooing.

"There," Carol says. "Mess that."

Jen does, slapping both hands down on the piles, rubbing everything back and forth. When she is done, she lifts her hands and waves them, sending particles of food onto herself, Carol, and the floor. One neat hunk of orange goo even makes it four feet away to the refrigerator. Jen laughs.

"You've got a good pitching arm," Carol tells her daughter. She gets up and takes a graham cracker from a box on the counter. "How about a cracker?" She hands the cracker to Jen. Still holding the spoon with her right hand, Jen grabs the cracker with her left. She brings it to her mouth and sucks on it. A large, saliva-moistened piece crumbles and falls onto the tray, but she succeeds in eating most of the cracker.

Carol pours some milk into a cup. Jen sucks bits of wet cracker off her fingers. "Do you want to try a cup now?" Carol asks. "I'll give you your bottle later."

Jen looks up at her and flashes her a puffy-cheeked grin. "Gabaha," she says. Carol carefully brings the cup toward her mouth. Jen lets go of the spoon and reaches both hands to touch the cup too. Carol holds the tiny hands in place. Jen takes a sip, acquiring a milk mustache. Carol tilts the cup against her mouth again, but Jen squirms, arches back, and with a sudden jerky motion pushes the cup away. A stream of white liquid tumbles out and splashes on the tray. Jen giggles with happiness at the sound.

Carol looks at the white liquid threading its way through the carrot and applesauce valleys. "Ugh!" she says. Then she begins laughing too. She puts a finger in the mashed food and rubs it over her upper lip. "How do I look with a mustache, Jen?"

Jen coos and reaches a hand toward her mother's face. "How about a carrot kiss?" Carol leans toward her daughter. Jen pats Carol's cheek, depositing more applesauce.

"Thank you." Carol dips a finger in again and draws a line of applesauce down her daughter's nose. Jen crinkles her nose and starts pushing everything on the tray to the floor. Carol lets her finish this task.

"Well, Sticky, maybe we should take a bath. What do you think?"

OBSERVATIONS

The World of Things

Jen now has sufficient manual control to play with food. She can pick it up, press it, squoosh it, throw it, and spread it. She can hold a spoon too, but she plays with it instead of treating it as a feeding tool. She can feed herself, however, if she uses her fingers. Tonight she ate applesauce off her hand and fed herself a cracker.

Jen used both her right and left hand equally (she will begin favoring one of her hands around the age of one). She is already beginning to use her hands separately. She held the cracker with one hand while still clutching the spoon with the other.

Jen mouths everything she touches. She uses her lips and tongue and gums not just to taste but also to feel different textures. Now that she is learning to use her hands more skillfully, she has become interested in distinguishing textures with her fingers too. Today she played with the applesauce and the baby carrots, which were mushy, the hard cracker, which grew soft as she gummed it, and the liquid milk.

The World of People

Carol finds Jen's eating habits rather revolting. To keep her composure and to keep her household in reasonable order, Carol usually tries to keep Jen from making too much of a mess with dinner. Sometimes she tolerates a bit of food play, but she almost never plays herself. Tonight she had a quirky, uncharacteristic impulse not only to let Jen play with her food, but to join in. She set up neat piles of applesauce for Jen to destroy, put a food mustache on herself, and gave Jen some applesauce makeup. Carol enjoyed herself; it was relaxing to stop worrying about keeping things in control and to be a little childish herself.

Ideas and Words

Carol's behavior tonight will not encourage bad manners. Jen is far too young to understand what manners are about or even to realize that there are different ways of eating.

For Jen, feeding herself, playing with food, and being close to Carol were all part of having dinner. She didn't distinguish the purpose—eating—from all the other activities.

Sense of Self

Jennifer is getting bolder and more active. Her new abilities to mash food, reach out and touch her cup, shovel with a spoon, and fling things off the table are making mealtime a different, less passive experience for Jennifer. Most important, Jen is learning to feed herself. She can eat, a little anyway, with her fingers. She is beginning, literally, to take her welfare into her own hands.

◆

ALEX
(Fifteen Months)

Robert is in the living room watching the news. Mike is on the living-room floor playing with his Transformer toy. Rita is in the kitchen making spaghetti and meatballs. Alex is sitting on the kitchen floor pulling cans of tuna fish and cat food out of the lower shelf of the cabinet. Barney, the cat, is sitting near Alex, staring at the bowl of spaghetti sauce on the counter.

Alex crawls over to the garbage pail with a tuna fish can, stands up, and drops it in. He toddles back, kneels down, picks up another can and carries it to the garbage. He makes a happy, gurgling sound as it falls in.

"No, honey," Rita says, going over and putting her arm around him, "let's not put the cans in the garbage . . . Barney! You fur-faced creep!" Rita leaps up to rescue the meatballs. Barney retreats delicately under the table. Alex drops another can in the garbage. "Listen," Rita says, feeling around in the garbage with her forearm, "would you like to help me set the table?"

Alex looks up at her, smiles, then turns back to the cans. He makes one roll. "Ca," he says, watching the can.

"Mike!" Rita calls. "It's time to set the table."

Mike trots in. "Mi," Alex says. He puts the can down and uses both hands to push himself up. Then bends down to pick up a can and walks over to Mike.

"Alex, would you like to help Mike and me set the table? You can put the napkins down."

Alex holds the can up to show Mike. "Put it away," Mike says. He reaches for a stack of plates on the counter.

Rita bends down and ties Alex's shoelaces. "Give me the can." She holds out her hand. "Thank you, Alex." She puts the can back on its shelf and hands Alex a small pile of napkins. "Here, you take the napkins, honey," Rita says. "Mike, please show him how."

Mike, bearing plates, confidently assumes leadership. "Come on, Alex," he orders, starting toward the dining alcove. Alex hurries after him, using his pigeon-toed trot. He holds the napkins carefully out in front of him. "Good boy," Rita says. Alex steps onto the rug, starts toppling, and catches his balance.

Rita is pouring the spaghetti into the colander when Alex shrieks. Since it is a shriek of indignation, not pain, she finishes pouring the boiling water before running out. "Where the hell is Robert?" she thinks. "Why doesn't he get up and do something?"

Rita finds Alex protectively clutching a shredded napkin. "He's messing it up," Mike complains. "He was ripping it up and dropping it all over."

Rita looks down: there is indeed a pile of shredded napkin at Alex's feet. "Yeah, it's a mess," Rita says, patting Alex on the back. "He's just a baby, so we have to be patient with him. Would you show him again?"

Mike hesitates, torn between the impulse to strike back at injustice and the desire to be mature.

"Alex, give me the napkin," Rita says. He hands over the mutilated paper. "Thank you." She stuffs it in her jeans pocket. "Where are the others, Mike?"

"Here." Mike has put them in the center of the table out of Alex's reach. He takes one. "Here, Alex," he says, opting for partnership with the adult world. Alex makes a grab for it. Mike holds it out of reach. "No!" he complains. "You fold it." He demonstrates. Alex looks at him, then tries to reach up to the table. The table is too high. Alex whimpers.

"I'll tell you what, Mike," Rita says. "I'll finish up here. Why don't you guys go get Daddy."

"Da," Alex says, perking up again.

"Come on." Mike holds out his hand. Alex takes it, and they go toward the living room. Alex watches his feet with deep interest as he walks.

When they are a few feet from the couch, Alex lets go of Mike and runs over to Robert. "Hi." Robert rubs his head. Alex clambers up on the couch, facing the TV like his father. He giggles. "How's it going?" Robert asks Mike, trying to listen to the TV at the same time. Alex hits the cushion on either side of him with his fist. It makes a gentle poof.

"Dinner's ready," Mike says.

"Okay." Robert eyes the anchorman one last time. Alex climbs onto Robert's lap and squirms against his chest.

"Want a ride?" Robert scoops Alex up. Alex giggles, then grows very quiet looking around from his elevated perch. Robert puts his hand on Mike's shoulder and they walk into the dining room. Rita is carrying the salad in. Barney is rubbing her legs hungrily.

"Smells good," Robert says. Alex looks down at the cat. Holding his son with one hand, Robert pulls the high chair over with the other. "There you go." He puts Alex in.

"Mike, you want to give me a hand with the milk?" Rita asks.

Alex cranes his head to see what Rita and Mike are doing. Robert picks a *piece of carrot out of the salad and eats it. "Here." He picks out another piece and gives it to Alex. Alex examines it.*

Alex starts bouncing and babbling in his chair when he sees Mike and Rita coming back. Mike hands Alex the cup with the balloons in it. He holds his own cup (dinosaurs) out to Rita, who is carrying a pitcher of milk and a basket of bread. "Can I have some milk?"

"Sit down first, Mike," Robert says. Mike sits. Rita sits too.

Alex holds out his cup the way Mike does.

OBSERVATIONS

The World of Things

Alex is constantly experimenting with objects to build up a mental picture of the physical world. He is fascinated by the way one object can fit into another. Today he experimented with putting tuna fish cans into the garbage pail.

Alex trips easily, partly because his coordination is still unsure, partly because he isn't good at estimating the space between himself and objects, partly because he doesn't yet know how to steer his course and think about something else at the same time. When he walked into the living room, he could easily have bumped into a piece of furniture. He was too busy watching his feet move to pay attention to obstacles in his path. When he was heading into the dining room he was concentrating on the napkins in his hand and almost tripped on the rug. He righted himself quickly, which he usually manages to do. Rita deliberately gave Alex napkins to carry because napkins wouldn't break and hurt him if he did fall.

The World of People

Alex senses that his mother values certain activities, like setting the table, more than others. He responded readily when Rita asked him to help and he obediently followed Mike around. He is learning that people work together to get jobs done. He is also learning that the people who work together sometimes quarrel but can make up, as he and Mike did tonight with Rita's help.

One of the ways Alex learns and tries to help is to imitate the people he loves. Since he doesn't realize the purpose of grown-up work, his efforts aren't always helpful. For example, when Rita was in the kitchen taking things out of cabinets and throwing empty packages away, Alex joined in by throwing the tuna fish cans in the garbage. It probably seemed to Alex that he was preparing dinner along with Rita.

Alex loves everyone in his family. He was happy to go into the living room and find Robert. When Rita and Mike left Alex and Robert alone in the dining room, Alex twisted around to see where they went. When they returned he was bouncy and excited, obviously pleased to have everyone gathered together.

Ideas and Words

Rita and Mike are trying to introduce Alex to a new concept about the relationships among things: order and arrangement. Napkins go in the same place at each setting. Alex doesn't realize yet that forks, plates, and napkins each belong in certain positions. He doesn't understand folding either. But seeing the set table every day from his high chair is one of the experiences that will help him develop ideas about order and shape as he grows older.

This evening and every evening, Alex learns a little more about language. He sees that people use language to communicate when they do things together. Though he says only a few words clearly, he does understand quite a bit of what is being said. He can sense, even when he doesn't know the words, the difference between questions, requests, commands, and explanations. He understands, for example, that when Mike says, "Come on," Mike wants him to follow.

Sense of Self

By giving Alex the opportunity to help her, Rita is telling him that he is a valuable member of the family. Tonight she gave him a special job of his own, carrying the napkins. He didn't understand what the job was, but that didn't matter. Working on his own special assignment alongside his brother and mother made Alex feel capable and important.

The only time Alex sees his father, mother, and brother all together on a regular basis is at the dinner table. Being with them every night at dinner is helping him to learn what it means to be a member of a family.

KATIE
(Twenty-eight Months)

Joe is humming along to a reggae tune on the radio, placing pieces of a roasting chicken in the baking pan on the downbeat. "Look!" Katie orders. Joe looks obediently. His daughter raises her arms above her head as though she were holding a giant beach ball, takes three precarious steps on tiptoe, catches her balance in a squat, and then goes off on tiptoe again. "Dancing," Katie explains.

Joe leaves the chicken to execute a clumsy cabriole. Katie giggles. "Show Mommy," she says, heading toward the kitchen door with neat little steps. Joe scoops her up. "No, Nutmeg, Mommy is resting, remember? You and I are going to make dinner tonight."

"No," Katie says. "No make dinner."

"Okay," Joe tells her, "you play while I cook." He turns back to the stove. Katie walks over to the kitchen table, reaches for an apple, and throws it on the floor. When her father doesn't react, she takes another apple and throws it down, too.

"Katie," Joe says. He picks up the apples, sits down, and pulls his daughter on his lap. "Calm down, will you?"

"No," Katie pouts.

"Do you want to help me make dinner?"

"No."

"Do you want to play by yourself?"

"No."

"What do you want?"

Katie squirms. She can't think of an answer.

"You don't know what you want, do you?" Joe says. He starts to tickle her, then realizes too late that he's made a big mistake. Katie is already overexcited. Now she's twisting and jumping like a puppy. Giggling, she escapes from his arms and clambers down, then crawls over, tugs on his sweater, and pulls her hand back suddenly, inviting him to catch her. Joe goes into the living room instead. He returns with her blocks.

"Here," he says. "Why don't you build a big apartment house? And I'll cook."

Katie, to Joe's relief, reaches for the blocks, and concentrates on them long enough for him to get the chicken into the oven. But when he starts washing the lettuce, she pushes her blocks away, scattering them around the floor.

"My want to—" she says.

"No, Nutmeg."

Katie pulls her chair over to the sink and climbs up, trying to reach past her father to the faucet.

"Katie, you're going to fall—"

"Hi." Sarah comes into the kitchen. She looks peaked.

"Mommy!" Katie yells, her tone a little accusatory. She scrambles down from the chair, trips, and screws up her face, not sure whether to cry. Sarah scoops her up. "Hello, darling."

Katie clings to her. "Mommy!" she says again, as though it were Sarah's fault she tripped.

"I'm sorry I couldn't play with you," Sarah explains. "I wasn't feeling well."

Sarah wishes she could explain that she is feeling very tired and that because of the pregnancy she can't take a pill for her headache. She can't explain because they haven't told Katie or anybody else yet.

Sarah strokes Katie's hair. "We've got to tell her soon," she thinks.

"How do you feel?" Joe asks, slicing potatoes.

"Exhausted. My head feels a little better. I just wish there was some way I could nap during the day."

Katie starts squirming in Sarah's arms. She wants Sarah to stop talking to Joe and just pay attention to her. Sarah tries to quiet her with a soothing pat. "Let me talk to Daddy for a few minutes," she says. "I think what's tiring me out," she tells Joe, "is feeling so moody."

"Look," says Joe, "maybe we should reconsider your taking a leave of absence. We could figure out a way to manage it."

"I'll lose the job," Sarah says. "I'll be able to get away with a few months after the—afterward. But they won't give me a year's leave. Besides, if it's like the last time, I'll feel better in a few weeks."

"Mommy!" Katie hits Sarah.

"Don't hit me," Sarah says. "Why don't you kiss me instead?"

Katie whimpers and hides her face against Sarah's shoulder. Sarah kisses her. "Come, we'll set the table together, okay?"

"No," Katie says, clinging harder.

Sarah sighs. She puts Katie down and starts getting out napkins, place mats, glasses, and silver to take into the dining room. Katie reaches for a glass. Sarah has a vision of the little hand bleeding and broken glass on the floor. "No, honey, don't touch that." She quickly moves the glass away. Defiantly, Katie reaches for another glass and manages to wrap her fingers around it. Sarah unpries them. "Here. You do the napkins."

"No," Katie says.

"Yes," Sarah says.

Katie grabs the napkins and starts flinging them on the floor one by one.

"Stop it!" Sarah shrieks.

Katie stops dead and stares at her mother. Sarah looks at the small, frightened face and bursts into tears. She sits down.

Katie crouches, very still. Then she timidly walks over. "Mommy," she says, hugging Sarah's knees. "Mommy." Katie begins crying too. Sarah strokes her hair, her own sobs fading.

◆

OBSERVATIONS

The World of Things

Katie is becoming adept at using tools. She likes to handle things the way her parents do. Tonight, for example, she wanted to turn on the faucet and wash the lettuce like Joe.

The World of People

Katie wanted to show how grown up she is by doing adult activities like washing the lettuce, dancing, and setting the table. Her repeated noes were another way of asserting she's a big, independent person with power. She stubbornly insisted on doing what she wanted to do. She would not take her parents' no for an answer without testing it first.

Sarah and Joe just wanted to avoid a confrontation tonight. They tried to placate and persuade Katie rather than establishing or insistently enforcing strict limits. Sarah only asserted her authority when Katie picked up the glass. Because Katie could hurt herself or break the glass, limits had to be set.

Katie now has a whole repertoire of social behaviors and is slowly absorbing more information about the relationship between what she does and how adults respond to her. Tonight, for example, she tried to get her parents' attention by being charming, by throwing apples and napkins, by clinging, by calling verbally, and by hitting.

Later, when Katie saw Sarah crying, she went over and hugged her. She may have been imitating the way Sarah behaves when Katie is the one who is upset, or she may have been telling Sarah, "Stop feeling bad and pay attention to me." Katie's behavior doesn't mean she was feeling empathy the way adults do, but she is beginning to learn that other people also have feelings.

As Sarah realized, she and Joe will have to tell Katie about the new baby soon. It's very difficult to keep a secret from a child. Tonight Sarah and Joe discussed the pregnancy in front of Katie, and this will probably happen again. If they don't explain what's going on, Katie will begin to sense that she's being left out of something important and feel anxious.

Katie won't understand exactly what's happening when they tell her. The mechanics of pregnancy will be impossible for her to conceptualize and nine months is almost a mythical time for someone her age. But as her mother's body begins to change and they begin to shop for the baby, the adventure of birth will become more real for her.

Ideas and Words

Katie is becoming aware that language has many complex functions. Tonight she heard her mother talking about how she felt. She has heard her parents talk about their feelings before. She doesn't understand these conversations, but she can hear the emotion in their voices.

Sense of Self

Katie is taking every opportunity to extend her control of her body. Lately she has been working on walking on tiptoe. She has a sense of what it means to perform with her body and be looked at. She learned about dancing from Sarah, who likes to put on records and dance around the house.

Katie likes to be held and stroked, but she also likes rougher touching games, which let her use all her strength to struggle and fight, like the tickling game Joe played with her. As Joe noticed, the tickling game excited her. Gentler touching soothes her.

Katie is experiencing a wide range of feelings that she can't sort out. For example, when Joe asked her what she wanted to do and she didn't know, and later when Sarah told her to kiss, not hit, Katie was clearly uncomfortable. Sometimes, when Sarah and Joe see Katie becoming agitated, they divert her attention as they did tonight. At other times, when Katie seems calmer, they try to give her words for what she might be feeling.

It will be many years before Katie fully realizes that her mother is a completely separate, fallible person, but the process has already started. When something happens that suggests Sarah has needs of her own and feelings that have nothing to do with Katie, Katie is uneasy. Tonight she became very edgy when Sarah wouldn't give her the attention she wanted. Sarah's independence worries Katie because Katie is so deeply dependent on Sarah's love.

Katie's attempts to get attention tonight backfired on her: Sarah yelled at her and then began to cry. Katie began to cry too. Sarah quickly assured her that she still loved her. Katie cannot analyze the experience, of course, but she has had another opportunity—and she will have many more—to see that people who love each other nonetheless get angry with each other. These experiences will make Katie less frightened when she sees other people becoming angry or when she feels angry herself.

8

---◆---

CLEANING THE HOUSE

Presented with the choice of playing with their child, playing with their spouse, snatching a little solitude, or cleaning the house, some parents decide that if they can find what they are looking for within five minutes and nothing sticks to bare fingers or bare feet, the house is clean enough. If a well-tended house is important to your peace of mind, this may be too extreme a compromise, but living with a small child probably will entail compromising your housekeeping standards to some degree. Children are messy, and since they are also time-consuming, parents have less time for cleaning than they did in their childless days. On the other hand, no one wants fungi growing on the rug. Even if you've always felt most at home with the sloppy look, you have to do a certain amount of cleaning, and sometimes you have to do it the slow way, when your child is there with you. Her participation will indubitably make the chore more time-consuming and nerve-jangling—but she will have a lot of fun.

When you clean, you manipulate all the objects and pieces of furniture in the room. You collect things (the things that don't belong) and move things (to clean under them). You may take things your child has never seen down from shelves to dust them. Watching or helping you take the room apart to clean it, then put it back together again gives your child a nice opportunity to make discoveries about the space she lives in and everything it contains. The tools you use to do the cleaning are interesting in themselves. You take out bottles and cans that spray liquid, you turn on a vacuum cleaner that buzzes and can be pushed around, you bring out feather dusters and rags. You open bottles and boxes that fill the room with the smells of bleach, ammonia, lemon, and pine.

Witnessing this activity from a blanket or chair invites a small baby to do one of the things she most enjoys—looking. Babies like looking at spaces from different angles. Most of the time your activities take place at two levels: five or six feet high when you stand and walk, three or four feet above the ground when you sit. But when you clean, you bend down to pick things up from the floor and reach up or even climb ladders to clean walls and cabinets and shelves. Following you with her eyes, your baby sees, literally, new areas of the room. Babies also enjoy focusing on small changes and small movements, and when you clean, you create many pleasing, tiny sights. The surface of a table sparkles when you pour furniture oil on it. A small red rattle emerges from under a pillow. A white rag falls over the TV.

The profusion of sights and sounds and smells can excite your baby. She may get restless watching you without being able to do very much herself and demand that you stop your work and give her your attention. You can put out a supply of interesting objects within her reach to keep her busy touching and mouthing, but you'll still have to be prepared to interrupt what you're doing from time to time to visit with her or keep her from putting something dangerous in her mouth.

By the time they can crawl, most babies will be unhappy staying in a pen while you are moving around the room, but letting a child who can crawl wander freely while you clean is not very practical. The baby will be zipping around, making noises to herself, reaching out to touch everything, including bottles filled with chemicals and the vacuum cleaner plug—and tasting everything she can pick up, including dirty rags and small mysterious things taken from the depths of the carpet. If you're not in a tranquil and patient mood, it's probably wisest to keep her in the frustrating pen (or if the cleaning can be put off, to do it when she is sleeping).

Toddlers can't be confined for long (the wailing would be unbearable), which means you will sometimes, somehow, have to keep an eye on your child and the dirt at the same time. Your toddler will imitate your activities in possibly strange ways and will discover tasks for herself that have some relation to what you're doing but perhaps the opposite effect. A toddler has a notion of moving things to a different place but not of putting them where they belong, of wiping but not of wiping clean. She may end up following you around the room undoing your work as fast as you do it or simply distracting you so much you can't get anything done. If you are collecting scattered toys, old papers, or stray articles of clothing, she will start making piles of her own or undoing yours. She will take a duster or rag, imitate your wiping movements for a while, then start climbing on the furniture or tottering dangerously on the rocking chair so that you have to drop everything and scramble to the rescue. She will pick up and examine all sorts of objects, including the delicate glass vase you took down and the bottle of ammonia. She may start unrolling all the paper towels or overturning the wastebasket you filled up. She might want to use the vacuum cleaner, even though it's too big for her, or try to sit on it when you push it. You can't stop this activity: toddlers are unstoppable. What you can do is steer your child—with words or demonstrations—toward tasks that will keep her safe and out of your way for a while. It may help you retain your good humor to remember that her apparently aimless play is, in its way, profoundly constructive. Your child is using her body to begin important investigations of differences like big/little, tall/short, light/heavy, front/back, wet/dry, right side/wrong side.

Cleaning with two-year-olds about is a little easier. Your two may set out to help you and then detour to empty out and examine all the things in the closet, or to figure out how the spray gun works, or to try the buttons on the vacuum cleaner. But twos can understand verbal instructions (sometimes, and when they choose to). They are aware, though they easily forget, that certain objects belong in certain places. They have a clearer sense than a toddler that there is a difference between play and adult work. And they can really help you. Twos do realize the purpose of very simple chores like wiping up a spill or sweeping up crumbs, and they like to achieve the goal. For them, achieving a goal is a new way of relating to the world.

If you give your two-year-old jobs of her own to do that can be completed in a few minutes, she will become absorbed in the work. She can plump pillows, collect scattered toys, dust something sturdy like shelves of books, bring you something you ask for. Like younger toddlers, she enjoys these activities because they give her a chance to practice physical skills and to manipulate different objects and materials. But the two-year-old's explorations have become more complex. She is asserting and practicing, in some conscious way, her new ability to maneuver spaces and objects in the room as adults do. When you invite her to help, you are showing her you appreciate her new grown-up accomplishments.

Katie helps Sarah change the linen, but after that, she insists it's time to play. Alex flings himself enthusiastically into cleaning and gets in everyone's way. Jennifer can't move around yet, but even sitting on her blanket she manages to make it very difficult for Carol and Sam to straighten up the living room.

◆

JENNIFER
(Six Months)

Jen is sitting on a blanket on the floor by the couch. "Aaaaabah," she says. She kicks her feet and shakes her yellow spoons through the air. The spoons fly out of her hands, landing on the floor beyond the blanket. Jen stares at them.

Sam's twenty-year-old son James and one of his friends have just left after a weekend visit, depositing litter in their wake. Carol is collecting glasses and empty beer and soft-drink cans. Sam is gathering up the scattered sections of two Sunday papers, which are mingled with Saturday's mail, playbills, magazines, and an assortment of books.

Jen leans forward and stretches her hand toward the spoons. They are too far away. She pulls her arms back, rumpling the blanket underneath her. She whines.

Carol turns to see what's happening. Nothing serious, she decides. Jen continues making cross noises. Carol takes the glasses into the kitchen.

Grunting, Jen extends both arms toward the spoons again. She loses her balance and falls forward on her stomach. Carol, returning, is greeted by a sharp, frustrated wail.

Sam goes over and squats down by his daughter. He puts the envelopes he's collected down at his side and pats Jen's head. She arches up, leaning on her elbows to look at him. "What's the matter now?" Jen stares at him, drooling. Sam leans his head a little closer and blows a little puff of air on her nose. Jen gurgles with pleasure. Sam purses his lips again. Jen closes her eyes. Sam blows. Jen laughs. Sam tickles her belly. Instead of giggling, Jen whines. "Okay, okay," Sam says. "Let me help you sit back up."

"Auhejah."

Sam hands Jen the spoons. She isn't interested anymore. Ignoring them, she turns to look at her father, falling backwards until she's leaning against the couch. "Aaabah, abah, abah," she babbles.

"Aaabah, abah, abah," Sam babbles back.

Jen cocks her head and smiles. Then she looks down and notices the envelopes. She gurgles and leans forward, stretching out her arms to touch them, fingers wide. She can't find a way to grip them. Sam pulls out a piece of junk mail and holds the envelope up so Jen is able to grab it. She closes her fist around it. "Ssabah," she squeals. She looks at Sam. "Yes," Sam says, "it crumples." Jen begins sucking on the crumpled envelope.

"That's been all through the postal system," Carol warns.

"No, Jen," Sam says, prying her fingers apart. "That's not good for chewing." He pulls the envelope away, but a wet piece rips off in Jen's mouth. Sam sticks his finger in to get it out. Jen cries.

"Come on, Jen," Sam says, exasperated.

Carol is wiping cream cheese off the end table. "Try the rattle," she suggests. "She seemed interested in that this morning. It's on the coffee table."

The rattle rustles when Sam picks it up. Jen looks toward the noise. She leans forward, kneading the blanket with her hands. Sam holds out the rattle. Jen's eyes widen and her mouth scrunches. She grabs it. It makes a noise.

Sam picks up the envelopes and stands up. Jen, still holding the rattle, gives a little cry of protest at his leaving.

"I'll put on the radio," Carol says. "Maybe that will quiet her down." Carol puts down the pile of plates with bits of bagel and drying cream cheese on them and goes to the stereo. "I wish she'd go to sleep." A trustworthy baritone is praising a bank. Jen stops whimpering and turns her head toward the sound. Carol slips the dial to a slow symphonic movement led by a yearning violin. Jen, staring in the direction of the speakers, smiles and begins swaying.

Sam, standing, has stopped to skim an article in one of the newspapers. "Did you see this? The piece about arbitrage?"

"No, save it," Carol says. She nods toward the basket where she puts papers and magazines she intends to read later. Since Jen's birth, the basket has been stuffed.

Jen drops the rattle and starts reaching toward something blue sticking out from under the couch.

Sam puts the paper in the basket. "I'll start loading the dishwasher," he says, picking up the pile of plates.

"Don't save the square inch of potato salad," Carol tells him. "We'll just let it rot."

"Okay." Sam goes to the kitchen.

Jen reaches out for the blue thing with one arm, holding herself up with the other. It doesn't work. She whines. Carol, wiping off the coffee table, ignores her. Jen shifts her weight forward, plops down on her stomach, and reaches again from her new position. She grunts. She finally gets hold of the blue thing.

"Good girl," Carol says.

Jen pulls it toward her. It's a sock. She puts it in her mouth.

"Damn." Carol puts down the rag, spilling the crumbs she collected on the floor. She goes over to Jen. "Jen, that's ucky."

Jen, still sucking, looks up at her mother, clutching the sock tightly. Carol unpries her fingers and pulls the sock away. Jen cries. Carol stuffs the sock in the waistband of her jeans. "Jen, that was filthy. It's been on someone's sweaty feet and under the couch. Do you want to sit up? I'll help you sit up." She lifts Jen up on her feet, holding her under the armpits.

Jen quiets at once, taking in her new position. She turns her head to one side, looks at her mother, and smiles. "Yes. You're standing." Jen coos. She reaches out to touch Carol's face, slapping her on the nose. "Gentle! I'm going to sit you down now." She lowers Jen. Jen's face remains fixed on Carol. Carol stands up and steps away. Jen, a still, Buddhalike expression on her face, watches Carol dust off the coffee table and rocks gently to the minuet from the radio. Then she lowers her eyes to look around her. She starts moaning and wiggling fretfully.

Carol goes over to her. "Where are your spoons, Jen?" She sees them on the blanket. "Here are your spoons." Jen looks at them. She doesn't take them. She whines.

"Jen," Carol says, "I've got to get this mess cleaned up." She stands up. Jen cries. "I just can't play with you now," Carol tells her, turning away.

◆

OBSERVATIONS

The World of Things

During her ten minutes on the living-room floor, Jennifer practiced looking at things from different angles, reached, grabbed, and examined several different objects. She shook, chewed, and flung her spoons. They made a clicking sound when she jangled them. The rattle made a different kind of noise. The envelope and sock were so thin that when she pressed them she could feel her fingers meet. When she made a fist, the envelope crackled and crumpled. It got wet and soft in her mouth. The sock felt soft all the time. No doubt it had a distinctive smell.

Jen doesn't have the physical skills to do all the things she wants to do. She can take something within reach, touch it with her fingers, feel it with her mouth, and shake it, but she is helpless when an object she wants is beyond arm's length. Today she worked hard to get the spoons but lost her balance and fell on her stomach without getting them. She was frustrated. Her efforts to get at things will begin to pay off soon, however. She is learning to coordinate torso and arm movements. Today she practiced stretching her torso out and sitting with her weight on her hands, a position she will soon use for crawling.

The World of People

Jen likes games in which she responds to something her parents do and they respond to her response. When Sam blew on her face, she giggled and then closed her eyes to invite him to do it again. Even when she is doing something by herself, Jen likes to have an audience. She is very skilled at using her eyes and facial expressions to engage people's attention. When she crumpled the envelope, for example, she looked at Sam for approval. He acknowledged her excitement by smiling and commenting on the crumpling.

Sometimes Sam and Carol decided not to go to Jen, but they still let her know they were aware of her. They kept glancing at her to make sure she was all right. Carol congratulated Jen when she found the sock and warned her before she went back to cleaning.

Ideas and Words

Jen is very attentive to all kinds of sounds. Even a soft sound, like the noise the rattle made when Sam picked it up, catches her attention. Listening helps Jen decide what to look at. When she heard the sound of the rattle and later the radio, she turned her head to where the sound was the loudest. She saw Sam moving the rattle at the same time it made a noise. She saw the speakers when she positioned her head to hear the sound better. These experiences will help her understand that sounds have causes.

Jen has a sense of rhythm and clearly enjoys rhythmic sounds. When the music came on she swayed. When she babbled, she repeated sounds rhythmically. When she said "Aaabah, abah, abah," she was pleased that Sam picked up the rhythm and said "Aaabah, abah, abah" back.

Jen can remember very short sequences of actions. For example, when Sam puffed his cheeks a second time she anticipated that he was going to blow on her face again and closed her eyes. But her memory and attention span are both very short. Jen forgets a project completely if she is interrupted, the way she lost interest in the spoons after Sam changed her position.

Sense of Self

Jen was in a restless mood. She couldn't focus on anything very long and was easily frustrated. When she couldn't reach the spoons, for example, she began whining right away. When Sam stood up after he gave her the rattle, she began crying for his attention again. The music diverted her but didn't break her mood. She fussed a lot in a very short period of time. Perhaps James's weekend visit left her tired and overexcited.

Carol and Sam were feeling impatient with Jen for being so whiny and demanding and for making it hard to straighten up. After several interruptions, Carol finally told Jen she couldn't play with her and just let her cry. This was not a bad thing to do. All her life, Carol and Sam have done their best to respond quickly whenever Jen has really needed something. Even if Carol won't play with her, Jen knows by now that she's safe when Carol is nearby. Being grumpy in itself won't hurt Jen. Sam and Carol can't devote all their attention to amusing and soothing her. Sometimes they have to leave her to her own limited resources. And her resources are increasing. Jen will gradually learn to comfort and amuse herself the same way she will learn to move her body to get to things she wants—by trying, on her own, with her parents' support.

◆

ALEX
(Fifteen Months)

Rita is getting the feather duster, ammonia spray, a wood cleaning and polishing fluid, paper towels, and a clean rag out of the kitchen cabinet and putting them on the kitchen table. Alex has just opened the doors under the sink. He bends down at the knees but ends up plopping on his bottom. He takes out the package of steel wool, the sink cleaner, and a sponge and struggles to get out the big spaghetti pot.

Rita hears the sound of things under the sink falling down. "No, honey, please don't take the pot out. Would you help me carry these things into the living room instead? Come over here and I'll give you something to carry."

Rita hands him the duster. "Would you take this into the living room, please?"

Alex takes the handle of the duster in one hand and runs the other through the feathers. Then he turns the duster so the feathery end faces him. He bends his head down, sticks his nose in the duster, and sneezes. He looks up at Rita, startled.

"Yes, it's got dust in it. Don't put your face in it."

Alex is looking at the feathers again. He gets hold of a bunch and pulls. One feather comes out and floats slowly in the air. "Ma!" *Alex calls Rita's attention to this enchanting phenomenon. He reaches for the feather; it moves sideways away from him before settling gently on the table.*

Rita picks the feather up and runs one end along Alex's nose. Alex crinkles up his face and giggles. He lets the duster go and grabs the feather.

Rita picks the duster off the floor. "Take this into the living room for me, okay?" *Alex drops the feather and takes the duster from Rita. When she picks up the rag, he holds out his other hand and babbles.*

"You want to carry two things? Here." Rita hands him the rag. Holding the feather duster stick in one fist and the rag in the other, Alex trots into the living room.

Mike is sitting on the living-room floor lining up Transformer figures in two rows for a battle. "Zzzp, zzzp," he says, as one toy lasers another to death. Alex watches for a second. Rita, carrying cleaning fluids and a roll of paper towels, arrives in time to see Alex catch Mike's eye, then take the duster and mow down the Transformers. Alex eyes Mike again.

"Hey!" Mike yells.

"Alex!" Rita says. He ignores her. Rita puts the cleaning stuff on the coffee table. She goes over to Alex, kneels down, and takes him by the shoulders. "Those are Mike's toys. You don't knock down other people's things that way." Alex looks down. "Did you hear me?" Rita takes the duster away from Alex and stands up.

Mike has been retrieving his Transformers.

"Mike, sweetie," Rita says, "I've got to clean the living room. Would you get your basket so you and Alex can collect your toys and take them to your room?"

Alex picks up the coffee can where Mike keeps the transformers. He turns it upside down.

"Mom!" Mike protests.

"You could get your new backpack and carry your toys that way."

Alex notices the receiver of his toy phone sticking out from behind the hassock. He drops the coffee can and goes for it.

Mike sighs. "Okay."

Alex is pulling on the receiver, trying to drag the phone out. He pulls the string taut and tugs, but the base of the phone doesn't appear. The cord is caught on the hassock leg.

"Come on, Alex," Mike says.

Alex looks at him. "Pho," Alex says.

"You can talk on the phone later," Rita tells him.

"Come on," Mike says, "we're going to get the pack."

Alex drops the receiver and half walks, half runs over to Mike. Mike takes his hand. They go off toward their room.

Rita is dusting off the shelves when the boys return. Mike is carrying the pack at his side, in one hand. Alex has reached up to hold an edge as though he is carrying it too. All he is doing is dragging on it, but Mike is tolerating the inconvenience patiently.

Mike puts the pack down. Alex picks it up, turns it upside down, and lifts it high. "We're going to bring all the toys here," Mike explains.

Mike starts by collecting his Transformer toys and dropping them back into the coffee can one by one. Alex puts the pack down and drops a toy in the can too. Then he starts to turn the can over. Mike snatches it away. Alex whines and reaches for the can again. Mike holds it above his head, out of reach. "Mom," he calls.

Rita hurriedly finishes the last shelf and turns. "What, sweetie?"

"Alex keeps emptying the can."

Rita puts the duster down and retrieves the toy telephone. She picks up the receiver and begins talking. "Yes? . . . You want to speak to Alex. I'll get him. Here, Alex," she tells her son, "it's for you."

Alex grabs the receiver, pulling the base out of Rita's hand. It bangs on the floor. "Hata roma a," Alex says into the receiver.

Mike has put the can in his pack and is gathering the other toys. Rita starts cleaning some flowery porcelain cups on an upper shelf.

"Yee! Yee! Yee!" Alex shrieks into the phone. He laughs. "Yee! Yee! Yee!" he shrieks louder.

Mike puts his hands over his ears. "Alex, stop it!" Rita says. "That's too loud."

"Yee! Yee!" Alex starts again.

Mike grabs the phone away from Alex. Alex lets out an angry screech and hits Mike in the chest as hard as he can. Mike punches him in the stomach, not as hard as he can but hard enough. Alex begins crying.

"Stop it!" Rita says. She descends on Mike. Alex retreats to watch. "Your brother is a baby. I know he can be a pain in the neck, but you mustn't hit him. Do you understand?" Mike looks at the couch, the backpack, the corner of the room. "Do you understand, Mike? Look at me!"

"Yes," Mike says.

"Yes what?"

"Yes, I won't hit Alex!" Mike shouts. Rita ruffles Mike's hair. "I know he hit you first," she says softly. "He's a drag sometimes."

Rita finds the duster and brings it to Alex. "Why don't you play with this?"

Alex waves the duster and giggles. He starts dusting the shelves, making big sweeping movements. Rita returns to the porcelain. Mike takes the toys into his bedroom, comes back, and asks Rita if he can have a cookie. "Yes," Rita says, reaching to put the last cup back in place. She begins spraying the coffee table and wiping it with a paper towel.

Alex starts climbing the shelves, trying to get at the porcelain. "No, Alex," Rita says. He ignores her. "Come." She takes his hand. Alex struggles to get away. Mike, eating a cookie, watches.

"Why don't you help me wipe?" Rita says to Alex.

Mike stuffs the rest of the cookie in his mouth and waves the roll of paper towels. "Here, Alex," he says.

Alex takes the roll and begins unrolling the towels.

"Easy," Rita says, going over to help him. She hands him one sheet and rerolls the rest.

"This way, Alex," Mike says. "You wipe like this." Mike squirts the TV and starts wiping. Alex wipes the floor. "Wi," he says. "Wi."

Rita begins polishing the wood chest. Alex notices the spray bottle. He picks it up. The liquid sloshes as he shakes the bottle. He giggles. He starts examining the top. Suddenly he cries out—he has hit the plunger and sprayed liquid into his face.

Rita flies over. "Are you all right? Let me see."

Alex looks up at her. His eyes are wide open and he is not touching them. Rita hugs him hard. "Thank God you didn't get it in your eyes. Here." She releases Alex and gets a clean sheet of paper towel. "Let me wipe your face." Alex clings to her leg, whimpering. "There, sweetie, it was just a bad surprise."

OBSERVATIONS

The World of Things

Alex is collecting information about all the objects in his house. He examines objects like the feather duster and the ammonia spray bottle very carefully, turning them to see and touch all the different surfaces, shaking them and smelling them. The feather he pulled out of the duster was especially interesting to him because it floated in the air.

Alex also learns about objects by using them as tools, to do things. He used the duster like a broom, sweeping the Transformer toys, and he used it the way Rita did, to dust the shelves. He likes unrolling the paper towels and he also likes wiping with them as adults do. Today he wiped the floor.

Alex has only recently learned to walk and carry things at the same time, but he is already working on a new skill: carrying two different objects, one in each hand. When Rita gave him the duster, he indicated that he wanted to carry the rag too.

The World of People

Alex likes to participate in family activities. When he is not given a chore, he assigns himself one. When he emptied the cabinet under the sink, for example, he thought he was helping Rita. When he is given a chore he understands, he tries hard to do it. Rita made good use of Alex's appetite for work. She got him to leave the spaghetti pot alone by asking him to carry the duster. She got him to stop trying to climb the shelves by asking him to wipe.

Alex seemed to know what he was doing when he knocked Mike's Transformers down: he made a point of getting his brother to look at him before he did it and he watched Mike afterward to see his reaction. He was experimenting to find out what kind of response he could get from Mike.

Ideas and Words

Alex is beginning to have mental pictures of objects and to understand relationships like part and whole. When he saw part of the telephone receiver, he realized the whole toy telephone was there. He knew if he pulled, the rest of the phone should appear. His reasoning powers are limited, however. When he tugged at the receiver and couldn't pull the phone out, he couldn't figure out that it was caught.

Alex can understand simple requests. He realized that Rita wanted him to carry the duster into the living room and that Mike and he were going to their room to get something.

Though Alex imitates adult activities, he has little sense of or interest in their purpose. He does each task for its own sake. After he dropped a toy into the coffee can, he emptied it out again. To Alex, emptying is just as important an activity as filling.

Sense of Self

Alex is pleased with himself because he can do so many things. He liked helping the important people in his life do their work. He did not understand that his screeching on the phone, emptying the can of toys, and climbing up the shelves made the job of cleaning the living room harder for Mike and Rita.

Alex is trying out his new social skills too. He was being nasty when he knocked down Mike's toys—but he was also testing his ability to make other people react, something he needs to know how to do to feel powerful in the world.

◆

KATIE
(Twenty-eight Months)

"Mama."

Sarah looks up. Katie, holding Franklin, is standing in the doorway of her parents' room.

"Hi," Sarah says. She continues stripping the bed. She had been hoping Katie would continue playing by herself just a little longer. . . .

Katie drops Franklin and jumps up on the bed. "Meow, meow," she says, crawling along the mattress. She rubs her face in the pillows, then begins burrowing in the pile of sheets and covers at the foot of the bed. She peeks out for a quick meow and then sticks her head back in.

Sarah knows her cue. She continues to strip the bed. Then she reaches to gather the dirty linen. "Hey!" she says running her hand over the toddler-size bump. "What's this? There's something in the bed."

A giggle wafts out of the bedding and is squashed midway.

Sarah very slowly picks up an edge of the rumpled sheets and peers in. "It's a little kitten." She reaches her hand in. "Here, kitty—" Katie tries to scramble out. Sarah climbs on the bed. "I'm going to catch that kitten." She stalks her daughter. Katie crawls backward, giggling. Sarah pounces and bundles Katie in her arms. "What a cute kitty," she says, rocking.

Katie cuddles for a few seconds, then squirms away. "Meow."

"No, darling," Sarah sighs. "I have to clean the room. I'm in a hurry." Sarah gets up and rubs the small of her back. Her lower back has been aching and chasing felines was probably a mistake.

"Meow," Katie calls loudly. She squirms and rolls under the sheets with frenzied enthusiasm.

"Katie, I mean it. I'm going to count to three and then pull the covers off, okay? One." Giggles bubble out from under the sheet.

"Two." Katie grabs hold of the sheets.

"Three . . ." Sarah pulls the sheets, dragging Katie across the bed.

"Come on, now." Katie is laughing and rolling around. "Honey, I mean it. I'm really in a hurry. You can help me shake the sheets."

"Okay," Katie says. Sarah smiles. It has been a long time since Katie's last "okay." Sarah holds out her hand to guide Katie off the bed, but Katie pushes it away to climb down by herself.

"First, let's take the dirty linen to the bathroom."

Katie tries to pick the pile of sheets and blankets off the floor and gets caught in one of the sheets. She starts spinning to wrap it around her.

"Here," Sarah says, unwrapping her, "you take this." She hands the pillowcases to Katie. Then she leans down to lift the rest of the linen. "Oh," she groans.

Katie stares at her, very quiet. Then she pulls at her mother's leg.

"Yes, Katie. I know you're there. My back hurts."

"Why?"

"It just does." She smiles. "Let's go."

Sarah and Katie dump the linen in the bathroom hamper. Sarah gives Katie two pillowcases from the closet and takes two sheets to carry herself. They walk back to the room.

"One," Sarah says, as she begins shaking one of the sheets open over the bed.

Katie runs over to the other side of the bed and grabs the sheet. "Two," Katie shouts.

"Three," Sarah and Katie say together, shaking the sheet.

Katie's side is twisted but she doesn't notice. She puts it down then picks it up again. "One—"

"No. Now we tuck it in." Sarah moves to the bottom of the bed and starts tucking the sheet in. "Look, Katie." Katie comes over. "I'll hold up the mattress and you push the sheet under." Katie pushes the sheet in. "Now we put the mattress down." Sarah quickly tightens Katie's tuck. "Now your side."

But Katie is sidetracked by the radio on the end table. She turns it on—very loud. "Radio," she says. She turns the volume knob all the way to the left until the sound is off, then all the way to the right so the radio roars, then left again, right again, left, right.

"That's enough!" Sarah snaps.

Katie looks at her, startled. The radio is bellowing the news. Sarah reaches over and lowers the volume. "I'll tell you what, we'll find some music that you like and leave it on." She fiddles for a rock station for Katie, who likes to dance to a strong downbeat.

"There." Sarah finishes smoothing the sheet.

Katie comes around to join her but notices the red lacquer jewelry box on top of Sarah's bureau. "Red," she says, pointing.

"Yes," Sarah says, "it's red."

"Toe toe," Katie says. On her toes, with her arms over her head, she can reach the brush on the edge of the bureau but not the jewelry box. She tries again, grunting with effort. She tries to pull herself up by grabbing hold of one of the drawer handles but can't get a good grip.

Sarah comes over. She doesn't want to give Katie the box because she knows Katie will empty it and one or two pairs of earrings will be widowed. Katie is still trying to get at the box, getting clumsier with each attempt. "No, me do," she says, trying to push her mother aside. Sarah, ignoring her, opens the box and takes out three fairly sturdy necklaces—fake pearls, little blue and black shells, and pink quartz beads. She hands them to Katie.

"Beads," Katie says happily. She holds them in one hand and fingers the beads individually with the other. She bends down her head and tastes the quartz. Sarah seizes the opportunity to finish the bed.

Katie puts the beads on. "Look," she says, starting to dance in front of the wall mirror. She runs in circles on tiptoes, waving her arms. "Look. Dancing."

"Yes," Sarah says, plumping the last pillow, "you're dancing." She moves quickly around the room, dropping old mail into the wastebasket, pulling a sweater off the back of a chair and sticking it in its drawer, hanging up Joe's robe.

"Look!" Katie demands again.

"You look very pretty in the beads." Sarah takes a glass from the end table to put in the "take down" pile on the floor at the top of the stairs.

"Katie, while you dance, I'm going to get the vacuum cleaner."

"No," Katie says.

"I'll be right back. Do you want to come?"

"No."

"Okay. I'll be right back."

Katie, no longer dancing, looks at herself in the mirror. She turns and runs after her mother. "Okay," Katie says. "Katie vacuum."

OBSERVATIONS

The World of Things

Katie can now move in most of the ways adults do. She can control her body well enough to move expressively, the way she did when she imitated a kitten and later when she danced.

Helping Sarah gave Katie the chance to do different things with the sheets. She helped shake the sheet out and stretch it so the surface became smooth and flat. When she clung to the sheet and Sarah dragged her across the bed, she used the linen as a rope and felt how strong it was. When she got twisted in the pile of linen on the floor, she wrapped the sheet around herself, making a kind of dress or cocoon.

The World of People

Katie came looking for Sarah when she got bored playing alone. She likes to play by herself sometimes and can keep herself occupied for fifteen minutes or so, but fairly soon she goes looking for one of her parents. Her parents' presence reassures her and also stimulates her.

Katie realized that changing the linen was a job, but she thought of it as a kind of game too. For Sarah, on the other hand, it was just a chore to get done. Her back hurt and she didn't really feel like playing, though she did for a while. Katie couldn't and didn't understand that Sarah would have liked to hurry. But though Katie can't perceive Sarah's needs and desires, she is very sensitive to Sarah's moods and feelings. When Sarah's back hurt, Katie noticed right away.

Some objects are particularly interesting to Katie because she connects them to people she cares about. The connection gives the objects their own emotional character. The red box, for example, interested Katie partly because Sarah keeps something she considers special there, her jewelry, and puts it up high, out of reach. Katie enjoyed holding and wearing the beads because they were bright and sleek to the touch, and also because they were Sarah's. Placing them around her own neck may have made her feel grown up and beautiful like her mother. Crawling over the big expanse of bouncy mattress was probably more exciting to Katie because the bed was her mother and father's. They sleep in their bed. She sleeps in her bed. Though she sometimes goes to their bed for early-morning snuggling, it's still theirs and sometimes off-limits to her. Today she was allowed to play freely on it and to twist herself up in the sheets that smell of Sarah and Joe.

Ideas and Words

Katie doesn't always want to, but she is able to understand and follow directions. She understood when Sarah asked her to carry the pillowcases, to shake the sheet, and to tuck the sheet under the mattress.

Katie understood that Sarah was taking the linen off the bed. She understood that she and Sarah were going to the bathroom to put the old linen in the hamper and get new linen. But she can't sustain a sense of purpose about the whole chore—changing the linen—very long. When she tried to pick the sheets up and couldn't, she became absorbed in the draping game and forgot about going to the hamper. She enjoyed tucking the sheets in but was distracted by the radio and the box on the bureau.

Katie's kitty game was a make-believe version of hide-and-seek. She was using her ideas about cats to imagine how a cat would move and behave.

Sense of Self

Katie knows that she is Katie and that she is pretending when she acts like a kitten. She may have pretended to be a kitten to help herself feel agile and graceful and lovable like a cat, or to enjoy her own small size more, or maybe just because she likes cats.

Katie was obviously pleased to see herself dance in the mirror. She called Sarah to watch too. She could see her arms and legs moving as she felt them move. She could see Sarah's beads on her neck as well as feel them. Looking at herself and trying out different outfits and different expressions and gestures in front of the mirror is helping Katie to picture herself in her own mind.

Though her main concern was getting the chore done, Sarah took the time to recognize and encourage Katie's growing competence. She asked Katie for help changing the linen and gave her specific tasks she could do. She straightened out Katie's side of the sheet without criticizing Katie.

Katie likes to control things in her environment. The radio is particularly obliging. With one small turn of a knob, Katie can create blaring music or silence. People are not always so accommodating. After playing with Katie a little, Sarah turned her attention back to cleaning the bedroom. She went to get the vacuum cleaner even though Katie didn't want her to go.

Katie is very attuned to Sarah and Joe. Their responsiveness energizes her and gives her confidence. When Sarah, distracted by physical discomfort or absorbed by her work, stopped giving Katie her attention, Katie became uncomfortable. She didn't want to go on dancing after Sarah left the room.

9

DOING THE LAUNDRY

Adults see doing the laundry as a dull means to the necessary end of having clean clothes. Many of us do it as infrequently as possible, waiting until we have nothing presentable to wear before accepting fate and organizing a wash.

Small children, unlike their parents, like to do the laundry. For them collecting clothes, sticking them in baskets and bags, dumping them out of baskets and bags, stuffing them into washing machines and driers, watching the machines shake and hearing them growl, taking the clothes out, wringing them, shaking them, gathering clothespins, hanging clothes on ropes and rods and pulling them down again is fun. They don't realize that the purpose of all these amusing activities is to end up with clean clothes. They don't think about clean clothes.

There's a conflict of interest here. When your child obligingly takes clothes out of the machine or off the line, they will end up on the ground or bathroom floor as often as in the laundry basket because, to her, getting the clothes, not keeping them clean is the point. After she does one helpful job for you—putting the clothes in the laundry basket—she may do what she sees as another helpful job by turning the basket upside down to empty the clothes out again.

Having your child with you when you do the laundry obviously means working out compromises between her commitment to serious play and yours to achieving a goal. It means doing the laundry very slowly.

Even though it slows them down, some people like to have their baby around when they do a wash. Her presence makes the chore a game for them too, and if they're not in a hurry, they enjoy the company. But many adults find that when they do the laundry with their child, they quickly start regarding her as a dangerous saboteur. Pulling a protesting toddler away from a cup of poisonous bleach, stopping her when she starts rifling through someone else's clothes in the Laundromat, saying no when she begins burrowing in the pile of neatly folded linen or pulls the clothes off the line into the mud can exhaust an adult and make both him and his child very irritable.

If you don't like having your child with you when you do the laundry, then of course it makes sense to wash and fold the clothes when she's out, asleep, or playing with your spouse or a sibling. But sometimes you won't have a choice: the laundry has to be done, and there's only one time to do it and no one else to watch the baby. If you try to look at the experience through your child's eyes, you can minimize the disruption by figuring out ways to involve her that you'll both enjoy.

To a small baby, doing the laundry, like every other household task, is simply a series of movements and noises her parents make. She doesn't understand that the movements are ordered and purposeful. She doesn't know what a purpose is. But small babies enjoy being near a parent, whatever the parent is doing. They also enjoy and need opportunities to exercise their senses. Being with you while you do the laundry gives them a special set of sensual opportunities.

The smell of bleach, detergent, and fabric softener are powerful and distinct. The washing machine is warm and the air around it is warmer than the air in the rest of the room. Clothes come out of the machine wet and cool. They are hot and dry when you take them out of the dryer or off the line on a sunny day. You create a stream of interesting sights as you work. A huge, multicolored mound of clothes rises in the air, moves down into the basket, and is gone. A bright red towel suddenly disappears under a blue sheet. The expanse of blue in turn disappears under an expanse of white. A small triangle of blue remains sticking out to one side.

If your baby is old enough to grasp and pull things, you can keep her amused while you do the laundry by giving her a sweatshirt to handle and cuddle. If you want to take a break, you can hold out different kinds of materials for her to reach for and finger—terry cloth robes, silk and rayon blouses, cotton tee shirts, and corduroy pants all have very distinct textures, and the differences (which she will want to taste) will intrigue her.

If you're going to be working mostly in one room when you do the laundry, you can just put your baby in her seat and let her watch you from there, chatting with her if she gets restless. If you're moving around from room to room, you can carry her with you against your body in her sling or backpack. (Remember to bend at your knees when you reach down toward a basket or bag so you won't hurt your back.) Carrying the baby will slow you down—you'll have to make more trips—but she'll enjoy being close to you, and won't need to call for your attention.

Toddlers have the skills and understanding to really help you do the laundry—and to undo everything you do as well. Doing the laundry involves a number of specific tasks that toddlers find very absorbing. Your toddler can help you carry clothes or clothespins or measuring cups and spoons. She will want to fill and empty bags, containers, and baskets (a favorite activity). She may try to lift the basket of wash or shake out wrinkles the way you do. Being able to do the same things you do is part of the satisfaction she gets from being with you when you do a wash.

Toddlers are also very interested in machines because machines move and make noises, two qualities they value highly. Your child will like the way the washing machine jiggles, and if the washer or dryer has a glass door and she notices the clothes moving around, she will be transfixed for a second or two. Toddlers are also agile enough to try to open the door of front-loading machines, to try to walk or climb on slippery surfaces, and to want to pour cleaning fluids which are dangerous; when you do the laundry with your toddler you have to stay alert. If you take her with you to a public laundry, you also have to watch to make sure she doesn't start playing with other people's clothes, cups, and detergent boxes.

Twos understand many of the individual tasks involved in doing the laundry, they just don't understand that they must all be done in a certain sequence to achieve the overall end, because they don't understand there is an end. They don't have the image of the final pile of clean clothes in mind. It's doing the separate little jobs that make up the whole process which interests them. Twos can get deeply absorbed in these jobs and do some of them quite well. By twenty-eight months or so, your child will be able to collect clothes, shake them to get wrinkles out, place them on a line or rod if it's low, and may even try her hand at folding. She will want to learn to do things the way you do, and she will be very observant of your personal rituals. Don't be surprised if, clothespin in your mouth, you look over as you take a sheet off the line and see your two-year-old pulling a pillowcase down, a clothespin in her mouth.

Doing the laundry gives two-year-olds a chance to practice intellectual as well as physical skills. Twos are beginning to identify colors and can help sort clothes into white and colored piles. (Their concentration is limited, however; a white shirt will end up with the navy blue towels after a few minutes.) Your two-year-old will want to practice finding and naming different articles of clothing. She has a concept of ownership and can help separate out her clothes from her parents' and her siblings'—at least until she gets bored and starts walking through the piles.

The allure of the washing machine is strong for twos (though they may go through a period when they find grumbling, vibrating machines scary). They understand that the buttons are what make the thing go. Since she likes to make things happen, your child may want to press the buttons and could interrupt the wash cycle if you don't stop her. She will want to do many other things herself, including things she cannot do without help, like lifting a heavy basket, and things she shouldn't do, like measuring bleach. (You can let her measure water and pour that in if you want.)

If her insistent *I do's* and your insistent *no's* start edging toward a shouting match, consider stopping and doing something else for a while. You can also try redirecting her energy and enthusiasm with a favorite toy or a job of her own to do—preferably a real one such as carrying the towels to the bathroom or wiping up water that has dripped on the floor.

Katie is very grown up about doing the laundry and actually does help Joe get the wash down from the line. Alex's way of being helpful is to crawl through the folded clothes. For Jen, doing the laundry is time to spend with her mother, watching and listening.

◆

JENNIFER
(Six Months)

Carol carries Jen to the bedroom, lays her on her back on the bed, and takes off her Hawaiian shirt, which has dried bits of lunch and spittle on it.

She stands up, takes off her own skirt and blouse, hangs them up in the closet, and puts on blue jeans and a green tee shirt. Jen shifts her head to follow her mother's movements, rapt.

The phone rings. Carol sits down on the bed and picks up the receiver. "Hello. . . . Hi, Mom." Jen is whimpering and reaching toward her. Holding the phone against her ear with her shoulder, Carol takes Jen onto her lap. "Pretty good. Sam takes Jen on Saturday afternoon now, so I had some time off. I had lunch with Victoria and then I went to the museum, just like a free person." Jen has reached for Carol's hair, succeeded in grabbing a handful, and is giving it a fierce tug. "Not so hard, darling." Carol unfurls the fingers. "Sorry, Mom. Anyway, I really enjoyed it. Only now I have to do another laundry or Jen won't have anything to wear tomorrow. It's amazing how someone so small can produce so much dirt. . . . No, Sam went downtown to pick up the stereo. It's in the machine hospital. . . . Wait a minute, Jen thinks I'm a trampoline . . .

"Jen," Carol appeals, as though Jen could listen to reason. She notices the yellow plastic measuring spoons on the night table. The spoons have become Jen's favorite toy. Carol lays Jen back on the bed and hands her the spoons. "Sorry, Mom. . . . Yeah, we're all doing all right. We're all tired except for Jen. How are you and Dad?"

Jen shakes the spoons. She giggles at the soft rattling sound. She makes it again.

"What did the doctor say?" Jen starts sucking the spoons. "How is he feeling now?" Jen drops the spoons and begins squirming and whining.

"Jen's squirming again. Let's talk tomorrow. We'll be over around four. I love you too." Carol hangs up.

"You're certainly making it hard for your mother to talk with anyone," Carol tells Jen, who has stopped squirming and begun smiling now that her mother is addressing her directly. Carol begins going through the clothes in the wicker hamper, deciding what to wash now and what to leave for another time. She pulls out Sam's blue cotton sweater and drops it on the bed. Jen laughs and rolls over on her tummy. She reaches out for one of the sweater's sleeves. She can't get to it and begins to whimper. Carol pushes it nearer. Jen manages to grab it and put it in her mouth.

After a few seconds, Jen, restless, tries to roll onto her back again so she can look at Carol. She can't. She cries softly. "What's the matter?" Carol asks. "Oh, your arm is stuck. Here." Carol leans down to free Jen's arm, which is pinned underneath her. Jen finishes rolling over and smiles.

Before straightening up, Carol notices three socks on the floor by the bed. "No wonder your daddy never has any clean socks," she tells Jen, leaning down to get them. Jen twists her head to watch Carol's back descend.

Carol stuffs Jen's shirt, the sweater, the socks, and a few other pieces of dark clothing into a pillowcase. "Okay, let's go to the kitchen." She bends toward Jen. Jen kicks her legs happily and reaches out to be picked up.

Carol carries the baby and the laundry into the kitchen. She drops the bag of laundry on the floor by the machine. "You can sit in your high chair while

I put the clothes in," she says. *Securing Jen against her hip with one hand, she lifts up the high chair tray with the other.*

"Would you like a rice cake?" *She takes one from the almost empty bag on the counter.* "We better put rice cakes on the shopping list." *She holds a cracker out to Jen, who takes it and begins gumming it.*

Carol puts the clothes into the washing machine. Meanwhile the rice cake falls apart. Jen drops a piece and peers over the edge of her high chair after it. Then she drops another piece. Carol measures out three quarters of a cup of soap powder from the box under the sink and sneezes. Jen, startled, forgets the rice cake and looks at her mother. Carol sneezes again. Jen laughs.

Carol turns the dial to cotton and pushes the on button. The machine begins to hum. Jen looks at it for a second and then turns her head to watch Carol.

Carol takes a peach from the bowl on the table and bites into it. She puts it down and fishes through the refrigerator, looking for something for Jen's supper. She settles on cooked potatoes and a small dish of yogurt. Carol lets Jen play with the soft pieces of potato with her fingers but spoon-feeds her the yogurt, keeping the dish out of reach. The potatoes keep Jen busy; she doesn't try to grab the spoon.

The washing machine stops.

"For dessert," *Carol says, retrieving her peach, biting off a piece, and holding it out for Jen to take. Jen grabs it and squishes it between her fingers.*

Carol washes her hands and transfers the clothes to the dryer. Jen watches her intently, then turns her attention back to her piece of peach. She drops it and peers over to watch it fall. She whines. Carol eats a bite of peach, then bites off another piece for Jen. "Here. You eat this while I look through the mail."

Jen squishes the peach and eats it off her fingers. She looks up and smiles at Carol, who is thumbing through a law review. She smears some peach on her tray and then starts whining and kicking. Carol looks at her. She has only been reading for a minute or two. Jen can't even go for two minutes without being the center of attention. Is she getting spoiled? Carol wonders.

Jen coos urgently and reaches out her arms. "Okay. Let's clean the mess off your tray and I'll check the laundry." Jen smiles in response.

Carol wipes off Jen's face and the tray. Then she pulls the dryer door open. The sweater and shirt are still damp but the socks are dry. Carol pulls them out.

"Feel this," she says, holding a warm brown sock to Jen's cheek. Jen coos. Carol holds the sock in front of her own face. She waits a couple of seconds, then peeks around the side. "Peek-a-boo," she says. Jen laughs.

"Here, you try." Carol holds the sock in front of Jen, blocking her view. "Peek-a-boo!" She pulls the sock away. Jen laughs. Carol kisses her on the head. "You are silly," she says.

◆

OBSERVATIONS

The World of Things

Three months ago, Jen looked at things around her but didn't reach out to get them. She manipulated an object someone put in her hand, but often she didn't look at it. Around two months ago, she began swiping at things—a hit-and-miss business for a long time. Now, through a combination of maturation and practice, Jen has learned to look at something, reach for it, take hold of it, and bring it to her mouth. Today she reached for her spoons, the sleeve of Sam's sweater, the rice cake, and the peach. Since Jen likes to practice reaching, Carol held the objects out for her to grab rather than putting them in her hand.

Jen practiced tracking objects with her eyes by dropping bits of rice cake and peach and watching them fall.

The set of yellow plastic measuring spoons is one of Jen's favorite toys. She seems attracted to the bright color. She particularly likes to shake them so they rattle. Her repertoire of actions is still very small, but she can produce this sound whenever she feels like it. (Everyday objects make good toys for small children: a wooden spoon with a short handle is great for banging on a high chair tray; cardboard tubes from rolls of paper towels roll easily; vegetable brushes make a curious sensation on the skin.)

Sounds of all kinds interest Jen in and of themselves. She thought Carol's sneezes were wonderful.

The World of People

When Carol was trying to talk with her mother on the phone, Jen kept interrupting her. Later, Carol gave Jen her spoons and then a piece of peach, hoping Jen would amuse herself for a while. Jen couldn't. She likes the spoons and she likes peaches, but after a few minutes she wanted Carol to play with her again. Carol is afraid she is letting Jen manipulate her—that she is spoiling Jen—by responding so quickly to her demands for attention.

Jen isn't asking for attention because she's spoiled: she really needs attention. She needs attention because her new skills are limited and tentative. When Jen's arm got stuck, for example, she needed Carol to straighten her out. When she wanted Sam's sweater, she needed Carol to push it within reaching range. Jen also needs help to keep from getting bored. She is interested in things that respond and change, but she doesn't have the physical skills to make things change very much herself, nor the mental ability to concentrate for very long. She needs adults to make new things happen for her. Jen could rattle her spoons and drop her cracker, but she needed Carol to give her a parade of bright falling clothes, to amuse her with the odd sound of a sneeze, to talk with her, to touch her cheek with a warm sock and play peek-a-boo. She needs people because she needs their help to play with things and also because playing with people is in itself her favorite activity. Their voices, their liveliness, their ways of responding to her excite her and make her feel good. Jen demands attention from Carol and Sam all the time because that is what she needs to help her grow up.

Carol, of course, has needs of her own. Jen doesn't know that. She has no sense that Carol exists in any way except to be there for her. The result is that Carol finds it difficult to talk to Sam, talk on the phone, do the laundry, look at a magazine, do anything at all when she is with Jen. On days when Carol is tired or needs to be inside her own thoughts for a while, she sometimes feels as though Jen is literally pulling all the energy out of her body.

Carol's needs are real whether or not Jen is aware of them. Jen does need a lot of attention, but Carol doesn't have to respond instantly every time Jen is feeling bored or fretful. Carol could have acknowledged Jen's cry with a word or a glance, for example, and gone on reading the law review. Jen is old enough now to begin stretching herself a little to find ways to keep herself amused.

Ideas and Words

When Jen rattles the plastic spoons, they always make a noise. When she holds a piece of food over the edge of her tray and lets go, it always falls. Repeating these games will help her develop a notion of cause and effect.

Jen didn't realize that she can't drop her peach and have it too. After she dropped it, she started fretting because it was no longer there.

Sense of Self

For now, Carol is the more active player in the peek-a-boo game. She was the one who held up the sock in front of her face and Jen's. Jen responded. Before long, Jen will learn how to initiate the games herself. She will be able to take control, making her mother and father appear and disappear. Her new power will make her more aware that she is a separate person from her mother and father.

Jen's demandingness, which is so hard on Carol, is healthy. Jen is asking for just as much attention as she needs. She is far too young to realize that she may be doing this at other people's expense.

◆

ALEX
(Fifteen Months)

Much to Rita's surprise, Robert volunteered to do the dishes with the boys after dinner, giving her a quiet half hour to sort the laundry and catch up on what is happening in the world. She carries the basket of clean clothes from the bathroom to the bedroom, turns the little TV on to the news, spills some of the laundry onto the bed, and begins sorting.

Alex's favorite pajamas—the ones with the blue cats on them—are right on top. Rita smoothes the wrinkles from them. Last time he wore them, she noticed they seemed a little small. They look very tiny and dear to her now. Her baby, her last baby, is growing into a little boy.

"Bah!" Rita hears Alex calling. I hope he doesn't bump into something, Rita thinks. Barney dashes through the door and scoots under the bed. Rita eyes the spot where the cat retreated with resentment. Couldn't he have chosen somewhere else to hide?

Alex bursts in on all fours. "Bah," he calls.

"Barney is taking a rest under the bed," Rita says. Alex scrambles over to the bed, plops down on his bottom, and tries to crawl under the bed frame, although it is just four inches up from the floor.

"Bah!" he says. He looks at Rita in frustration.

Barney sneaks out from the far corner of the bed. Alex lunges, but the cat scurries out of the room way ahead of him.

"Leave Barney alone for a while. I don't think he feels like playing." Alex is staring at the space where the cat was last seen. Rita leans over and puts her hand on Alex's shoulder. "I'm folding our wash," she says. "Why don't you go back and play with Daddy?"

Alex smiles. The cat is forgotten. "Aabahda," he says, looking at the bright fabrics on the bed.

He tries to pull himself up on the bed by tugging at the bedspread. A pile of folded towels slips to the floor. He pulls on the bedspread again.

Rita helps him up and retrieves the towels.

Alex sits next to his mother, who begins folding a sheet. He points to one of the cats on the pajamas Rita just folded. "Bah," he says.

"Yes," says Rita. "That is a kitty cat just like Barney."

Alex picks up the folded pajamas and laughs. He drops them and looks around. He glances at the TV, then spots a green washcloth. He picks it up and begins wiping his face with it. "That's right," says Rita. "You use that washcloth to wash your face when you take a bath."

Alex tosses the washcloth off the bed and begins climbing down. His foot gets caught in the sheet Rita is folding. "There you go," says Rita, untangling his foot and lowering him to the floor.

Alex pulls at the sheet and giggles. Rita puts the sheet over him so he is completely covered. "Where's Alex?" she asks.

Alex squirms.

"Where's Alex?"

Alex sticks his head out, then pulls it back, giggling.

"What's this?" Rita touches the sheet. She slowly lifts the corner up. "Why, it's Alex!"

Alex, laughing, begins crawling away, dragging the sheet with him. Rita catches him. "That's Alex." Laughing, he hugs her legs.

"Where's Daddy?" Rita says after a cuddle. "Why don't you go find Daddy?"

Alex looks at her. "Da," he says, stepping pigeon-toed but briskly toward the door.

"Good boy." Rita turns back to the bed to untangle the sheet. Alex notices the laundry basket and forgets where he was going. Rita turns around and sees Alex dumping the clothes in the basket on the floor. He lifts the empty basket and grunts the way Robert does when he lifts an air conditioner at the shop. He looks very proud of himself. He takes two steps and then drops the basket.

Rita considers and rejects the idea of carrying him off to the living room and tying him down. So much for the quiet half hour, she thinks.

OBSERVATIONS

The World of Things

Alex doesn't understand how to estimate the size of an object or a space. He doesn't have a sense of his own size either. He often tries to fit into spaces that are too small, the way he tried to crawl under the bed tonight.

When Barney ran away, Alex went to look for him. He has learned that when things and people disappear, they can be found again.

Alex dumped the laundry on the floor. Filling and dumping containers, both big ones like the laundry basket and small ones like empty Band-Aid boxes are among his greatest pleasures.

Alex showed Rita he knew what the washcloth was for by wiping his face with it. He is working hard to understand all the objects and places that are part of his daily routines.

The World of People

Rita wanted Alex to leave her alone tonight so she could relax and get the laundry sorted out quickly. After trying unsuccessfully to get him to go back to Robert, she gave up and resigned herself to putting up with Alex's "help."

Barney is an important member of Alex's family. Sometimes Alex ignores him for a couple of days, sometimes he plays very sweetly with him, and other times he pesters or pokes him or tries to pick him up in ways that do not appeal to cats. Tonight, Barney made it clear he wanted to be left alone, but Alex determinedly went after him. Rita tried to explain that Barney didn't want to play now. Alex didn't understand. He is too young to realize that cats, or other people for that matter, have feelings he must respect.

Ideas and Words

For Alex, playing is learning, and learning is moving and making noises. He is too busy moving to concentrate on the TV for long. He glanced at the set tonight but quickly turned away to do something more active.

Alex is aware that pictures represent something. He pointed to the cats on his pajamas and said "Bah." He realized that Barney is a cat and that the pictures on the pajamas are images of cats.

"Reading" a book still means turning pages to him, but lately Alex has been stopping longer to look at pictures and sometimes tries to name the things he recognizes. Naming pictures is a skill which will help him learn to read.

Alex understands more than he can say. He can't name his washcloth, but he recognized it and used pantomime to identify it by its function.

When Alex tries to do something the way his adults do, he imitates their actions and gestures. He grunted when he lifted the basket the way Robert grunts when he lifts something heavy. To Alex, making this noise is part of doing the job.

Sense of Self

Alex wants to do everything he can do, all at once. He wanted to climb on the bed, to examine and name things on the bed, to dump the basket, to lift the basket. He saw all these activities as part of putting away the laundry and helping Rita. He worked really hard to do them: he is very demanding of himself.

Alex expects and usually gets Rita's praise for exercising his new skills. She smiled at him tonight when he pointed to the pajama cats and said "Bah" and when he showed her what a washcloth was for.

Her encouragement increases his pride in his ability to learn.

Alex toddled away from Robert and went off on his own after Barney. He began going off on little trips by himself as soon as he learned to crawl. His sense of his own separate individuality has come to a considerable degree from his ability to separate himself physically from his parents and go exploring independently. He has enough of a sense of himself now to feel whole and confident when he's away from his parents, and enough of a sense of his parents' continued existence to feel sure they won't disappear while he's gone—as long as he's only gone a little while. He comes back to his parents or calls for them to find him after a few minutes away. He recharges emotionally by being near them, and then—so predictably he sometimes reminds Rita of a wind-up toy—he's off again. His little excursions sometimes make Rita nervous. She is glad he feels confident and independent, but she worries he may hurt himself, the way she worried he would bump into something tonight.

Tonight Alex chased Barney and played a hiding-under-the-sheet game which combined elements of catch-me and peek-a-boo. Alex likes chasing and hiding games partly because they let him play with his separateness. In the games, he can control the appearances and disappearances of himself and others. There is a slight edge of controllable danger in that moment before a safe, friendly face emerges that Alex finds exciting. The games always end in capture or discovery and the cuddling that refuels his growing sense of self.

◆

KATIE
(Twenty-eight Months)

Katie, Sarah, and Joe are sitting on the sofa, looking through the photo album. Sarah has just added the roll taken last month.

"Dog," Katie says.

"No," Joe says. "That's a picture of Mommy and me playing badminton with the Birches—oh, I see." Joe notices the Birches' dog on the sidelines in the lower left. "Yes, that's Ralph, the Birches' dog. You were just a baby then."

Katie, excited, starts turning the pages. "Baby." She points to herself in the next picture.

"Yes," Joe says. "That's you eating a cracker."

Katie smiles at him, her finger still on the page.

"You were just beginning to talk then," Sarah tells her. "Cracker was your first word." Katie looks at Sarah while she talks, then studies the picture. She turns to the next one. It is a photo of Joe's sister. Katie, impatient, starts turning the pages a few at a time.

"Wait, stop!" Sarah puts her hand down to hold the book open at the last page Katie turned. "That's you and me feeding the brown ducks at the pond, remember?" Sarah points to the top picture. Katie stares for a moment, then laughs in recognition.

"Did the ducks say 'woof, woof'?" Joe asks.

Katie looks at him, beginning to smile. "Nooo," she says.

"Did they say 'meow, meow'?" Sarah asks.

"Nooo." Katie grins.

"No?" Sarah asks.

"'Quack, quack,'" Katie shouts.

"And speaking of ducks," Sarah says, "I think it's time for Katie's bath."

"No. My look pictures."

Katie, who has recently declared war on going to bed, realizes what comes after her bath. Joe looks at his watch. It's seven-thirty. They've been trying to get Katie into bed by eight-thirty. "I'll tell you what," Joe says. "You help me take the laundry down and then you'll take a bath and go to bed." He takes off his reading glasses and puts them in his shirt pocket.

"Laundry down," Katie says, scrambling off the couch.

"And then—" Sarah says, holding her daughter still. Katie giggles and looks away. "And then it's time for bed."

"No bed," Katie shouts.

"Katie," Joe says, "after we bring the laundry in, you'll go to bed. That's the deal."

Katie scowls. She picks up Franklin. But she meets her father's eye. Joe gets up and takes Katie's hand. "Come on." Katie changes her mind and puts Franklin back down.

Joe picks up the laundry basket on the back porch. "Can you get the clothespins in the can over there?" Joe says, nodding toward the corner table.

Katie picks up the coffee can with the clothespins. "Red," she says.

Joe looks: he doesn't see anything but tin. Katie points to a tiny speck of red paint near the rim on one side. "You're right," Joe says. "That's red." Katie shakes the can to make the clothespins rattle.

They walk down the four steps into the twilit yard. Joe goes over to the line, puts the basket down, and starts taking off the clothes. Katie walks over and puts the tin down next to the clothes basket.

Joe is shaking the wrinkles out of one of his tee shirts before dropping it in the basket. "Daddy's shirt," Katie says.

"Yes," Joe agrees. He takes the clothespins he has stuck in his pocket and hands them to Katie. "Will you put these pins in the tin?" he asks.

Katie takes the pins. "Pins in tin," she says, dropping them in. "Pintin, pintin, pintin," she repeats to herself.

Joe looks at her. She is starting to take all the clothespins out of the tin now. "Keep them in the tin, please," he tells her.

Katie puts them back.

Joe has gotten everything down but a sweatshirt, two pairs of Katie's pants, and Sarah's robe. "My help," Katie says, trying to reach her pants, which are two feet higher than her hand.

"You can reach Mommy's green robe," Joe tells her.

Katie walks over to the robe. "Toe toe," she says, standing on the same. She reaches the end of the robe and pulls it down so it lands on the ground. She picks up one end and starts to give it a good shake.

"Let me help you," Joe says, quickly grabbing the end dragging in the dirt. "You hold the sleeves, that's right. And I'll hold the bottom. We'll count to three and shake."

"One, two, three, shake," Katie and Joe say together. They give the robe a hardy shake. Katie likes shaking and wants to go on.

"Hey, enough," Joe says. He folds the robe in half and places it in the

The World of People

Katie is learning about who does what kind of work. In Katie's house, Sarah and Joe share the household work. Sometimes Sarah takes down the laundry. Sometimes, like tonight, Joe does it.

Katie recognized Joe's shirt and Sarah's green robe. Katie knows that different articles of clothing belong to different members of her family.

Katie is beginning to understand that social actions have social consequences, but she does not have a firm hold on this idea. She couldn't quite absorb the "no bed, no book" statement.

Katie is learning to joke and tease. Joe likes to tease her and his pleasure in their joking game encourages her sense of humor and her flirtatiousness. She knows when her father is being serious and when he is deliberately saying or doing things that aren't right, such as asking if a duck goes "woof."

Ideas and Words

Katie can joke with Joe about what dogs, cats, and ducks say because she knows the right answers. She enjoys wearing her shoes in the tub because she understands that it is not something people usually do.

When Katie looked at the picture of herself and Sarah with the ducks, she was able to remember the experience. Looking at pictures and listening to stories about things that happened are important to Katie. She is learning to make sense of experiences by reviewing them and making pictures of them in her mind.

Katie is noticing colors all the time now. Her parents are helping her learn colors by pointing them out and naming them. Tonight, Sarah called the ducks brown and Joe described Sarah's robe as green.

Katie can recite *one, two, three*. She doesn't understand what the words represent yet, but she understands that one follows the other in sequence. (This doesn't mean that she always says them in the proper order.) She is developing more of a concept of sequence in general. She knows, for example, that after she has a bath she will have to go to bed because that's the routine in her household. Joe and Sarah were helping Katie think about sequence by telling her that first she would take down the laundry, then take a bath, then go to bed. Telling Katie it was almost bedtime, letting her say "No," and then rehearsing the routine with words, may have made it easier to get her into bed.

Sense of Self

Katie likes hearing about herself when she was a baby. She was deeply interested in her baby picture and in Sarah's story about her first word. She is working to conceive of herself as someone who has a past and a future, who changes but is still always Katie.

Katie often got distracted from the chore tonight. A sudden impulse to practice running or play hide-and-seek was enough to make her momentarily forget the laundry. But she really wanted to help Joe take down the wash. She wanted to do everything she could—to get the clothes down and shake them and carry the robe. She is proud to be able to do real chores.

Sometimes Katie isn't really helping: she's getting in the way. Today Joe had to tell her to keep the clothespins in the tin and to stop shaking the robe. If Joe had done nothing but criticize her mistakes, Katie would have felt unappreciated and unsure of herself. He didn't make her feel that way. Most of the time, he encouraged her to help as much as she could. He gave her a task of her own—carrying the clothespins. When she tried to pull down the pants, which were too high for her to reach, he suggested she get the robe, which was lower. When she let the robe fall to the ground, instead of scolding her, he picked up the dirty end himself and suggested they shake it together. Joe's willingness to make Katie a kind of partner made her feel capable.

Katie is very stubborn about doing things she wants to do and doing them by herself. Sometimes she wants to do things she isn't capable of doing. She realizes she isn't, but she can't stop trying without feeling humiliated and she doesn't want an adult to stop her. She just keeps going, getting more and more frustrated. This might have happened when she tried to lift the basket tonight. If Joe had told Katie she couldn't lift the basket and had taken it from her, she might have felt embarrassed and gotten angry. Instead, he just picked up one handle without saying anything.

Katie likes getting her own way. She also likes testing her parents' authority (though of course she needs and wants them to really be in charge). Tonight, when Joe told her she had to take a bath and go to bed, Katie said no and then hit him. Once she takes a stand like this, Katie doesn't know how to back down. She can't control the situation anymore. Often she wants to retreat and is relieved when her parents assert themselves. Joe did this tonight—without humiliating her. When Katie was confused by his threat not to read the book, Joe took the decision out of her hands by starting to take her shoes off.

Words like *embarrassment* and *humiliation* may not be the most accurate way to describe Katie's feelings. There's no way to know if Katie has the same kind of feelings adults do: she hasn't learned how to sort out or describe or name her feelings herself. But it is clear from Katie's expressions and behavior that she's building up her sense of herself by asserting her desires and abilities. Her successes at achieving her goals and the way others respond to her self-assertions determine her feelings about herself to a large degree. When Katie fails at a task she sets herself, or adults dismiss her efforts to help, or she gets caught in a win/lose conflict with her parents—and when she simply can't make sense of things—she feels small in some way.

Part Four

------------------- ♦ -------------------

THE OUTSIDE
WORLD

10

GOING TO THE SUPERMARKET

By the time she is three or so, a child knows her house or apartment inside out, literally, having taken everything inside something out of it a hundred times. She knows which room has the tickly shag rug, which chair is the bounciest, which closet is best for hiding, and how to put pillows on the floor to make a place for jumping. The rooms she lives in with her family are the center of the universe for her, a bright island in a broader world of which she may be only sleepily aware but which becomes a little more visible to her every day. First one place brightens and begins to become familiar, then another: the place where she goes for day care, the homes of her relatives, the homes of her parents' close friends and neighbors, the streets and roads she rides or walks through regularly, the places filled with strangers where her parents take her to do errands.

The supermarket and grocery are the first public places to become familiar to many children. Trips to gas stations, department stores, hardware stores are once-in-a-while events, but most families do a big food shopping once a week and stop at the local store once or twice during the week as well for extra milk or eggs or bread. Working parents often buy the newspaper and go to the bank, the cleaner, or the pharmacy on the way to or from work or at lunch—when the children are somewhere else. But they usually go marketing nights or weekends when the children are around. Since small children can't be left alone, they often get to come.

Supermarkets, like all stores, encourage shoppers to look around. Package designers try to ambush the eyes with bright colors and pictures and patterns. Store owners display the packages as seductively as they can. Adults become skilled at ignoring the whole consumer show and steering straight toward the items they want; they tend to regard much of the display around them as roadblocks. But to a small child for whom looking is still discovery, a supermarket is delightful. There are boxes of different colors, shapes, and sizes covered with pictures and designs. There are all sorts of cans with pictures on them too, pictures of peaches, tomatoes, artichoke hearts. There are glass jars holding long pointy asparagus, round white onions, red spaghetti sauce. There are shelves piled with oranges, grapefruit, lemons, yellow bananas, green peppers, purple plums.

The shelves form long, canyonlike aisles. Moving through them lets children experience space in a special way. The smell and feel of the space changes as they move. The air around the rotisserie in the deli section is hot and smells pungent, the bakery has a sweet, yeasty odor, the air is cool above the low shelves containing packaged strips of red beef, pale veal, pink and tan pork. The boxes with pictures of vegetables, pies, cakes look sharper when the freezer door is opened and cold air comes out. And throughout the supermarket a child sees faces. She sees that the world is full of people she doesn't know. When her mother or father stops to find an item or wait on a line, she has a chance to examine the adult faces close up and unhurriedly.

Food shopping is basically a matter of collecting and dumping, which are among children's first focused activities. A child may not understand why her parents are picking some objects and not others, but during her second year she will quickly realize that her parents are taking things and putting them in a basket or cart, and she will want to do the same. Later, she will be equally happy to take things out and help put them on the checkout counter (if she can reach). The carts are great toys in themselves. Children like riding in them, and if they are old enough, they want to push the cart themselves or try, at least.

The easiest way to take a small baby to the store is in a backpack. Your baby will enjoy traveling this way. Usually she has to look up from a crib or blanket or couch or playpen to see you and the things around her. But in her backpack she gets to look down at the floor from a full five or six feet above and to view close up rows and rows of jars and boxes and cans and fruits that constantly change as you move along. While she is looking, she is enjoying the sensations of being close to the thing in the world that interests her most—you. She can feel the texture of your shirt on her skin. Your hair brushes her cheek when she turns her head to look at something. She can smell your smell and feel the muscles in your back move when you reach for something. She hears your voice when you speak and if she leans her cheek against your back she can feel the vibrations of your words. The smells, the changing air temperatures, the sounds of clanking carts, the brightness of the sunlight through the window or the dull clearness of the fluorescent lights add interesting layers to the experience.

As she gets older, your baby will begin to distinguish different sights and sounds and to use whatever resources she has to examine the things that catch her attention. Sometimes she will sit in her pack observing with regal passivity (or even doze), but other times she will squirm around and try to touch the bright oranges or the toilet paper with the picture of the baby. You will have to pay attention to make sure she doesn't succeed in knocking something down or getting herself twisted in the pack. At about six months or so, she may start paying attention to strangers, staring at them with curiosity or hiding her face against your back if they come too near.

For a baby, the supermarket remains perpetually new. It will take many trips before she will remember and recognize it. Toddlers who are experienced shoppers recognize the supermarket when they get there and have the mobility they need to investigate it fully on their own. Your toddler will pick up jars, pieces of fruit, anything she can reach, pull down a box and try to open it, run her hand along the edge of the dairy shelf, feeling where the cold part ends and the warm outside begins. She may become absorbed in examining cans, feeling and smelling and licking them, or she may systematically take all the cans off the lower shelf and put them on the floor.

The division of space into aisles is particularly pleasing to a toddler, who has just acquired the ability to move herself. When she trots toward an interesting bin of sale items at the end of the aisle, she can see her progress and get a physical sense of covering a distance much more easily than she could in the living room at home. She will enjoy helping you push the shopping cart down the long paths.

Your toddler will also enjoy going for a ride down the aisles in the cart, particularly if you race and joggle it a bit to make the trip more exciting. If she is in a quiet mood, she may be happy to stay in the cart observing or maybe just sucking her fingers. If she's feeling more active, she'll want to get in and out, in and out, and you may have to insist she stay in one place or another long enough for you to get some shopping done.

Your toddler doesn't understand that you go to the market to get the food you eat at home. She doesn't realize the food in the refrigerator comes from somewhere, much less that hard, raw brown potatoes are the same food as the diced, white, soft boiled potatoes she eats. But she will recognize pieces of fruit, cartons of milk, and other familiar items. She may start eating them in the store. She may start imitating you by putting items in the cart and she will be particularly pleased if you specifically ask for her help. When you ask her to take down the red can, she will probably take down the first can she sees instead, but if you hand her the right one, she can put it in the basket for you and later take it out to put it on the checkout counter. She can add a pear to a plastic bag you are filling. She can carry something to the car or, if you are walking, hold it on her lap in the stroller.

The supermarket may be the place where your toddler is first introduced to money. She won't understand what it's for, but she'll be interested in examining the coins and bills you take from your bag or pocket. If you give her some change at the checkout counter, she'll be pleased, though she won't realize she's supposed to give it to the person at the register.

Though toddlers will rarely ignore a dog or a cat, they sometimes act as if they don't see people. Your child may walk right into a stranger in the store, oblivious to his warnings or attempts to move out of the way, and pay no attention when a fellow shopper smiles and says hello. But other times—staying close to you for safety—she may stare fixedly at strangers as if hypnotized by the patterns of noses, eyes, and mouths. Very social toddlers may even go up to strangers and stand near them to see what happens.

Two-year-olds enjoy all the activities toddlers like, but they have a clearer understanding of what you are doing in a supermarket, and they play in ways that are easier for adults to understand. For example, a two will enjoy running down an aisle, realize she has run down a kind of path, and run up and down again, or turn the corner, discover there's another aisle, and run down that one. (Twos are also very good at getting lost, even in small places.) When she is in the cart, a two-year-old may ask to be pushed faster, and if you pretend you're driving a car she may help you with the motor noises.

Your two knows you are going to the supermarket to get food, although she may not make the connection between the food you get there and the food you take out of the refrigerator later. Language will help her make that connection eventually. She will want to reach out for the things she sees in the supermarket with words as well as with her hands. She will name items that she recognizes, ask the names of others, notice and point out verbally and with her hand every object in the store that's blue or green or whatever color she is learning that week. She will also realize that cans, jars, and boxes have something inside, and she may discover that the pictures on the outside have to do with what they contain. The word *pancake* may be the first relationship she discovers between the box you buy and the soft round things she eats.

Your two is beginning to be familiar with your shopping routine, and she will be pleased to help you out. If you ask her to get the carton of strawberry yogurt as you go by the dairy section, she won't know what to do, but if she knows what the carton looks like and you pull up right by the yogurt cartons and point, she may come up with the right one. You can also try asking her if she would like you to get orange juice or apple juice. If she isn't in the mood for juice right that minute she won't know what to say, but she will gradually begin to get the idea that you make choices when you shop.

Two-year-olds don't understand what paying means, but they sense that money is important to adults. They are aware that people give money to other people in stores. If you hand your two some coins at the checkout counter, she will probably realize she's supposed to give them to the person there.

Twos sometimes like to watch the strangers in the supermarket. A shy two will stick close to her parents and even hide if a stranger looks back at her, while an outgoing child may practice social skills the same way she practices physical ones. She might smile at a stranger to see if she can get him to smile back, then do it again and again. She may even try a game of peek-a-boo, sticking her head out from behind a bin, catching a stranger's eye, and then retreating quickly.

Today Katie, an old hand at supermarkets, gets her first shopping list. Alex shoplifts a peach and helps his mother carry the hamburger rolls. Jennifer is giving her father's back a hard workout.

JENNIFER
(Six Months)

Sam is burning with culinary enthusiasm.

"Lemons," he tells his daughter, writing lemons down on a pad, "tomatoes, maybe those hothouse ones, fresh basil—we're going to grill the tomatoes." He gets up and peers into one of the cabinets. "We need capers. How about some good dried mushrooms for a pilaf?" He turns to Jen, who is sitting in her high chair gumming a banana and watching the doors open and

shut. "Okay, we won't get carried away." He goes over to a pad hanging by the refrigerator and looks at the shopping list kept by Mrs. Semple and Carol. Jen kicks her feet and babbles. "Nothing here we need tonight."

Carol's work load this week is gargantuan. Sam, doing his best to be supportive, has managed to get home early and has decided to greet his wife with a special dinner.

"How are you doing, banana face?" Sam pats his daughter's nose. Jen bounces in the high chair and gurgles. Sam wipes banana off her face and hands. "Do you want to go to the store?" Jen rubs her newly cleaned hands in the banana bits on the tray. Sam takes this for a yes.

Twenty minutes later, Sam pushes open the door of the twenty-four-hour gourmet grocery and they step into the fertile smell of coffee beans and flowers. Jen bounces up and down in the backpack, excited to be going for a ride. A ceiling fan is humming. A man to their left is taking bunches of pale green grapes out of a carton and placing them on a shelf. Jen stares at the man and begins bouncing with new determination, pressing her feet against the metal bar at the base of the pack. Each time she bounces, the strap pulls at Sam's shoulder. "Jen," Sam says, "take it easy on your father's back." Jen touches his ear and coos. Sam bends to take a small basket from the pile by the door. Jen uses her arms to press away from him, arching her back slightly. This brings her face directly opposite the face of the man unpacking grapes. He nods at her. Jen whines and pulls at her father's shirt.

Sam straightens up with the basket and starts down an aisle lined with bins of fruits and vegetables. Jen looks around from her perch, sucking on the edge of the pack. She looks to the right at slender orange carrots with green tufts, deep purple cabbages, creamy pointed endives, dusty potatoes. Then she holds her head back and looks at the ceiling. The spinning fan catches her attention. She opens her mouth, drooling a little.

"We need some of these." Sam stops at a pile of tomatoes near the end of the aisle. Jen begins pushing against the metal rod with her feet again. Sam notices a carton of presumably fresher tomatoes just underneath the bin and bends at the knees to choose from the new arrivals. Jen suddenly reaches both hands to the left and lurches out. Sam almost falls. "Easy," he tells Jen, recovering his balance. Jen gurgles. Sam notices a display bin holding a neatly arranged pyramid of imported crackers towering above them.

"Did you want to knock the crackers over?" he asks Jen. "Huh?" Jen bounces enthusiastically.

Sam takes a tomato, lifts it up behind his shoulder, and rubs it along Jen's cheek. Jen quiets down at once, concentrating on the smooth touch of the tomato skin. She reaches for it. Sam lets her touch it, but doesn't let go. "Let me put it with the others," he says, stroking Jen's fingers and slowly pulling the tomato away. Jen, diverted by a patch of bright yellow ahead, lets go without bruising the tomato. Sam continues to the yellow patch and starts picking out lemons. Jen grabs hold of his hair with both hands and tugs.

"Ouch!" Sam reaches back to pry her hands off. "Do you want to make me bald?"

Sam pauses at the tall, cabinet-style freezer, thinking about the gentle admonitory pat Carol gave his stomach last night. "How about some ice cream?" he asks Jen. "What do you say?" Jen gurgles. "Okay, you're the one who insisted, right?" He opens the freezer door.

Jen blinks as a blast of cold air hits her face. She shifts her weight slightly and burrows her right foot into Sam's side. "Barara," she says.

"Strawberry or chocolate chip?"

"Ahhh bahhh," Jen says.

"Okay. We'll get both."

Sam puts the two containers of ice cream in the basket with the produce and closes the freezer door. He reaches back to put Jen's right foot up on the bar of the p⌐k. Her leg is chilly. "That was cold, wasn't it?" He rubs her legs. She grabs hold of his hair again and pulls. "Ow," he says sharply. "Jen, that hurts!"

Jen blinks, startled by the sharpness in Sam's voice. Her head flicks to the right. Her face grows still.

Sam goes back an aisle to get a package of rice cakes. He opens it and hands a piece of cracker over his shoulder to Jen. "Ahh," she says, making an immediate recovery. She grabs the cracker, takes a bite, and then drops the rest. She bends her head to watch it land on the floor. She takes another handful of Sam's hair.

"Hey you!" Sam says, undoing Jen's hand and tickling her leg. "You're not playing by the rules. Your mommy told me that when she gives you a cracker, you eat it and stop pulling her hair."

Sam breaks off another piece of the puffed rice circle and hands it back. "Aaeee," she says with delight. She squeezes the cracker a second and then begins chewing on it. Sam feels a wet crumb landing on his neck.

◆

OBSERVATIONS

The World of Things

A grocery store is an exciting place for a sensualist like Jen. Hearing the hum of a fan, smelling ground coffee, feeling the silky touch of a tomato on her cheek or a lick of freezer-cooled air are rich events for her.

From the crib, the stroller, the couch, and the playpen, Jen has to look up to see what adults see. In the backpack, she can see the world from adult height and she can look down. Today she saw the fruits and vegetables stretched out below her like a carpet and was able to look directly at the items on the high shelves.

Jen covered a lot of ground on Sam's back, which she can't yet do on her own. As Sam moved, the world around Jen changed. The red tomatoes and yellow lemons appeared as patches of color, then slowly grew bigger as Sam walked toward them. Every time Sam turned a corner, a new scene appeared.

Jen can't creep or crawl, but lately she has been moving more and more, getting ready to go places. Sometimes she sat quietly in the backpack tonight, looking and listening, but often she was physically busy, bouncing, reaching, bending, stretching, pulling at her father's hair.

The World of People

Jen was close to Sam's body for a full twenty minutes. She was close enough to smell his special odor, to touch his ear and his hair, to feel his back move as he walked and reached.

Jen doesn't realize that bouncing and hair pulling are unpleasant for Sam. She does not understand that Sam's body is Sam; she treated his hair and earlobes as though they were objects.

When Sam discussed buying the fattening ice cream with Jen, he was making her, in a mock way, his conspirator in indulgence. Jen is too young to understand him now, of course, but Sam is already establishing his own special relationship with her. In a few years' time, indulging each other in special treats will be one of the things Sam and Jen do together. Jen and Carol will have special ways of being together too. Long before she starts making friends of her own, Jen will have learned a great deal about different kinds of relationships simply by being a member of a family.

Ideas and Words

Sam played a game with Jen and himself, fondly discussing all his shopping decisions with her and pretending her gestures and babbling sounds were responses to his comments and questions. He is introducing Jen to the idea that people share an experience by talking together.

Today Jen saw the tomatoes as a splash of red in the distance. As she was carried closer, the red area got bigger. Sam touched it and pulled out a single red tomato. He held it to Jen's cheek. She felt a pleasant smooth sensation.

Over the next two years, Jennifer will learn the name of the color red and the word *tomato*. By then she will have touched many tomatoes. She may have discovered that she likes the taste of tomatoes. She will have watched her father cut tomatoes in pieces and put them in green salads or chop them into red bits and put them in a pan with creamy white specks of garlic and shiny, stinging onion strips. Perhaps one day she will visit a garden and see tomatoes hanging from low plants on strings of green. The first time Sam asks her to pick a tomato from the shelf, she may hand him an apple. He will show her the tomato and she will compare the apple and the tomato with her hands and eyes. Bit by bit she will learn more about what tomatoes are and about what the word *tomato* means—to everyone and to Jennifer in particular.

Sense of Self

Jen was an explorer today even from the confines of her backpack. She listened, smiled, touched, tasted, and looked as hard as she could.

ALEX
(Fifteen Months)

"Just a minute, honey." Rita, one hand in Alex's, is riffling through her shoulder bag with the other hand, looking for her shopping list. They have stopped at a convenience market on their way to pick up Mike at school.

Rita lets go of Alex to free both hands for the search. Alex steps away. He rubs his hand back and forth along the plastic wall, staring at the assortment of faces going past.

A few feet away, a woman is struggling to pull apart two shopping carts. They clatter. Alex heads toward the carts, barely missing a man who is packing cartons.

"Hey, buddy," the man says. "Keep your eyes open."

Rita looks up. "Alex, I told you to wait by me." She steps over and takes his hand again.

"Ahdoban reee," Alex says, tugging gently to free his hand. He is watching the man pack a carton. The man grins at him. Alex looks at Rita. She is busy going through her bag and doesn't notice. Alex steps closer to her, puts his tongue on his upper lip, pulls it in, then gives the man a full-blast smile.

"Okay," Rita says, list in hand. "Let's go." She takes a cart. "Do you want to help me push?" Alex, rising on tiptoe, reaches for the handle. "Why don't you hold on lower down, honey?" Alex looks up at her.

"Here." Rita indicates a good spot. Alex runs his hand down the edge of the cart to touch Rita's. "That's right." She starts off toward the produce, Alex trotting along at her side. "First, let's get the lettuce."

Rita feels a head of lettuce, puts it back, feels another one. Alex walks over to the peaches a few feet down. He reaches up and takes one. All its neighbors begin slowly rolling down. Rita's early warning system goes off. She drops the head of lettuce in the cart and arrives at Alex's side just in time to prevent the peach landslide.

"Come on, Alex." She goes back to the cart. Alex follows, almost bumping into a display of pink grapefruit in the middle of the aisle. He stops and stands still with an absentminded air, squeezing the peach in his hand. He takes a bite. He licks around his lips to catch the juice running down his chin.

"Alex," Rita says. He blinks and looks up at her. "Did you just take that peach? Give it to me."

Alex hands it to Rita. "Pea," he says, smiling.

Rita wraps it in a tissue and drops it in the cart. "We're not getting anywhere," Rita tells Alex. "How would you like to go for a ride in the cart?"

"Up," says Alex, holding up his sticky hands. The small cart doesn't have a child's seat. Rita pushes the lettuce out of the way and sits Alex down facing front.

"Okay, on to the hamburger rolls." She makes an engine sound: "Vrrooom!"

Rita gives Alex the rolls to hold, fills the space around him with juice, milk, and peanut butter, and pushes toward the checkout counter. There are two people on line ahead of them. Rita leafs through a magazine. Alex begins squirming and tries to stand up.

"Is that cart hurting your heinie?"

Alex raises his arms. Rita lifts him out. He starts taking magazines out of the racks.

"No, honey. See, it's our turn now. Will you put these up on the counter, please?" She hands him the hamburger rolls. He squeezes them. "Up there." Rita taps the counter. Alex reaches as high as he can and puts the rolls on the edge of the counter. They fall off. He sits down on his rear and picks them up, but he can't stand up again with full hands. Rita squeezes around the cart, lifts him up, and hands him the rolls. The cashier leans over to take them this time. Alex stares: it's the same man who was packing cartons.

"Thanks, buddy."

Alex smiles.

Rita has emptied the other items in the cart. "This is a peach," she says, gingerly picking up the peach-juice-soaked tissue with two fingers.

OBSERVATIONS

The World of Things

Alex's hands are always working to bring him information about things. Sometimes he handles things deliberately to find out about them. Sometimes his fingers seem to go about feeling things on their own, the way they felt the wall of the supermarket while he was looking around.

Alex is still learning how to move from position to position and from place to place. He tried rising on his toes to reach the handle of the cart and to put the rolls on the counter, but he isn't very steady on his toes yet. Sometimes when he bends down to pick up something on the floor, he ends up sitting down the way he did when he reached for the fallen rolls. He needs to use his hands (when they aren't filled with rolls) to push himself back up. He bumps into things frequently, not because there's anything wrong with his eyes, but because he's easily distracted and often doesn't realize that the things he sees are in his path.

The World of People

Alex now makes a sharp distinction between people he knows and strangers. Though he is interested in adults and their activities and is quite outgoing, he doesn't approach unfamiliar people on his own. He relies on Rita to guide his social adventures. For example, when the man packing boxes smiled at him today, he looked to his mother for some cue about how to proceed. Rita, busy looking for the list, didn't notice. Alex stepped closer to her to give himself confidence, studied the man a few seconds, then said hello with a generous smile. He was able to recognize the man when he saw him again at the counter several minutes later.

Ideas and Words

When Rita told Alex to hold the shopping cart lower, she pointed to the spot she had in mind. He found the right spot by running his hand down until he touched her hand. Rita was helping Alex learn, through his own motions, what *lower* means. He already knows the word *up* and raises his arms when he says it.

When something catches his attention the way the faces caught his attention in the supermarket, Alex can concentrate so hard on looking that he becomes oblivious to everything else. Other times, Alex seems absorbed in absolutely nothing. He stands still, staring blankly. It's impossible to guess what's going on inside him at these times.

Alex's picture of the world is locked into the immediate. He can't analyze people's actions and anticipate what they will be doing next.

For example, though Alex saw the man packing a carton near him, he didn't realize he might get in the man's way because he could neither measure the space between them nor anticipate that the man's work would require him to move and reach.

Sense of Self

Alex feels good when he thinks that what he is doing is useful. Rita gave him several opportunities to be useful today: he pushed the cart, he held the rolls, and he handed them to the checkout man.

◆

KATIE
(Twenty-eight Months)

Sarah is sitting at the kitchen table writing on a pad of paper. Katie, standing by her side, watches closely.

"Here's the list." *Sarah tears the top sheet from the pad.* "There are some coupons in the blue bowl. See if we have any for the things we're getting."

Joe takes his reading glasses from his shirt pocket and puts them on to look over the list. He shuffles through the bowl. "Wheat crackers and toothpaste," *he tells Sarah. He puts the list and coupons in his back pocket.*

"Ready, Nutmeg?" *he asks Katie.*

"My want list," *Katie says, looking solemnly at Sarah.*

"All right," *Sarah agrees, catching Joe's eye. In large letters, she prints the word* milk *on the pad and tears the page off. She holds the piece of paper out to Katie.* "This is your list. It says 'milk,' m-i-l-k."

Katie takes the paper and looks up proudly at Joe. "My have list," *she says, holding it out carefully.*

"Let's see what this says." *Joe takes it.*

"Milk!" *bursts out Katie.*

Joe studies the list. "You are right. You'll be in charge of getting the milk today." *He takes his glasses off.* "Why don't you put your list in your pocket like Daddy does so you won't lose it?"

Very carefully Katie half folds, half crumples her list. She wipes her hand down the side of her shorts, but misses the pocket.

"Here." *Sarah reaches over and holds Katie's pocket open. Katie stuffs the list in and pats her pocket closed.*

"Let's go," *Joe says.*

"Bye," *Katie says. She steps up and hugs Sarah.*

"Good-bye, darling." *Sarah strokes her daughter's back.* "I'll see you later."

Joe takes Katie's hand, but before he can start for the door, Katie notices Franklin sitting in the corner behind Sarah. "Franklin," *she says, reaching out toward the stuffed dog.*

"What do you say we let Franklin stay here with me?" *Sarah asks.* "You can see him when you get back."

"Okay," *Katie agrees, much to Joe's relief.*

As soon as they arrive at the supermarket, Katie runs over to the line of stacked carts. She turns and tells her father, "My push cart." *She pulls at the first one. It doesn't budge.*

"I'll help you," *says Joe. He pulls the cart out and starts toward the far aisle. Katie jumps up next to him, reaches her arms high, and begins pushing too. She pushes hard to make the cart go fast.*

"Whoa," *says Joe, pulling the cart to a stop at the shelves with cookies and crackers.* "We need some wheat crackers." *He puts on his glasses and takes the coupon out of his pocket to check the brand. Katie, still deeply absorbed in the cart, continues to push.*

"Katie," *Joe says sharply, but too late to stop his daughter from hitting the elderly woman walking past.*

The woman's lips purse in anger. Then, realizing her attacker is a toddler, she manages a grim smile. "You better watch where you're going, young lady," *she says.*

"I'm sorry," *Joe tells her. He turns to Katie.* "You have to be careful where you push this cart."

Katie looks up at Joe. She tries to straighten out the cart. The right wheel passes over Joe's toes.

"Ouch," Joe says. Katie looks confused. "I have an idea," Joe tells her, dropping the crackers in the cart. "What if I give you a ride?"

"No," Katie says. "My push cart." Katie starts pushing again, tense with determination—but one of the wheels jams. She sniffles angrily.

"You can't push the cart," Joe says. "It's too big." Katie tries pushing the cart again. Joe lifts her up and puts her into the seat in the front of the cart. She doesn't struggle, but she doesn't help out either. She sniffs, her eyes narrow, and the corners of her mouth tighten. Then suddenly she reaches out and grabs Joe's glasses off his nose. Her face relaxes into a big giggle.

"Hey," Joe says, looking around. "Where are my glasses?" He holds the list at arm's length as if he were trying to read. "I need my glasses to read this list. Katie, have you seen my glasses?"

Katie giggles and holds them out. "Daddy's glasses," she says, smiling.

"Thank you." He looks down at the list. "That's better." He leans over and kisses Katie. "Now we'll get some vegetables," he says.

Joe pushes Katie over to the produce. He picks up a pepper, notices a large soft spot and puts it back.

"String beans," Katie says, pointing at a clear plastic box of long green beans.

"You want some string beans? They're not on the list but they do look nice." Joe hands Katie the package. "So you're a string bean lover just like your mother."

Katie smiles. She tries to open the beans. She can't. She holds the box up to Joe. "Daddy open," she says.

Joe makes a hole in the plastic wrap covering the box and hands it back to Katie. She pulls a bean out and begins eating it.

Katie crunches on the beans and surveys the market while Joe makes his way down the aisles filling the cart. Finally he pulls up to the dairy section. "Here's the milk, Katie. I think I'd better get you down so you can check your list."

Joe puts Katie down on the floor. She pulls her list out of her pocket and holds it out for Joe to see. Joe smooths out the paper. "Milk," he reads. "Mommy wrote 'milk' on your list so we would remember to get some milk." *The milk is too high for Katie to reach. Joe takes a quart and hands it to her.*

"My have milk," *she says.*

"You sure do," *laughs Joe.* "Why don't you carry your milk over to the checkout counter so we can pay Mr. Wilson for it?"

"My carry," *says Katie, walking alongside Joe and the cart. Joe steers to the checkout counter where Mr. Wilson works. There's a woman on line ahead of them. As soon as a space is cleared, Katie reaches to put the milk up on the counter. She has to tip it on its side and give it a shove to get it all the way up.* "Money," *she says to Joe. He hands her a dollar bill.*

"Hello," *the woman behind the register says, smiling down at Katie. She is definitely not Mr. Wilson. Katie looks up at her and ducks, head down, behind her father's legs.*

"It's okay, Nutmeg," *Joe says, stroking her head and neck.* "It looks like Mr. Wilson isn't working today, so there's someone else at the counter instead."

Katie peers out cautiously from behind Joe's legs and gives the cashier a look-over.

"Hello," *the woman says to Katie again.* "Is this your milk?"

Katie rubs her head with her fist, steps out from behind Joe's legs, reaches up, and puts the dollar bill on the counter. She glances quickly at Joe and turns back to the woman. "My buy milk," *she says shyly.*

◆

OBSERVATIONS

The World of Things

Katie has seen her mother and father writing and using shopping lists all her life. Today she noticed the list in a different way: she wanted one of her own.

Pockets fascinate Katie. When the list was in her pocket, she could no longer see it, but she knew it was still there. All she had to do was reach into her pocket and pull it out.

The World of People

When Katie pulled the cart over Joe's toes, he said "Ouch." She didn't quite understand what had happened. She doesn't have a sure sense of the boundaries of other people's bodies, and her capacity to imagine the sensations of others is still limited.

Katie feels close to her parents when she does the things they do—when she uses a list or pushes the cart, for example. She noticed the string beans right away because Sarah snacks on raw beans at home and shares them with Katie. Eating string beans is one of the activities that connect them. When Joe said Katie was like her mother because they both like string beans, Katie was pleased.

Katie was expecting to see Mr. Wilson, whom she knows, behind the register. When she saw a strange woman in his place, she was disoriented. It took her only a few seconds to recover and deal with the situation.

Ideas and Words

An adult wouldn't be disoriented if he didn't find a familiar clerk at a checkout counter. Katie was flustered partly because she couldn't figure out right away what had happened: she thought of Mr. Wilson as always being at that counter. Joe gave her an explanation: Mr. Wilson wasn't working, so someone else was there. The explanation helped Katie relax.

Katie has some memory of the supermarket. She knows they get food there. She remembered the cart and Mr. Wilson. She remembered that before they leave, they give money to Mr. Wilson.

Katie knows the stories her parents read to her are somehow "in" the book. Today she had a more intimate contact with writing—her own one-word list. Sarah said the word *milk* to her. Then Sarah made marks on the paper that Katie knew contained the word. Katie took the paper, held it in her hand, and put it in her pocket. When she took it out later, Joe found the word *milk* still there. She ended up holding a carton of milk in her hand. Katie is learning that marks on paper mean specific words and that the marks can be used to save a meaning and carry it around.

Sense of Self

When Joe first asked her, Katie didn't want to ride in the cart. She wanted to go on pushing it instead. She let him lift her up without making a fuss, but she was not amused. There may have been a touch of revenge in the way she grabbed Joe's glasses. The gesture at least let Katie establish her independence.

Though she often refuses help when it is offered, Katie is learning to recognize a job she can't do and to ask for the help she needs. Today, for example, she handed the box of string beans to Joe to open. For Katie, asking an adult to do something for her is a very different matter from having an adult interrupt and take over a job she wants to do herself. Asking for help to do something she wants to do is a skill; exercising it makes Katie feel competent.

11

VISITING FRIENDS

New parents often find they are seeing less of their friends and of each other than they did in their childless days. Taking a child along to visit friends can be a lot of trouble. It's hard to have a good conversation with a small child about: when a baby needs attention, she needs it and demands it immediately, even if an adult is deep into an impassioned explanation or halfway through the punch line of a joke. Paying for a baby-sitter to enjoy friends undistracted is expensive. Besides, parents, especially working parents, are jealous of their time alone with their child. They are also often very tired. Why bother to see friends at all, some parents find themselves thinking, when arranging to see them feels like yet another chore?

Going visiting with your child does require a certain administrative effort and, like doing anything else with your child, patience. Along with the baby you have to carry her life-support system—diapers, wipes, a toy or two, a bottle. Once you arrive you have to rev both halves of the parental split brain into high gear so that one half can enjoy the company while the other keeps watch to make sure your child doesn't hurt herself or do something awful to your friend's house. (You and your spouse might agree in advance to divide up child watching so that each of you has a period of time just to relax with the grown-ups.) You may have to make an effort not to talk too long about toilet training, finding a baby-sitter, and the intricacies of crawling, especially to childless people, who will only find these things interesting for limited periods of time.

Other parents of small children of course will often be happy to have long conversations about child rearing. They are used to living with interruptions and are less likely than childless people and parents of older children to have delicate objects within easy reach, open electric sockets, and tables with swordlike edges. Don't be too distressed if you find, as many people do, that you are withdrawing a bit from some friendships you value and spending more of your time with new friends because they are also new parents. If you explain, the people you care about will understand why your friendship is less active at this time.

Even if they generally prefer to see you unencumbered by progeny, all of your friends will still want at least to meet the new member of your family and welcome her into the world. Some of them will want to have her over often. Children do sometimes make social occasions tense, but they can also make them especially warm and merry. Despite all the potential emotional strains and logistical wear and tear, taking your child to visit friends can be enjoyable for both of you—a chance for you to enjoy friends and family together and for your child to have a small adventure.

Trips to banks and stores and post offices, walks through the streets, and pictures in books give your child opportunities to look at new things and sort out strange people—but they don't give her the time for thorough hands-on, close-up, over-and-over-again explorations, which are the way she learns best. She needs to touch objects and examine spaces again and again to fully familiarize herself with them. She needs time to learn about people too, time to watch them and listen to them and touch them and be near them. When you take her to a friend's home, you are giving her a few hours to inspect a new place at leisure, to investigate people close up, and to see you playing your way.

Children are extremely interested in things, things in general. Your friends' homes are filled with things to handle just like your home—furniture to climb on, cabinets and drawers to open, objects on the low coffee table which can be picked up and carried around, dining tables to crawl under, halls to explore. Every time you take your child visiting with you, she will happily examine everything she can. By the time she is four or so, she will know, well enough to furnish a doll house, for example, that all the places where people live, not just your home, are supposed to have kitchens and bathrooms, living rooms with couches and chairs, and bedrooms with a bed. She will have learned from visiting your friends that all families set the table before dinner and clear it afterwards, eat off plates and drink out of cups. She will have begun learning about our customs, the way children do everywhere, by participating in them.

Those customs, of course, include courtesies, rules of social behavior. Each time you take your child on a visit, she'll hear you and your friends say hello, explain how glad you are to see each other, and say please and thank you. Long before she's old enough to be told to say please and thank you herself, you will have begun teaching her good manners simply by being courteous yourself.

You will also be giving her a model of friendship and an opportunity to learn how to make friends herself. If you visit certain people repeatedly, your child will learn to distinguish and remember them, to get to know them in her own way. For example, your child might notice that one of your friends has glasses and warm hands, another has a ripply voice, while a third laughs a lot and likes to tease. She might distinguish people too by the way they play with her. She may remember the man who always puts her up on his shoulders for a ride or the woman who played hide-and-seek with her.

Watching your child learn about other people will help you learn about her. A child's social style seems to be, in part, inborn: any child can go through a period when she's timid with strangers, but some children seem basically sociable by nature, while others seem to have shyer or more reflective characters. Does your child enjoy playing with people, even unfamiliar people, or would she rather play by herself for now and watch others from the sidelines? Does she become especially quiet or especially babbly with company? Is she easily affected by the moods of people around her, or do her own moods seem relatively independent of the social situation? Observing your child when she's with your friends will help you support her first efforts to form relationships of her own. When she's feeling wary or shy, staying close by can give her the reassurance she needs to feel bolder and more at ease. If she enjoys playing with people, and likes showing off her games and skills to your friends, you can help make the experience a happy one by intervening before she does a trick one too many times and begins annoying the adults she expected to please.

For very small infants, of course, socializing is a limited business. They can't distinguish one environment from another very well, so new places don't make them uneasy, and they usually fall asleep after eating no matter where they are. When they're awake, they enjoy watching moving figures and listening to the sounds people make as they talk. Some babies seem to love a party, while others prefer their social stimulation in small, easily digestible doses.

Older babies have a sense of the familiar and unfamiliar. They not only recognize their parents, they can pick their faces out of a crowd. They may worry if they are separated from them and are sometimes frightened by strangers. They can get whiny or clingy, grouchy or restless, but they can also be much gayer and more social than tiny infants. If they are comfortable with a strange adult, they will enjoy playing games the stranger initiates—bouncing, peek-a-boo, or a take-this-object game. They can look and listen to activities around them in a focused way, though after a period of attentiveness they may drift off into a sleepy trance or take a nap.

When you take your baby visiting, she may lie contentedly on her blanket while you talk with your friends and need very little attention. If she needs you, though, she will let you and everyone else know it. A bawling child can make a large group of adults uncomfortable or irritable in very short order. If your baby starts crying seriously when there's company around, you might want to retreat with her to another room for a soothing session. You and your child will find it easier to concentrate on each other away from the party—and your friends will appreciate the quiet.

Crawling babies are fun to take visiting because almost everyone thinks they are adorable, and the age in general is a good-humored one. Crawlers can move with astonishing speed; you'll have to case the area and keep an eye on everything dangerous or delicate within your baby's reach. The main problem will be making sure she doesn't gnaw an electric cord or eat the Sunday paper.

A crawler is usually more interested in exploring the room itself than in getting to know the people in it, but if one of your friends kneels down and holds things out for your baby to touch or plays wrestling or tickling games, she will be pleased.

Your toddler may hide behind you when your friends approach. On the other hand, she may decide to get in the middle of the room and entertain everyone. She can also amuse herself. Toddlers want to go everywhere and take apart everything, and they can get stubborn if you try to stop them. A toddler can keep herself busy examining an object or even just playing with some sheets of paper for a few minutes and will climb, open and close things, fill and dump for a bit longer. But if your toddler feels you have become too absorbed in the conversation and have forgotten about her, she may come back and try to get you interested in her activities. You might find, for instance, that your lap is suddenly filled with her or her toys.

Two-year-olds are already part of society. They are sensitive—intermittently—to the ways people behave in social situations and to how adults perceive them. Many twos have enough language to say hello and good-bye, please and thank you, and to ask and answer simple questions.

You can begin to show your two how to use good manners to make things easier for herself. If she is timid, for example, the ordered formulas of introductions and greetings can embolden her. If she's very high-spirited, you can teach her to use please, thank you, and excuse me as brakes on her own impulsiveness. She won't learn this all at once, but now is the time to start by giving her a model to imitate.

When the strange place and strange people are making your two-year-old uneasy, she may insist on being treated like a baby again. She may want you to hold and carry her and help her eat, even though at home she prefers to do things by herself. Then again, your two may rise to the social occasion when you go visiting and show you how very grown up she has become by being polite and self-possessed. If she is in a grown-up mood, she may get very annoyed if your friends treat her like a little baby—for example, if they try to pick her up or if they hold the cup for her when she wants to drink some juice by herself.

Twos are often happy to leaf through books, scribble, and explore by themselves. Some will also sit still for a few minutes and try to follow the conversation. They probably won't understand what the adults are saying, though a single word or short interchange may stick in their minds. What keeps them listening doesn't seem to be the meaning of the words so much as the movement and drama of the conversation. They can enjoy talk as a kind of music, with fast back-and-forth passages, long emotional sections, and periods of cacophony.

Because twos are learning so much about language, concepts, and people, they may actually demand more attention in a strange place than younger children. Your toddler doesn't need your help to climb over the couch or empty your friend's kitchen cabinet, but your two will need to ask you, "What's this?" Also, because they are more social than younger children, twos are more likely to get bored and restless in social situations that exclude them.

Katie, on the whole, is being quite a grown-up two with Sarah's friends. Alex, as usual, is busy investigating and dealing with the constant cry, "No, Alex," that follows him everywhere. Jennifer is not feeling altogether relaxed in a strange place and does not want to let Carol out of her sight.

JENNIFER
(Six Months)

"Maybe if we're lucky she'll nap while we're eating," Carol says to Sam, who is carrying Jen in his arms.

They step out of the elevator and start down the hall to Dan and Cynthia's apartment, where they have been invited for brunch.

Just about everyone they know dropped by in the first few weeks of Jen's life to meet her, but Carol and Sam have been too tired and busy to see many of their friends since. This is only the third time they have taken Jen out visiting. Carol is hoping Jen will be quietly charming. Dan and Cynthia have two children, but their daughter, Sandy, is fourteen and their son, Paul, ten. They've probably forgotten how domineering infants can be.

"It looks promising," Carol adds, looking at the very relaxed baby nestled against her husband's chest. Jen's eyes close for a second, open a few millimeters, then close again. Carol rings the doorbell.

"Hello!" Cynthia embraces Carol. Conversational noises spill out from behind her. Cynthia turns to kiss Sam, but coos at Jennifer instead.

"That's Jennifer!" she says leaning over. "God, she's gotten big and gorgeous."

"Jen, this is Cynthia," Carol says.

Jen's eyes open wide. She blinks and focuses on the face hovering above her. Then she whimpers and buries her face against Sam's chest.

"Shhh," Sam says, stroking her back. "It's Cynthia. Cynthia is nice."

"We'll get acquainted later," Cynthia says. "Come on in."

"Are the kids here?" Sam asks as they walk down the narrow entry hall to the living room.

"Sandy is at a friend's. Paul is here. He's doing his homework. He'll be out later."

"I'm sorry I'm not going to get to see Sandy," Carol tells her. "She sounded so grown-up on the phone."

Jen, wide awake, has turned her upper body away from Sam and is watching the rectangle of light at the end of the hall grow bigger. They step *into it.* Andrea and George and a couple Sam and Carol don't know are seated around a coffee table holding drinks and munching small things with melted cheese on them. Andrea and Carol exchange smiles, but before Carol can start over to her, Dan comes up. "Hi, good to see you." He kisses Carol. Sam shifts Jen to hold out his right hand for a shake. Jen peers down at the meeting hands.

"Hello," Dan says, patting her on the stomach. Jen looks surprised. She wiggles forward and reaches for Dan's sleeve. She grabs it and tugs hard. She tries to get it to her mouth.

"That's tweed, Jen," Carol says. "Do you like tweed?"

"Let me take that stuff." Cynthia indicates the baby paraphernalia. "Then I'll introduce you to the Shines."

Jen lets go of the sleeve. Her nose crinkles. Her face turns red. She grunts. The unmistakable odor of excrement rises in a cloud about her.

"Does Jen need changing?" Carol asks. Sam is blushing. "That was a rhetorical question." She holds out her arms to take Jen. "I'll do it."

"I'll help you," Cynthia says. "That will give Jen a chance to get used to me. Which would be easier: we could lay her on the toilet seat or I could clear a space off on the bedroom bureau..."

Carol, Cynthia, and a dry Jennifer emerge a few minutes later. Carol goes over to the couch and sits down next to Andrea.

"Hi," Andrea says. "You look great!"

"You too. I'm so glad you're here. I hear all these dramatic things have been happening to you." Jen is sitting upright in Carol's arms, looking intently around.

"Here, darling." Sam comes over and hands Carol a drink. Jen makes a swift grab for the glass just as it touches her mother's lips. Bloody Mary lands on Andrea's skirt. "Oh, Andrea," Carol says, "I'm sorry!"

"Don't worry," Andrea says unconvincingly. She dabs herself with a napkin with no effect. "I better see if I can get this out in the kitchen." She gets up.

"I'm really sorry," Carol repeats. She takes a napkin and wipes Jen's hands. "Jen, I wish you knew how to be careful."

"Aaah," Jen complains.

"Here." Carol hands her the napkin. Jen takes it and looks up at her mother, thrilled. "Yes, a napkin."

Jen crumples the napkin in her right hand. Then she lets go and watches it fall. She looks up again and sees Paul, who has come out to say hello to his parents' friends. She follows him with her eyes.

"Hello, Paul," *Carol says when Sam brings him over.* "How have you been?"

"Okay." *Paul leans over to kiss Carol on the cheek. Jennifer reaches her hand up and pats his face. Paul giggles. Jen giggles too.*

"I think she likes you," *Carol says.* "She's been watching every move you make." *Jen grabs Paul's shirt and starts pulling on it, babbling.*

Sam leans down, puts his hands under Jen's armpits, and lifts her up. "How's my girl?" *Jen squeals happily. Sam sits down next to Carol, putting Jen on his knee.* "This is Paul."

Jen tilts her head and says, "Ahabaahh gamoo." *She is staring at Paul's face like an artist planning a portrait. Paul smiles.*

"Would you like to hold her?" *Sam asks. Paul hesitates.* "Here, sit next to me and you can hold her the way I am. She won't break." *Sam hands his daughter over.*

Paul looks at the baby in his arms with some astonishment. He bounces her gingerly. Jen giggles.

"I'm going to run to the bathroom while Jen is busy," *Carol tells Sam. As she starts away, Jen begins squirming in Paul's arms.*

"All right, all right, shhh," *Sam says, taking her.*

OBSERVATIONS

The World of Things

Jen used to sit placidly in Carol or Sam's arms like a lovable lump of butter, but she's become more active and less cuddly. She moved a great deal today. When Cynthia looked at her, she turned her body to hide her head against Sam. She wiggled forward to get at Dan's sleeve. She managed to get to Carol's glass with one swift slap. Jen's new squirminess is making it harder for her parents to take her places.

Jen is more active partly because she is alert more of the time she is awake. But being alert doesn't always mean moving. Sometimes she sits very still as if she is engrossed by everything going on around her, the way she sat when Carol first took her to the couch.

The World of People

When Jen was drowsy or her attention was absorbed by an object, she didn't seem to notice the people around her. She didn't pay any attention to Andrea, for example. But she is definitely beginning to react when a strange person approaches her. She hid her eyes in Sam's shoulder when Cynthia first said hello. She was startled when Dan touched her.

Carol and Sam encouraged Jen to get to know the new people by introducing them and by staying close. Carol introduced Cynthia and Paul to Jen. Sam had Paul sit next to him before he handed Jen over.

Paul caught Jen's attention as soon as he entered the room. She followed him with her eyes. She let him hold her and even bounce her without protest. Maybe she was attracted to him because he was young: babies often show a special interest in older children. Maybe she just took a fancy to him—babies do seem to get crushes on people (or, conversely, to find that someone rubs them the wrong ways for no apparent reason).

Jen was enjoying Paul's attentions, but when Carol walked away to go to the bathroom, she became tense. She watched Carol and began squirming in Paul's arms. Perhaps she only felt relaxed with Paul because her mother was at her side, or perhaps, after several minutes of meeting new people and moving around a new place, she just wanted her whole family to stay put with her on the couch for a while.

Ideas and Words

Jen is aware now when people and places are strange, another sign she is developing memory.

Jen was aware that when Carol headed toward the bathroom, the distance between them was increasing. She was able to anticipate Carol's going away.

Jen is using sounds and gestures more subtly than she did when she was younger. She used to whimper when she was tired or bored. Today, she whimpered as a way of warding off Cynthia and a way of calling Carol.

Sense of Self

Jen was sometimes nervous today but her uneasiness didn't make her passive or withdrawn. She acted on her feelings very firmly. She moved away from the adults she didn't want to touch her and toward the ones she did.

Jen's growing awareness of strangers reflects her developing self-awareness. Her sense of herself and sense of others are both sharper now.

◆

ALEX
(Fifteen Months)

"Don't, Alex," Tracy says. Alex is pulling out one of the pages of her dinosaur book. Tracy unpeels his fingers. "Give it to me."

"It has this great scene with Tyrannosaurus rex," Eric, a five-year-old, tells Mike. "Tyrannosaurus rex is the biggest of all."

"No, it's not," says Tracy, who is seven and knows better. "The brontosaurus is bigger."

"It is not."

"It is too."

"Liar!" Eric grabs Tracy and starts tickling her.

"I'll kill you!" Tracy screams.

Rita, Robert, Mike, and Alex are visiting Marian, Ed, and their two children, Eric and Tracy. They've just finished dinner. The adults are still at the table in the alcove of the living room, talking. The children have been excused and are playing on the living-room floor. Marian has told them they can watch Fantasia on the VCR later, and Eric, who has seen it three times, has been telling Mike about the dinosaur sequence.

When she hears Tracy's death threat, Marian leans back her chair and peers into the living room. "They're all right," she tells Rita, who gets up anyway to take a look.

Eric and Tracy are wrestling. Alex and Mike watch from the sidelines. Alex reaches out to touch the squirming figures. Tracy's flailing arm hits him by accident. He whimpers and backs off. "Alex." Mike pulls him away.

Tracy gets serious and succeeds in pinning down her brother. Alex, who has lost interest in the fight, wanders over to the rocking chair. Rita watches as he puts his hands on the seat to pull himself up. The chair rocks toward him and then away. Startled, he lets go. After a few more tries he succeeds in pulling himself up on the swaying seat. He giggles with satisfaction. Very cautiously, he turns around so he is facing forward.

"Good for you," Rita says to herself before returning to her place.

"Alex," she hears Mike saying behind her, "you want me to rock you?"

Alex shrieks happily as Mike rocks him. His eee eees follow a pattern which he repeats over and over again in time with the rocking. Then there is a real yell. Rita leaps to her feet.

Mike gave the chair too hard a push and Alex slid off, landing on his hands and knees. He is crying. Mike has stepped back, frightened. Alex, Rita realizes, is crying more from shock than pain.

Tracy runs over to him. "Alex, are you all right?" Alex holds his arms out to the little girl. She kneels down and hugs him.

"Sit down," Robert tells Rita. "They're okay."

A few minutes later the adults move into the living room with their coffee cups. Ed goes to put Fantasia on for the kids in the bedroom.

Mike comes running out of the room. Alex follows him at a trot. "Could we have some cookies, Mom?"

"Ask Marian. This is Marian's house."

"Could we have some cookies?" Mike asks Marian.

"What do you say, Mike?" Rita reminds him.

"Please."

"Help yourself. They're in the red tin on the counter next to the stove."

Mike heads for the kitchen, Alex two paces behind. Mike takes down the cookie tin and offers Alex a cookie. Alex smells it. He closes his fist around it. Still holding the cookie, he tries to reach the top of the counter the way Mike did. He stretches his arms all the way up and almost manages to get hold of a china cup near the edge.

"No, Alex!" Mike yells, more loudly than necessary. He rescues the cup. "Mom! Alex is trying to get a cup."

"Can you find a plastic one?" Rita calls back.

"In the cabinet below the sink," Marian adds. "You can take some juice."

"Just a few drops," Rita warns.

Mike gets the orange juice out of the refrigerator, fills the plastic cup, and gives it to Alex. He starts back toward the bedroom with a pile of cookies in each hand. Alex follows, holding his cup very carefully in front of him, spilling juice over the sides each time he takes a step.

Rita looks over at them. "Mike, wait." She gets up and gets Mike a plate. "Put the cookies on this, and thanks for helping with Alex." She takes the cup from Alex and drinks some juice to lower the liquid level. "Alex, sweetie, I want you to stay here with the adults." She brushes some cookie crumbs off his pants and gives him back his cup.

"Let him play with the other kids," Robert says. "He's not going to break."

"I don't like having to jump up and down all the time to check on him," she explains, steering Alex back with her to the sofa.

"I think there's a squashed cookie somewhere," she tells Marian. Marian shrugs. Rita sits down. Alex stands next to her leaning against her legs. She strokes his head. "I'm going to my tenth high school reunion next week," she says. "I'm really nervous about it. . . ."

"Mine was two years ago," Ed tells her. "Everyone was the same."

Alex listens awhile. He watches Rita take a sip of coffee. He points at the cup. "Abarema."

"Yes, I have a cup too. I'm drinking coffee."

Alex holds his juice cup up to her.

"You want some coffee?" She pours a tiny drop into his juice. He sips it. He puts the cup down on the coffee table and puts his arms around Rita's thighs. After a brief cuddle, he goes off exploring again.

Rita hears noises from the kitchen. "Can you see what he's doing?" she asks Robert.

Robert gets up and goes into the kitchen. "Alex, you shouldn't mess around in the garbage." Actually the damage isn't bad: Alex didn't get to the coffee grounds and eggshells. He is chewing on the corner of an empty cornflakes box.

"Give me the box, Alex. I'll give it back, come on." Robert turns the box over the garbage to get out any crumbs. "Okay, now you can play with it." Alex heads back toward the garbage.

"Not here. Come on. Alex, I said come on." Robert picks Alex up and deposits him—still holding the box—in the living room. "There you go."

Alex heads toward the wall opposite the couch. Holding his box in one hand, he drags the other along the surface of the big wall unit. He spots a photograph of Tracy and Eric when they were babies on one of the lower shelves. He drops the cornflakes box and stretches his arms to get the picture. "Bay, bay, bay," he says to himself. He can't reach the photo. But there is a small door within reach. He pulls out wrapping paper, envelopes, record books, and Scotch tape, dropping them on the floor.

"Alex," Rita suggests, hopefully, "why don't you put the paper and envelopes back in the cabinet?"

Alex looks at her. Leaving the things where they are, he toddles over to the adults and begins to examine the objects on the coffee table.

"It's okay," Marian says to Rita. "I'll put the stuff back later."

Alex picks up a large piece of quartz Marian keeps on the table for decoration and turns it around in his hands. Then he starts hitting the table with it.

"Alex, cut it out!" Robert says. Alex smiles and bangs again. "Alex!" Robert holds out his hand. Alex bangs it again.

Robert pulls the rock away from him. Alex hits Robert's arm and starts crying. Everyone has stopped talking.

"Oh, come on, Alex," Robert says. He gets up and puts the rock on a high shelf of the wall unit. He notices the cornflakes box by his feet, where Alex dropped it.

Alex continues to cry, hugging Rita, though he's working his way down to a sniffle. "Alex," Robert says, coming over, "look. Here is your box."

Alex looks up. He stops crying. He turns to the coffee table and reaches for the ashtray. "Alex—" Rita grabs it. Alex whines. Robert rips the box part way along one of the edges. "Alex." Robert puts the box on his head. "See my hat?" Alex giggles. "Here." Robert puts the cornflakes box hat on his son's head.

———————————◆———————————

OBSERVATIONS

The World of Things

Alex's many physical skills allow him to entertain himself. Climbing on the rocking chair, opening the cabinet and taking out the things inside, rooting in the garbage, and examining the objects on the coffee table kept him quite busy tonight.

The rocking chair presented Alex with a new set of problems: how to climb on something that moves when you touch it. He persisted in experimenting until he found, by trial and error, a way to climb up. Once he had succeeded in getting on the chair, he was delighted by the rocking movements.

Rhythm, in general, pleases Alex. When Mike rocked him, he began repeating a pattern of sounds in rhythm with the motion. Alex often makes up nonsense phrases and repeats them over and over again, almost as though he were rocking himself with his voice.

The cornflakes box he found in the garbage became a toy for Alex. Kids, Rita and Robert have learned, are good at recycling garbage. Alex likes to play with empty boxes, the cardboard cylinders from plastic wrap and aluminum foil, and empty plastic bottles. Mike likes to play with broken machine parts Robert brings home from the shop.

The World of People

Alex is not a considerate houseguest. He doesn't understand that he's not supposed to dig through the garbage. He doesn't understand that the objects inside the cabinet belong there and should be returned if they are moved. He doesn't know you shouldn't drop squashed cookies on the floor. Marian and Ed were quite tolerant, but Rita and Robert know Alex's behavior would irritate many of their friends. Recently, they haven't been seeing much of those other friends.

Alex likes to be with people, but much of the time he doesn't pay attention to them. He is more interested in physical activity. When he became absorbed in climbing on the rocking chair, going through the garbage, examining the wall unit, he seemed indifferent to the people around him.

When Alex's attention is caught by people, he is not content to just watch them for long; he tries to imitate them. Alex followed Mike around. When Mike reached for the cookie tin, Alex wanted to reach for something too and tried to get hold of the cup. When he saw the adults drinking coffee, he wanted some of Rita's coffee in his cup.

Alex was in a sociable mood tonight. He was pleased when Mike rocked the chair for him. When he fell, he was very willing to accept solace from Tracy. He obligingly joined the adults when Rita asked him.

When Alex is doing something he shouldn't, Rita usually stops him rather gently or tries to distract him. Robert is more straightforward: he just tells Alex "Stop it" or "No." Alex doesn't seem to find his father's scolding either alarming or discouraging. When Robert took his rock away, Alex was not afraid to protest vehemently and hit his father.

Ideas and Words

Alex uses gestures adeptly. He let Rita know, for example, that he wanted some coffee by pointing to her cup and babbling. He is beginning to say more words as well. He said "bay, bay" to himself when he was trying to reach the photograph, as though saying the word could extend his arm and help him get a hold of it.

Alex doesn't have any sense that different social situations demand different types of behavior. He went through the garbage and emptied out the cabinet at Marian and Ed's exactly the way he roots through things in his own home.

Sense of Self

Alex likes to bang things, the way he banged the rock on the table tonight. He feels powerful when he can make something dramatic happen and a bang is a very dramatic happening.

At fifteen months, Alex's abilities fall considerably short of his aspirations. He can't, for example, reach a cup on the counter or a photograph on a high shelf or pour himself a glass of juice. He can't do the vast majority of things he tries to do without help, and often he isn't even allowed to try. But Alex doesn't seem discouraged when he can't do what he is trying to do. He just keeps on trying anyway or goes on and tries to do something else. When he accomplishes a task, however, Alex is triumphant. He was delighted with himself today when he succeeded in climbing on the rocker. (Rita, who witnessed his struggle to get up, quietly applauded him too.) He was satisfied when Rita figured out he wanted coffee and let him have a drop. Alex's admirable ability to be energized by small achievements and unfazed by rather large shortcomings is part of his natural drive to grow up.

Rita was worried about leaving Alex alone with the other children. Robert felt she was being overly protective. Rita wasn't being overly protective—but Robert wasn't being careless either. Rita probably would have enjoyed some time off tonight, as Robert thought. Alex probably would have had fun playing in the bedroom, but then again, he might have gotten hurt trying to keep up with the older children. Rita decided it would be too dangerous to leave Alex alone with children as young as Eric, Tracy, and Mike. She didn't feel like getting up every few minutes to check on him. Robert accepted her judgment. On another occasion, they might decide to give Alex a chance to be a little more on his own. Balancing Alex's need for independent adventures, his need for supervision, and their own needs is a delicate operation; Rita and Robert usually end up dealing with each situation as it comes up.

Alex tries to maintain his own balance between safety and adventure. When he touched the rocker it moved. He let go at once. He approached it again—but carefully. He figured out how to climb up without a single practice fall.

KATIE
(Twenty-eight Months)

Katie is turning the knob on the door that leads out of the apartment and pushing. The door is locked. Katie has realized the door isn't going to open, but she keeps turning and pushing anyway.

Sarah is a few feet away in the living room talking to Joanna and Wayne. Franklin, abandoned by Katie, is sitting next to her.

"I'd better see what Katie is doing," Sarah says. She walks down the hall to the door. "Hi."

"Out," Katie says, her hand still on the knob.

"We'll go out later. First we are going to have lunch."

"No," Katie scowls. "Out now."

It's Saturday morning. Sarah and Katie are in the city for the weekend visiting Wayne and Joanna. Tomorrow they will pick up Sarah's grandmother at the airport and drive her back to their own home. Katie, who sat quietly with Franklin on the trip down, sucking on his ear, sucking on her fingers, staring out the window, and occasionally asking about something she saw, is evidently running out of patience now. This morning she scrambled out of the bathroom as soon as Sarah helped her brush her teeth and began darting back and forth around the apartment. She quieted down and looked through Wayne and Joanna's picture books for a while; then she started getting restless again.

"Katie, you can't go out now. We'll go out later."

"Now!" Katie shouts.

Please don't be a terrible two today, Sarah prays silently. "Katie, you can't go out now. You can go out after lunch. Do you want to stay here and turn the knob?"

"Go out," Katie says, sniffling a little.

"Later," Sarah says. "In about two hours. After lunch." Katie offers her mother her best sulky look, then turns her attention back to the door. She turns the knob as far as she can to the left, then all the way to the right. She repeats the motion faster and faster.

Sarah goes back to the living room. "She's feeling a bit cooped up," she explains.

"Let's start making lunch now then," Wayne suggests. "I could eat." He looks at Joanna.

"Yeah," Joanna says, "I'm starting to get hungry."

"Katie," Sarah calls, "we're going into the dining room."

They hear Katie's feet pattering down the hall. She arrives running with both her arms spread out. "Flying," she explains, waving her arms as she circles the room, then lands in the center. The adults laugh. Pleased at their reaction, Katie gets up and repeats the routine. Joanna and Wayne's response is not quite so enthusiastic this time.

"Let's fly into the dining room and help set the table," Sarah says, getting up.

Katie, arms out, zooms ahead and spins around the dining room. The adults follow her in. Katie's flight takes her by the desk on the far wall. She lands and starts examining the pens and pencils on the desk.

Joanna is clearing papers and odds and ends off the table.

"Can I help?" Sarah asks.

"No. I know where this stuff goes. Just sit down and talk with me while I straighten up."

"Katie," Sarah says, "please stay away from the desk. That's where Wayne and Joanna keep their private things. Would you like some paper and your crayons?" Katie ignores her. "Katie, did you hear me?" Katie goes back to flying again.

"How old is your grandmother?" Joanna asks.

"Eighty-two," Sarah says, "or maybe eighty-three. She's in really good health, though." Katie's zooming hum gets louder and louder, approaching supersonic levels. Joanna raises her voice. Katie raises hers. When Sarah asks, "What?" for the third time, Joanna shakes her head.

"Katie," Sarah says. "Quieter, please." Katie ignores her. "Why don't you come over here?" Katie zooms over and crashes into Sarah, laughing. Sarah hugs her. "Is this an airplane or a little girl?"

Katie raises her arms to be picked up. She cuddles while Joanna and Sarah pick up their conversation. "I never knew my grandparents," Joanna says, putting a pile of papers on the desk. "They all died before I was born. I was jealous of the other kids because they had more people to give them presents." She lays a white cloth down.

"Let's help Joanna set the table," Sarah says. She gives Katie a kiss and lowers her to the floor. "Come." Sarah takes her hand and walks into the kitchen, where Wayne is making a salad.

"Where's the silverware?" Sarah asks.

The phone rings.

"I'll get it," Joanna calls from the dining room.

"The other side of the sink," Wayne tells Sarah.

Katie has gone over to the windowsill. "Grass," she says, reaching for a small pot of green.

"Don't pull it, Katie," Sarah, who is collecting silverware, warns. "Pulling hurts it. Be gentle."

"Gentle," Katie says. She touches the plant lightly, then pulls her hand back and looks up at her mother.

"It's dill," Wayne tells her. "It's an herb. It's a kind of plant with a nice taste that you can eat." He puts his knife down and goes over to Katie. She looks at him cautiously. He breaks off two little pieces. He puts one in his mouth and makes exaggerated chewing motions. "Mmmnnnn. Here." He hands Katie the other piece.

She takes the little green sliver and rolls it between her fingers, studying it intently. She smells it and finally bites off a tiny piece. Then she takes it out of her mouth and puts it down on the sill.

"Didn't care for it?"

Katie shakes her head.

"Here Katie," Sarah says. "Would you please take these napkins in?"

Sarah comes into the dining room with plates and silver a few seconds later. The napkins are in a pile on the table. Katie is not in sight.

"Katie?" she asks. She hears a giggle from under the table. "Where could Katie be?" Sarah asks the table. The side of the tablecloth rises up and Katie's head appears.

$$\blacklozenge$$

OBSERVATIONS

The World of Things

Katie was able to recognize objects in the strange apartment at once, and in a single morning she familiarized herself with the various rooms and their functions. Because Katie now has a great deal of control over her body and a good basic understanding of the things in a house, Sarah was willing to let her play near the door, out of sight.

Katie has become very capable with her hands. There was a time when Katie would have had trouble touching a plant without uprooting it, but she was able to touch the dill delicately today. (She might not have thought to be gentle, however, if Sarah hadn't suggested it.)

She knows how to open an unlocked door. If one of the adults had showed her, she could probably have learned to unlock the locked door quite quickly.

Katie used to use her sense of taste to help herself become acquainted with new objects, but she no longer automatically puts everything in her mouth. In fact, she has become quite hesitant about tasting something strange, like the piece of dill.

The World of People

Katie made a bit of trouble at the door, but when Sarah let her know that she understood her desire to go out, Katie accepted a postponement without making a big fuss. She was definitely getting edgy, however. When Sarah and Joanna started a serious conversation in the dining room, Katie made louder and louder noises until it was impossible for the women to talk and her mother had to notice her. Katie probably didn't decide to do this deliberately. More likely she felt neglected and found herself using her voice to call for attention.

Katie didn't make overtures to Joanna and Wayne, but she was not shy with them either. She enjoyed their applause when she did her flying dance. She accepted the dill—and the explanation—from Wayne.

Sarah said please to Katie whenever she asked her to do something. By being polite to Katie, she is showing her in a very direct way that courteous words are signs of appreciation and respect.

Ideas and Words

Katie is now truly living in the world of ideas and words. She is beginning to use words to control herself. When she said "gentle," the word helped her rule her hands and touch the plant gently. Words also help Katie make believe. Making believe for Katie is a way of thinking about things. Her flying game, for example, was a way of exploring the idea of flying. The idea may have been on Katie's mind because Sarah had explained that her great-grandmother was flying into the city.

Katie doesn't understand that her great-grandmother is the mother of Sarah's mother, or that Sarah was once a little girl too. The passage of biological time is not something she can grasp. She is trying to sort out much simpler, more immediate kinds of time. When Sarah said she could go out "later," Katie understood she would go out some time but not now. She also has a concept of before and after. When Sarah said "in two hours," the phrase didn't mean much to Katie, but she understood when Sarah added "after lunch."

Katie understands that some things are good to eat and some things are not good to eat. She may have been cautious about tasting the dill because she thinks people don't eat plants; she probably doesn't think of fruits and vegetables as plants.

Katie has developed some ideas about privacy and possession. She also understands that she is allowed to play with some things but not with others, though she doesn't always comply. When Sarah told her today that the desk was private, she left it alone.

Sense of Self

When Sarah told Katie she couldn't or shouldn't do something, she gave an explanation. She told her not to touch the desk because it was private and not to pull at the plant because she might hurt it. Katie may not have understood everything Sarah was saying, but she probably understood some of it. Over time, her mother's explanations will help Katie understand rules and learn to apply them herself.

Katie was in a strange apartment today with two strange adults. Her mother was paying attention to her friends instead of to Katie. Katie went a long time without any chance to get outside and run around. Under these rather trying circumstances, she was remarkably good-natured and grown up. She demanded that Sarah pick her up and baby her once when she needed it, but most of the time she was able to keep herself amused.

12

---◆---

TAKING A WALK

The outdoors is too vast and various for a small child to take in all at once. Children learn best about the world outside their home exploring it foot by foot. Walks are important for them.

In this book, we've been interested in the discoveries children make as they participate in the routine activities that are part of most families' day or week. This chapter is the exception. Going outside is part of everyday life for virtually everyone, but in many parts of the country, going for a walk is not. If you live in a place where cars, not feet, are the usual means of transportation, you might consider making the time to take your child for an occasional walk. A ten-minute excursion down the road before or after dinner, a brief walk through the streets next time you go downtown to do errands, a weekend foray to a nearby patch of woods, or a stroll through a shopping mall would all be real pleasure trips for your child.

Walks with a child are necessarily leisurely. Your child can't walk as quickly as you do and she wouldn't want to if she could. Merely looking around is not enough to satisfy her curiosity. She needs to use her whole body to make herself at home in the very wide world of city streets and open fields, woods and shopping centers, beaches and parks. If she is walking in the woods and comes to a fallen log, she will have to touch it and maybe try to climb over it. If she passes the automatic banking machine she has seen you use, she will want to stop and press the buttons. Over months and years, these very particular investigations will help her build up a feeling for different outdoor spaces, a sense of space and distance and location.

Meanwhile, she will slow you down. Taking your child with you when you go on a walk intending to get somewhere and get something done can be a very frustrating experience. Small children really don't understand what it means to get somewhere. Though your child may like the idea that she will be at the destination you've described, she still may not quite grasp that arriving there is the purpose of your walk.

Even when you take your child on a recreational walk with no purpose in mind but pleasure, you may find that your child's idea of pleasure conflicts with your own. Since everything is bathed in freshness for them, children have no sense of "sights." They don't realize that certain features of a place are thought to be more exceptional or beautiful or important than others. This can be exasperating. You might, for example, take your child on a trip to a special park to show her the pond with toy sailboats and then find yourself unable to pull her away from a big puddle twenty yards away. To compensate, there will also be days when your child will lend you some of her sense of discovery and for a moment, puddles and sticks, stoops and curbs, mailboxes and ditch drains will become new and intriguing to you.

An infant, of course, won't ask you to wait while she investigates something on the side of the road. A walk for her is a sensual journey. Her first notions about outdoors and indoors come from her eyes, ears, nose, and skin. Lying in her carriage or sitting in her backpack, she can see the clarity of sunlight, the weight of shadows, the openness of the sky, colors, shapes, patterns tumbling out around her. She can feel the differences in temperature between inside and outside, the coolness of a passing cloud, the wind on her skin. Leaves rustle; awnings flap; cars grind, sigh, crank, buzz; birds cry; dogs bark; music grows louder, then softer as a girl carrying a radio walks by. Odors color everything—musty garbage smells, tickling smells of trees and grass, unctuous gasoline smells, wisps of perfume and sweat trailed by passers-by.

The most interesting thing about the outdoor world for your baby is probably its motion. Most of the things she sees indoors are still, but everything in the outside world is always changing. People, cars, leaves, clouds move around her, and when the person carrying her or pushing her carriage goes forward, even still things move. The buildings, grass, parked cars, benches, trees change continuously as she is taken through them. A person, a lamppost, a shrub become bigger and bigger and bigger and then, as she is moved past, disappear. Even if your baby is too young to put these experiences together, she'll be learning something on her walk: that the world is rich and delicious. As she gets older and can reach and grab, sit and twist, she will begin to bring some order to her sensations. She can turn her head to follow noises and link them with sights. In the stroller, she can choose to look down at the ground or up at the sky.

Your baby will enjoy walks on which you do errands. The changes in temperature and light as you go in and out of the grocery store or post office and the new things to see inside will add to the interest of a trip for her. When she reaches crawling age, however, try to plan some walks to include a stop in the park or playground, so you can take her out of the stroller and put her down on the ground. On her hands and knees, your baby can go for a walk by herself and experience the outdoors in another way. She can examine the ground below her, picking up bits of slate from a gravel path, pulling at grass, digging in sand. She can touch a bench, a tree, a trash can.

When your child learns to walk, the world becomes three dimensional for her. Her vantage point is two or three feet high, but as a walker she can easily look up and reach and climb to rise higher, bend down and squat to study things on the ground. She will want to take full advantage of her new physical skills to touch and climb everything that interests her—trees and fences, shrubs and rocks, ledges, cars, bikes, lampposts—but simply walking on different types of ground is a tactile experience for toddlers too. Your toddler will enjoy the distinct sensations of gravel or dried leaves, mud or concrete under her feet.

Your toddler's perpetual investigations and lack of concern with progress can be a problem when you are in a hurry and trying to get errands done. You can, of course, try to persuade her to ride in a stroller. She may fuss at first since she is big now and likes to walk on her own two feet. But toddlers expend such a huge amount of energy on their explorations, they are ready for—and need—some time off after a while. In the stroller, your child may peer around, looking and pointing and babbling, or slide into a dreamier mood and let the sights and sounds wash over her. Sometimes she will lose interest in the outside world altogether and become absorbed instead in examining her hat or stroller toy. She might even take a nap.

Two-year-olds are learning new ways of moving: hopping, jumping, balancing, leaping. A walk outdoors gives them the space they need for athletics. Like toddlers, they need to touch and climb and pick up interesting things to thoroughly enjoy a walk. Twos are also learning to use adults' knowledge to expand their own. They ask questions. They want to know what things are called and what they do as well as how they look and feel. They enjoy learning what a mailbox is for (and may peer in to look for letters if they understand the explanation) or that birds live in nests or that clouds go with rain. Twos can understand that the point of a walk is to get somewhere, even if they can't hold on to the idea for long. They have some inkling of what it means to hurry.

Twos, like toddlers, have mixed feelings about the stroller. Your two-year-old will refuse to use the stroller, even when she's dragging her feet from fatigue, if she's in the mood to be grown up. She knows big girls walk. But most twos get tired of being grown up from time to time. After weeks of making a fuss whenever you ask her to get into the stroller, your two may refuse to walk one day. Another day, a month after you've abandoned the stroller altogether and when you're tired and carrying two packages, your two may even decide she wants you to carry her in your arms. And the day after that, she may offer to carry your packages for you.

Jennifer has just graduated to a stroller; her parents are using it for the first time today. Rita and the boys are going to the park with a neighbor who has a son Mike's age, and Alex makes a number of interesting discoveries along the way. Katie, in the city for the week-end, is fascinated by the odd things she sees in the streets.

◆

JENNIFER
(Six Months)

"Don't fuss," Carol tells Sam. "She's fine."

Sam is bending down over the stroller, adjusting the strap around Jen's middle.

"She's a little droopy." He brings his face closer to Jen's. "Aren't you, Jen?"

Jen looks at him, wide-eyed.

Sam and Carol got Jen a stroller last weekend. It rained and they didn't get to take her out in it themselves. Mrs. Semple initiated her on the follow-ing Monday. Though she was ashamed of the feeling, Carol nursed a sharp dislike of Mrs. Semple for being the first to show Jen the world from a moving chair. But today is a shiny, limpid spring Sunday, and Sam and Carol are taking Jen and the Sunday paper to the park.

"A little drooping isn't going to hurt her," Carol says. "She needs to be able to move."

"Just a little snugger." Sam repositions Jen upright. When he stands up she turns to look up at him, twisting to one side but remaining erect.

Sam starts pushing again. Jen leans forward, gripping the bar in front of her with both hands. She is very still and wakeful, though she doesn't seem to be looking at anything in particular; she is letting the sights roll past her eyes, swaying slightly in her seat. After a few minutes, she twists and looks down intently.

"What is it, Jen?" Carol asks, looking to see if there is anything of interest on the sidewalk. There is nothing special—except, Carol realizes,

the sidewalk itself. Jen, enthralled, is watching the knobby carpet of concrete unfold, the shiny metallic bits glinting in the sun.

"Sidewalk, Jen," Carol says.

The interesting sidewalk has a bump in it. Jen babbles. She starts sliding down. Sam reaches over to straighten her.

"No, see if she can do it," Carol insists.

Jen doesn't try. She ends up half slouched against one of the corners. She seems to like this new position. She tilts her head and sucks her hand. In her half recline, she can see the tops of the trees lining the park. The leaves turn in the breeze and shuffle the sunlight. Jen's eyelids sink down.

"Okay, Jen, we're here." Jen opens her eyes to see her father leaning over her. She smiles drowsily.

Sam kisses her hand and unstraps her. "Up we go!" They have stopped on a grassy hill in the park. Carol is laying a blanket out on the ground, securing two corners with her shoes and one top corner with the paper. Sam holds a still sleepy Jennifer over his head. She giggles, but then starts whimpering. He lowers her. "Here's your mommy," he says.

Jen coos as Carol takes her. Carol kisses her forehead. "Did you like the stroller?" Jen snuggles on Carol's chest a second, then throws her head back to look coyly at her mother. "Yes," Carol says, kissing her on the nose. "Now I'm going to put you down on the blanket. You can nap some more if you'd like."

Carol and Sam stretch out on the blanket, placing Jen on her stomach between them. The adults begin dividing up the paper. Jen, no longer sleepy, lifts her head up to look around. She whimpers.

"You want to sit up?" Carol lifts her up. "Here, you can lean against your father. Let me get you a toy." Carol retrieves a red and white ball from the stroller bin. She gives it to Jen, then stretches out again with the paper. Jen uses two hands to hold the ball. She drops it and watches it roll toward Sam. She stares at it.

Some boys are shouting somewhere off to the left. Jen turns her head toward the sound, then turns back to the blanket and begins plucking absentmindedly at it with her hands. She catches sight of Carol's shoe at the edge. She reaches for it, both hands stretched out, and falls forward onto her palms. A bit of grassy ground is exposed in front of her where she pulled the blanket up. Grunting, Jen reaches out her right hand, fingers wide, and hits the grass. She pulls her hand back, looks at it, and starts to bring it to her mouth.

"Hey," Carol says. "What do you have there?" She sits up and grabs Jen's hand before it reaches her mouth. A dead caterpillar is stuck to Jen's palm. "Jen, no, don't eat squashed caterpillars." Carol sits Jen up, still holding Jen's hand, which Jen is trying to pull away.

Carol looks around for a tissue. There are none in reaching distance. She wipes the caterpillar corpse off the little hand with a corner of the blanket. Jen whines. "There'll be other things to squash."

Sam sits up to help. "Where's your ball?" he asks, looking around. "We'll play ball." The ball is next to him under a piece of newspaper. He digs it out and holds it in front of his whimpering daughter. "There it is."

Sam rolls the ball toward Jen, who stops whining to watch. The ball rolls halfway under a fold of blanket. "Ah!" says Jen, reaching both hands toward the red and white half circle.

◆

OBSERVATIONS

The World of Things

Carol and Sam have introduced Jen to a new form of transportation, the stroller. In the carriage, Jen had to lie down. The only direction she could look was up. She sat up in the backpack, but had little freedom of movement. Her torso was held fairly firmly against the back of the person carrying her. Though she could peer over her carrier's shoulder or look to the side or down, her view was blocked from many angles. In the stroller, Jen has much more freedom. The straps provide her with some support, but enough freedom to lean forward and back and twist and turn. She can easily see all around and up and down. Jen seemed to be enjoying this new freedom of vision. She bent over to look at the sidewalk and tilted her head to look up at the trees.

When she is sitting, Jen can use her arms to explore the area around her by herself. Today she discovered the ground underneath the blanket. When she hit the grass she felt something—a dead caterpillar—on her palm. She wanted to mouth it to learn more, but Carol wouldn't let her.

Jen can hold, drop, and hit a ball, and when it rolls she can follow it with her eyes.

The World of People

Sam wanted to adjust the stroller strap so it was just right, and later he wanted to help Jen straighten up. Carol told Sam not to make the strap so tight that Jen couldn't move and to let Jen try to straighten up herself before volunteering help. The proper degree of stroller strap tautness isn't a crucial child-development issue, but this small difference in the way Sam and Carol handle a daily routine does reflect differences in their attitude toward Jennifer. Sam seems to enjoy being able to do things for Jen—for example, arranging her stroller straps —while Carol seems more concerned with encouraging Jen's independence.

Often on the weekends one of Jen's parents takes care of her, while the other uses the time to attend to personal or family affairs undistracted. Today Jen got to spend the morning with both her parents together, which she probably enjoyed. The three of them were physically close on the blanket, but each of them was absorbed in his own activities.

Ideas and Words

Jen reached for her ball when it was half covered by the blanket. She has enough of an idea of the ball to look at part of it and recognize the whole, something she couldn't have done two months ago.

Though Jen can't understand them, Carol and Sam automatically tell Jen the words for things that interest her, like sidewalks and grass. Gradually she will begin to realize that different sounds are associated with each different thing.

Sense of Self

In the stroller, Jen is sitting by herself. She can move in place and look where she will. The stroller is helping her experience the world, from her own point of view, as an independent person.

◆

ALEX
(Fifteen Months)

Mike and his kindergarten mate Stuart are trying to wrestle and walk at the same time.

"Stop it," Rita says. "If you fall on the sidewalk, you'll hurt yourselves." Mike gives Stuart one last poke. "Mike!"

Rita and Stuart's mother, Jean, are taking the kids to the park. Rita and Alex are pushing Alex's stroller. Alex has stretched his hands over his head to reach the handle. He is using his whole body weight to push hard, swinging his legs out a little to the side when he steps and sticking his tongue out to increase his strength.

"Race you to the corner," Stuart says. Mike sprints.

"Remember to stop at the square before the curb," Jean calls after them.

Alex has let go of the stroller. He starts to trot after Mike. "No, Alex," Rita says, "you stay here with us."

He runs forward another few steps, then stops. "Ca!" he shouts, point-

ing to a combat-hardened gray character who has emerged from a parking lot and is jogging along near the wall of a building.

"Yes," Rita says, "that's a cat, like Barney. A gray cat." Alex starts following the cat. Rita decides not to worry: Alex doesn't stand a chance.

"Ca!" Alex repeats. He bends down to grab the cat, but it shoots behind a garbage pail and disappears. Alex bumps into the garbage pail, making a great bang and stumbling. Rita is ready for a rescue, but Alex rights himself. He examines the pail. The cover, attached to the side of the metal barrel by a chain, is hanging down. It's almost as big as Alex himself. Alex picks it up and pulls it until the chain is taut. He can't hold on. The cover slips out of his hands and tumbles back against the barrel with a bang. Alex laughs. Then he grips the edge of the barrel and tries to pull himself up on tiptoe to peer in. The barrel teeters.

Handing the stroller to Jean, Rita walks over to extricate her son. "Come on, Alex, enough garbage pail."

Alex looks up at her compliantly, but his fingers seem glued to the barrel edge. Rita undoes them. "Come on." She takes his hand and walks with him along the side of the next building. They are nearing a main shopping and business area surrounding the park. The detached brick and wood buildings have given way to prewar buildings of stone. This one has a relief skirt of granite around the base about Alex's height. He reaches out his hand and draws it along the narrow stone shelf.

"Mom." Mike runs over to Rita. The older boys have gotten tired of waiting for their mothers to catch up.

"Hi," Rita says. Mike reaches up seemingly to hug her, then makes a disgusting splat noise in her ear and laughs.

"Mike! I told you not to do that. I don't like that noise!" She glares at her son. Jean represses a smile.

Mike barely resists doing it again. "Let's go," he says instead.

"We're trying, Mike," Rita says. "Come on, Alex, let's try to hurry. He's been making that noise all week," she tells Jean. "I hope he doesn't teach it to Stuart."

Alex has been trying to pull his hand out of Rita's so he can walk up the three stone steps leading to the double entrance door of a little office building. Stuart starts walking along the lowest step.

"I'll take him," Mike says. "Come on, Alex." Mike holds out his hand. Alex takes it. "Let's go to the corner," Mike says, beginning a very slow run. Alex laughs and trots along as fast as he can.

Stuart hops down and takes Alex's other hand. "Away we go!" he shouts.

"Take it easy," Jean warns.

"Mike," Rita calls. "Mike!" Mike stops. "I don't want Alex to go near the curb. Stay here and walk with us."

Mike obediently slows down. Stuart starts walking along one of the lines in the sidewalk. "Tightrope!" Mike says, following another line. Alex trots back and forth between the two boys watching his slightly pigeon-toed feet.

Rita relieves Jean of the stroller. "What did you think about the new principal?" Jean asks. "I mean besides being cute."

As they near the corner, Alex heads for the lamppost. He walks around it, dragging his hand along the surface. Then he lets go and starts to step down into the street. "No, Alex!" Mike shouts.

Rita lets go of the stroller and grabs Alex. She bends down and holds him tightly by the shoulders. "Alex, never, never step into the street! Do you hear me?"

Alex cries. "Here," Rita says standing up. "You hold my hand while we cross the street."

Jean takes Mike's and Stuart's hands. Rita, holding Alex's hand, resumes her place behind the stroller. They wait for the light to change. Alex, still crying, watches the cars. He points to a red one as it goes by. "A go!" he says, sniffling, using his word for motor vehicles.

"Yes," Rita says mechanically. "It's a red car.

"See, Alex," she says a few seconds later. "Now the light is green. That means the cars have to stop and the people can go." They cross the street, Rita and Jean enforcing a fast, no-nonsense pace. Alex stares at the line of waiting cars.

The park on the other side of the street is surrounded by a low stone wall. The group turns right to walk toward the entrance a block away. Mike and Stuart only last a few feet before they run up to the wall and start trying to climb. "Hey, you guys," Jean says. "I thought you were in a hurry to get to the park."

Alex has let go of Rita's hand and is starting to stagger a little. "Are you getting tired, sweetheart?" Rita asks, indicating the stroller. "Do you want to get in?"

Alex shakes his head.

Stuart and Mike are spinning in circles. Alex wanders over to the wall and squats down. He picks up a small stick lying in the dirt and starts poking the ground with it.

"Mom, can we have ice cream?" Stuart is asking Jean.

"No, you can have an apple. I brought fruit."

"Alex," Rita says, "we can play in the park. Take your stick and come on."

Mike goes over to Alex, bends down, and makes the horrible splat sound in his brother's ear. Startled, Alex falls backward, landing on his rear. He wails.

"Mike," Rita says, "you get over here and take this stroller." She goes over to Alex. He lifts up his arms to be picked up. Rita obliges. "There," she says as he cries softly. "You're going to be fine."

◆

OBSERVATIONS

The World of Things

Alex investigated various things he encountered along the street just the way he investigates different objects at home. He chased a cat, tried to look inside a garbage pail, walked around a lamppost, felt the side of a building, picked up a stick and poked dirt with it.

Alex doesn't realize that if he steps down into the streets when the cars are moving he will be hurt. Rita pointed out the green light today as she has many times before, but even if Alex noticed the traffic lights, he wouldn't yet be able to connect them to the traffic and his safety.

The World of People

Rita pulled Alex back when he stepped off the curb, bent over him, held his shoulders to make him look at her, and screamed at him. She didn't offer any explanation, she just told him never to step into the street. Alex may not have realized his step off the curb was what angered her, but he understood Rita was truly upset and angry. He became upset too and cried. Rita knew that Alex couldn't understand everything she said. She was hoping that he would make the right association and stay away from curbs.

Rita and Robert don't enjoy running and climbing, but Mike enjoys many of the same physical activities Alex enjoys. Alex would like to be able to move in all the ways Mike can move. When Stuart and Mike were racing, he wanted to follow. He didn't understand what the boys were doing when they tried to walk on the cracks in the sidewalk, but he tried to do whatever it was anyway.

Mike seemed to enjoy being older and more capable. He was willing to let Alex be his playmate today and he tried to be protective. When he took Alex's hand, he deliberately ran slowly so Alex could keep up. But later Mike took advantage of his superiority to tease Alex: he made the awful splatting sound in Alex's ear. The sound startled Alex, but it didn't irritate him the way it irritated Rita. No doubt he will work hard someday to make disgusting noises himself.

On this walk, Rita wasn't trying to do any errands, so Alex's explorations didn't create any real problems. She had Jean to talk to so she didn't get bored. At the curb she spoke very angrily to Alex, but her other No, Alexes were good-humored, not cross. She was enjoying the walk and was being attentive to Alex without getting in his way or telling him what to do too often.

Ideas and Words

Alex is developing ideas about objects and relationships at the same time he is learning to speak. Though he isn't setting about the task consciously, he is clearly figuring out how to group individual things into categories. He knows the word for cat and he knows that it refers to all cats, not just Barney. Fire trucks and motorbikes and cars and trains don't look alike, but he calls them all "gos" because they all go. This is a good idea, but it isn't English. Alex will soon learn how we group and name different types of vehicles.

Alex understands the idea of containers. He quickly realized that there might be something inside the garbage pail. He tried to look and see. He has played with many similar kinds of objects before, very small ones like jars and yogurt containers and bigger ones like the round straw hamper. He is learning that the same shape can come in many different sizes.

Sense of Self

Sometimes Alex wants to be Mike and Rita's partner. Sometimes he wants them to take care of him. Today, he wanted to push the stroller with Rita. He wanted to play with the older boys. But when he fell, Alex raised his arms so Rita would pick him up and comfort him.

The walk to the park is an adventure for Alex. Each time Mrs. Weiss or Rita takes him to the park, Alex discovers things that are new to him, and on each walk he applies his physical skills with real determination to investigate the unknown.

♦

KATIE
(Twenty-eight Months)

"Press one for the first floor—on the bottom." Sarah indicates the button labeled "one." Katie reaches her hand up and presses it.

"One," Katie says. The light goes on. She presses another button.

"That's enough, Katie. The elevator will stop at all the floors and then we'll never get outside." Katie giggles and tries to press another button. Sarah grabs her for a mock struggle.

The elevator stops at five, the second floor Katie pressed. The doors open. Katie starts to go out. "No, this is five," Sarah explains. "We want to go to one. Now when I say 'now,' jump up, okay?"

Katie nods. Just as the elevator is about to move, Sarah says, "Now jump!" Katie jumps. Because the elevator floor begins to descend while she is in the air, Katie has the sensation of having jumped very high. She laughs and tries it again. "It's best when you jump just as the elevator starts," Sarah explains. But Katie keeps jumping anyway.

It's Sunday morning. Yesterday Wayne and Joanna had talked about taking Katie for her first big-city walk together. But after breakfast today, Sarah realized that her hosts and her daughter were starting to get on each other's nerves. When Sarah suggested she and Katie go out alone, Wayne and Joanna were visibly relieved.

Sarah and Katie step out onto the sidewalk and start for the park two blocks away. Katie takes Sarah's hand. She stays close to her mother for a few minutes. She has never seen buildings like the ones here, thirty-story apartment buildings on the corners, brownstones with stairs leading to an above-ground entrance in the middle of the block.

"Stairs," Katie says, pointing to one of the more ornate stoops.

"Yes," Sarah says.

Lions are carved in relief in the stone at the base of the balustrade. Katie lets go of Sarah's hand and goes over to inspect. She touches one of the lions.

"Dog," she says.

"No," Sarah tells her. "They're lions. Remember in your book?"

"No lions," Katie says.

"Well, they don't look like the lions in the book," Sarah concedes. "But see the mane? Put your hand higher—that's the mane."

Katie has doubts. She climbs two stairs. The steps are adult-size of course, so she steps up with her right foot, then brings her left foot up to the same step. When she is about a third of the way up, she walks over to the banister and tries to climb up on the stone base supporting the posts.

Sarah is about to say "careful" but stops herself. Actually, Sarah notes with something like pride, Katie is being pretty careful. She adjusts her grip on the post several times to make sure it's safe before pulling herself up. "Up," she says. She stands on the stone, holding the banister firmly for support and looking around.

A man in a business suit comes out of the front door. "Hello," he says.

Katie is very quiet for a second, staring at the man hard. Then she says, "Hi!" very loud and bold.

The man smiles and trots down the stairs, straight out into the street. He holds one hand up in the air and waves it agitatedly. He scowls, lowers his arm, then a few seconds later raises it and waves again. Katie watches.

She goes down the stairs, dragging her hand along the posts, and starts after the man. "Katie," Sarah says, going over to retrieve her. "Leave the man alone." Katie stops moving but continues staring. "He's getting a taxi."

"Taxi," Katie says, looking at her.

"When people don't have a car of their own and they want to go somewhere in a car, they can pay someone to drive them in his car."

Katie notices a pigeon pecking at something on the edge of the curb.

"They give the driver money and he takes them where they want to go." Sarah is aware this explanation is getting awkward, but she doesn't know how to straighten it out. "The cars you hire to drive you are marked in a special way. We have them at home and they have little things on the roof."

Katie steps toward the pigeon. It speeds up huffily, then flies away.

"Here they're yellow."

Katie turns her head to look back at the man. He is waving his arm again. Katie pulls at Sarah's arm. Sarah looks back. A yellow car has pulled up. Katie watches the man get in. The yellow cab drives off, passing Katie and Sarah.

Sarah takes Katie's hand at the corner. "See that red light?" Katie nods. "The red light means the cars can go and the people have to wait. The same way it does at home. Remember the light by the department store? When the red light goes off and a green light comes on the cars will stop and we can go."

Katie looks at the red light. It doesn't change right away. She looks down and notices the grating covering a hole in the street.

"Hole," she says.

"Yes," Sarah explains, "when it rains and the streets get filled with water, the water falls down the hole."

Katie squats down to look into the hole.

"No, it doesn't stay there. I think there are pipes in the hole that take the water to the sea." Sarah realizes Katie can't possibly be absorbing all these explanations.

Katie tries to get down on her hands and knees so she can reach her hand into the grating. Sarah pulls her up. "Come on, the light's changing. We have to hurry now."

"Let's try to go a little faster," Sarah suggests when they get to the other side. Except for three brief stops, one to pat a labrador, one to investigate a fire hydrant, and one to examine the awning in front of an apartment building and the uniformed doorman underneath, Katie does move faster. The street is more crowded and Katie stays close to her mother, staring hard at the procession of faces passing by. They cross one more street and arrive at the park.

After a few yards, the path leading into the park turns into long, low steps. Katie can take four regular steps along each level before she comes to the step down. When she gets to the second step, instead of putting one foot down, she jumps with both feet. She laughs, takes three running trots to the next step and jumps again, continuing the run-run-run-jump! exercise until they reach the bottom and turn off into a small playground.

Sarah finds a bench in the sun, sits down, and slouches back a little, letting the sunlight warm her face. Katie bends down to examine a stone.

"I'm going to sit here, Katie," Sarah says, "while you play. I'll swing you later if you want."

Katie, carrying her stone, goes off to explore the playground. She heads first toward a rocky knoll right next to the fence. Sarah watches her clamber up the rocks. She puts her hand on her belly where the new child is growing. When Katie was born, she remembers, she seemed so fragile, so breakable. Sarah was afraid if she rocked Katie too hard she'd fall apart, and when Joe bounced her up in the air her heart nearly exploded. But Katie could certainly handle a few rough bounces. Look at her now, picking herself up from a fall . . .

◆

OBSERVATIONS

The World of Things

Yesterday and today were Katie's first walks in a big city. An adult visiting a big city for the first time might deliberately try to orient himself by noting the type of buildings, their arrangement, the location of subway or bus stops and the names of the streets. Katie began to make herself at home simply by examining whatever happened to catch her attention: an interesting stoop, a man hailing a cab, a street drain, an awning.

Katie liked pressing the elevator buttons because by touching them she could make the buttons light up. She understood that touching the buttons had to do with making the elevator go.

Katie enjoys sensations in and of themselves, so she was excited when Sarah showed that she could get a special sensation by jumping in the elevator. She jumped again and again, trying to keep hold of the feeling. Later she discovered a run-run-run-jump pattern down the steps in the park which made her body feel good.

Katie went over to the rock in the park, not to the slide or sand-box. Real things and places are still just as alluring to her as play-things and places designed for play.

The World of People

People, especially people doing things, are one of the most interesting parts of the environment to Katie. She isn't used to seeing so many people, so many different kinds of people, and so many hurried people as she saw today in such a short period of time. She couldn't take them all in. She just looked at them. She didn't smile at anyone or study anyone closely with the exception of the doorman, who was standing still and wearing a smart uniform, and the man who came out of the brownstone.

The man from the brownstone initiated a relationship with Katie by saying hello. After a moment's hesitation, Katie said, "Hi." Because he spoke to her and because his activities were so mysterious, she became very curious about the man.

Katie knows how to tease now. Sarah told her not to press more elevator buttons, but Katie realized this was not an important prohibition: she pressed another button, inviting a mini catch-me game. After sharing Sarah with Wayne and Joanna all weekend, Katie may have wanted the physical contact.

Ideas and Words

Katie of course has no idea why she felt the particular sensation she did when she jumped in the elevator. But in about ten years, one of her teachers may very well refer to the experience while explaining inertia.

Katie saw that the carvings on the stone stoop were animals, but she thought they were dogs, not lions. She does not know enough about lions to recognize an unusual lion. Sarah tried to call her attention to the mane as an identifying characteristic of lions.

Katie still needs to touch, move, look, and listen to get information about the world, but now she can also get information from people through words. When she learns the name of something, she repeats it to help herself remember. She is beginning to want to know why people do the things they do and what things are for, which means she is beginning to develop a notion of purpose.

When Sarah tells her to do something specific, Katie can usually follow what she is saying. She understood that she wasn't supposed to press the elevator buttons. She jumped in the elevator when her mother said "now jump." She understood that Sarah wanted her to hurry and later that Sarah was going to stay on the bench.

Katie doesn't understand all of what Sarah tells her about the nature and purposes of things like taxicabs and street lights. Sarah tends to go into too much detail when she explains things to her daughter. But Sarah's explanations are still valuable for Katie. Explanations are about the way things are related to one another. When she tells Katie about the objects and events they see around them, she is helping Katie make connections in her mind. Katie probably does make some of the connections. She may have realized, for example, that the reason the man stood in the street had something to do with yellow cars or that the hole in the street had something to do with water.

When she explains something, Sarah is also helping Katie connect language with what is happening around her. She is showing Katie how to use language to understand the world better. Katie already uses language to help herself think. When she was climbing the stone balustrade, for example, she said "up": she was using the word to think about what she was doing.

Katie experimented with a greeting word on her own, with a stranger. When the man from the brownstone said "Hello," she said "Hi" back.

Sense of Self

During their walk this morning, Sarah was very conscious of how independent and capable Katie has become. She demonstrated her faith in Katie's abilities and good sense by staying on the sidewalk while Katie climbed the stoop and later by telling her she could play in the park by herself, however she wanted. Since Katie's sense of self is closely tied to Sarah's sense of Katie, the respect Sarah felt and showed today was an important gift to her daughter.

Katie was a good companion for Sarah today. She didn't need to be carried or pushed. She didn't have to be made to do anything or to be persuaded to stop doing something she shouldn't. Katie's curiosity made the walk more interesting for Sarah. When they arrived in the park, Katie, like Sarah, wanted to play alone for a while.

Until recently, Katie was too much of a baby to be good company for Sarah. She's still too much of a baby to be good company very often. But as she grows older, companionship will become a more important element in her relationship with her mother.

Part Five

◆

OTHER ADULTS

13

SAYING HELLO AND GOOD-BYE

Every day, several times a day, whenever we leave our family, arrive at work, leave work, make a phone call, go to an appointment, or pass a friend on the street, we say hello and good-bye. Though they are part of our daily routine, we usually don't think of these greetings and leave-takings as tasks or jobs, as activities which accomplish something, like taking a bath or doing the laundry. But saying hello and good-bye are activities, complicated and important ones, so important that in the joy and exhaustion of having given birth, the first thing many women say to the wet, squiggling baby on their stomach—the first word their baby hears—is "hello."

The baby doesn't answer. She isn't aware yet that she's someone to be introduced or that the warm skin to which she's clinging is another person. But within a few months, she will be smiling and squealing when a familiar person or object comes into view—a first gesture toward greeting—and disappearances will begin to disturb her. By the time she is three, hellos and good-byes will have become vital daily rituals for her, rituals that help her manage her feelings and that help her understand separation is not abandonment.

Parents say hello and good-bye to their child many times during the course of a day—in the morning, at bedtime, every time they play peek-a-boo or hide-and-seek with their child, every time she checks back after an excursion on her own. Most children go through periods when they are so distressed by separation that their parents don't even go into the kitchen to fetch a glass of water without saying an elaborate set of good-byes first. In the three scenes that follow, however, we will focus on one particular set of hellos and good-byes: the good-byes working parents say to their children when they leave them in the morning and the hellos they say when they pick their children up later in the day. We decided to focus on these good-byes and hellos because they are a regular part of the week for so many people and because so many adults find them difficult.

Morning good-byes are difficult for working parents partly for practical reasons: working parents are always rushed in the morning. Adults see the early morning as a transition time between home and work, a kind of extended, sometimes strained, good-bye. They are concerned with getting themselves and their children dressed, fed, and ready to go, efficiently, in a short period of time. They want to gear up for the day. Children don't have to gear up. They don't have much sense of what it means to prepare emotionally for something that isn't happening yet. They live very much in the present. Even if they're old enough to realize the family is getting ready for their individual daytime activities, they don't understand the point of rushing or what it means to be on time. A nine-month-old may want to spend a leisurely five minutes crumbling and examining toast, when her father just wants to get some food into her stomach so he can get to the bank before work. A two-year-old may decide she wants to "read" a book, stick a tape in the stereo, or play with her train on the morning her parents are running late. By the time they arrive at day care or the caregiver arrives at their home, both parent and child may be cross. Shifting to a tender good-bye at this point is sometimes impossible.

There's no way of getting around the problem of the morning crunch altogether. If your usual response to the dawn of a new tomorrow is to roll over in bed hoping it will go away, you are sometimes going to find getting your child ready for the day an alarming prospect. Getting up earlier to make some play time is one solution, but not a happy one, since parents of small children are usually chronically short of sleep anyway. It might be reasonable for you and your spouse to get up a little earlier on alternate days to have some extra time with your child. It might also help to invent some kind of special activity to mark the transition between getting ready and going to day care. It could be five minutes of reading, a find-the-baby game, a game built around packing the lunch box or walking down the hall to the door. If the activity is repeated daily, it can become a signal that it is time to go to day care or time for the caregiver to arrive.

When you finally leave your child with her daytime caregiver, it's important that you do say a proper good-bye—even if you dread farewell scenes. Morning good-byes are difficult for parents partly because they can hurt. There's something truly desperate about the way a child, particularly a child in her first two years, cries when her mother or father leaves. It's very hard for a parent not to feel the frightened child in himself reach out in sympathy—and the baby may cry louder and cling harder if she senses her parent is upset too. You may be tempted to hand your child over to the caregiver and then just slip off when she isn't looking to avoid the tears and screams.

That's a mistake. Your child will trust you more if you warn her before you go. She may cry with anguish when you leave, but if you say good-bye, at least your absence won't take her by surprise. She'll know you're going—and more important, she'll know that when you're with her, you're with her. She won't be afraid that she'll turn around and suddenly find you've disappeared.

Making an effort to distinguish your feelings about separating from your child from her feelings about separating from you can make good-byes easier to handle. It's natural for you to want to stay with your child and savor her love and protect her with yours. It's natural for you to want to get away from her sometimes too. It's natural for your child to want to have you near her and available to her whenever she wants you and to feel unhappy when you leave. But you can't stop working because your child doesn't want you to leave her—and you needn't think it would necessarily be better if you could.

Adults empathize so readily with a clinging child because all of us (including those who were raised by doting mothers who stayed home) have felt abandoned at some time or other as children: it's part of growing up. Difficulties, including unwanted separations, are an inevitable part of life. Everyone, whether he's eight months or eighty years, has to learn to deal with difficult times himself. You can't spare your child separations or the distress that sometimes accompanies them: what you can do is support her while she invents her own ways of dealing with the experience.

One way you can support her is to arrange your schedule so you can take a few minutes to help her adjust to being at day care each morning. Help her hang up her coat, put her extra diaper in the bin in the bathroom and her bottle in the refrigerator; take a few minutes to watch while she tosses a beanbag or pushes the wheelbarrow. Your presence will make it easier for her to relax. Even if she pulled away as soon as you arrived to rush to the caregiver or get going on a favorite activity, she'll appreciate having you around for a few minutes.

Another way you can support your child is to develop your own good-bye ritual, a sequence of words and gestures you repeat every morning just before you leave. You'll probably find yourself doing this naturally: maybe you'll give your child three kisses and a brush on the nose one morning and that will turn into your particular way of saying the morning good-bye; maybe walking to the door, where you hug her and say "See you this afternoon," will become your morning farewell ceremony. By saying good-bye in a special way, you're showing your child that your feelings about her are special. Repeating the ceremony every morning helps her understand what's happening. Over time, the daily repetition makes the meaning of the good-bye clear—afterwards you always leave—and it makes the separation predictable, part of a regularly recurring sequence of events that ends with your return. When you say good-bye in the morning the way you always do, you're reassuring your child that you'll be back at the end of the day, the way you always are.

Your child will quickly become familiar with your good-bye ceremony, and if she's a toddler or a two, she'll begin to join in herself. When a child says good-bye herself, she's no longer just being left behind. By participating actively in the ritual, she's gaining some control of the situation. Children, like adults, feel happier when they feel in control of their lives.

"Happier" isn't necessarily happy. Parents naturally want to feel reassured by the morning good-bye. They want to feel that their child knows they love her, likes the day-care arrangement, and doesn't mind being left. The child doesn't always oblige by offering them sufficient reassurance. Some mornings your good-byes may indeed be warm and relaxed. Your child will turn with enthusiasm to the business of play and you will go off to work peaceful and energetic. (That may disturb you too: everyone likes to feel a tad indispensable.) Other mornings you will leave a weeping child and carry something twisted in your stomach away with you.

When your child is upset about your departure, you and the caregiver can show her you respect her feelings by letting her express them. Your child should feel entitled to cry when you leave: crying is a natural thing for a child to do when she feels bad. The fact that your child cries when you go doesn't mean she will never like day care. It just means she wants you to stay. She'll probably feel better if she's allowed to feel sad a while and show it. It's really not fair to distract her and try to get her to stop crying. (You might feel better if she stopped, but that's not the point.) When she's ready—very often after you're gone—she'll stop crying and get on with her day. Being allowed to cry won't prevent her from feeling sad or anxious the next time you leave, but it will show her that she can get through hard feelings. They don't last forever.

Sometimes there will be weeks when your child weeps in despair every morning—but there'll be other periods when she accepts your departure cheerfully. Children have different vulnerabilities at different times. Saying good-bye is, of course, going to be hardest for them during clingy periods when they like to stay near their mother and father and are wariest of strangers. There is more than one clingy period. Separation isn't something a child learns to handle once and for all time. It's something children (and adults for that matter) feel in different ways at different stages of their lives. (There will be times when your child is the one who wants or has to leave and you will do the clinging.)

Circumstances will influence your child's feelings about separation too. The morning good-bye will be most difficult for your child when she's not used to a daily separation, when she is being cared for by someone new for the first time, or when she is changing from one day-care arrangement to another—for example, if she's been staying with a neighbor and begins going to a day-care center for the first time or when she returns to day care after a vacation. It's unrealistic and unfair to expect your child to say good-bye without some distress if she's accustomed to having you around all day or is getting used to a new situation.

Even when your child likes and looks forward to day care and is going through a period when she relishes her independence, there will be occasional mornings when she wants to stay with you. Maybe she just doesn't feel like going to day care the way you sometimes don't feel like going to work. Maybe she wants to be babied again for a day or two or three. Maybe she's anxious because work or marital or health or money problems are making you anxious (your moods affect your child's).

When your child is having an especially hard time saying good-bye, she needs more help from you. The first problem is simply realizing when your child needs a bit of extra support: it's not always easy to tell. Every child has her own individual ways of expressing her feelings. When your child makes a big fuss, it may mean she's upset, but it may just mean she's making a fuss. Healthy children naturally try to figure out ways to get adults to do what they want. What children want very often is everything—day care and having their parents with them and being left alone when they feel like it. Your child will do her best to get it all. She may even make a fuss just for the pleasure of having power over you or to win a few extra minutes of play or a promise of a future treat. A bit of fussiness may also have become part of the good-bye ritual, the way demanding a glass of water can become part of a child's going-to-bed ritual.

On the other hand, a child who is very quiet and compliant when you first take her to day care isn't necessarily making a beautiful adjustment. Maybe she is taking to day care right away. But it's also possible she's too anxious to make the scene she'd really like to make. Babies sometimes become subdued when they're worried, and it's easy to assume a quiet baby is feeling fine. Older children who are beginning to get a feel for what is socially desirable may choose the cautious path of being obedient and sweet if they're unsure of a situation. Sometimes children who handle good-byes with seeming ease at first, start crying and struggling after they've been in day care a few weeks, when they feel relaxed enough to be heartily difficult.

You know your child's emotional style better than anyone else. If you feel your child's morning protests are a kind of game, play with her awhile, but make the good-bye ritual part of the game too, the part that firmly ends it. If your child is genuinely anxious, however she shows her anxiety, try to spend a few extra minutes with her and her daytime caregiver before going. Make it clear that the extra time is limited, that you'll stay long enough to read her a book or hit the xylophone with her, and then you will have to go. Give her a clear warning and repeat your good-bye ritual when you do leave. You're explaining something to her this way: separations are an unavoidable part of relationships, not something she can negotiate away.

To help her feel less anxious, you can give your child something of hers from home to keep when you are gone (a favorite toy or pillow or blanket) or something of yours (a scarf or a glove). Having a familiar object close by will help her feel emotionally in touch with home. Since many toddlers and twos like to look at pictures, you can try pasting a family photo to your child's lunch box so she can look at it whenever she wants. You might also want to leave her a love note that the caregiver can read to her, to remind her that even though you are not there, your love still is. When you give your child a note or a photograph or a favorite toy to keep with her, you're not giving her a pacifier. She will use these objects actively to keep you and her home present in her mind even though she is physically far away.

At the same time you say good-bye to your child in the morning, you have another job: helping her say hello to the caregiver. A good way to do this is simply to say hello to the caregiver yourself and ask how she is. When you greet the caregiver, you are giving your child an example of courtesy and also showing her that you trust this other adult. If your child is feeling shy, she may stick close to you until she's ready to say hello to the caregiver herself. A brief morning conversation with the caregiver will also give the two of you a chance to exchange information about your child.

Even when you're in a hurry, it's important to say a quick hello to the caregiver and let her know you're leaving so she can keep an eye on your child. If your child is upset when you leave or becomes upset after you've gone, the caregiver can comfort her, confirm your promise that you'll be back later, and remind her of some of the interesting things she will be doing during the day. You may have to wait a few minutes until the caregiver at a center or family day-care home is available. Other parents will be dropping off their children at the same time you are. The caregiver can't comfort someone else's crying child and yours at the same time.

When you are concerned about your child, tell the caregiver you'll call later to see how she's doing. Chances are she'll be fine.

You might expect that if morning good-byes are difficult, evening hellos should be easy as melted butter. They're not. Many parents complain that the hours between 5 P.M. and 7 P.M. are the most acidic of the day.

The time when you pick your child up may be precisely the time when what you need most is to sit quietly by yourself for a few minutes to put the strains of the working world behind you and make your own transition from work to home. You don't get your quiet half hour. You have to summon yet more energy to jump right back into your job as a parent. The thought of a loving reunion and tranquil domestic evening is sustaining but not always realistic. However skilled and affectionate the people who care for her during the day, your child will still guard her deepest feelings of the day until she is with you again. When you arrive at the end of the day to pick her up, the emotions your child held in reserve may suddenly overwhelm her—and get dumped on you. Instead of a warm hug, the child you have been thinking of every now and then all day with tremors of adoration may sometimes greet you angrily or turn away in a conspicuous sulk. Or she may reach or crawl or run toward you and cling as if you are rescuing her from the direst circumstances.

When you find your child in a bad mood at the end of the day, it may have to do with something going on between you. If she greets you angrily, for example, she may be initiating another skirmish in an ongoing battle you've been having. Perhaps she has leftover feelings of resentment because you rushed her in the morning. On the other hand, her greeting might reflect something that happened during the day: maybe her toy was broken or she scraped her knee or one of the day-care workers went to help another child when she wanted the attention herself.

Most evenings, of course, your child will radiate delight when she sees you. Sometimes she may be sleepily affectionate, but more often she will greet you with a rush of pent-up exuberance. When she sees you, her energy level will soar. Though you probably don't feel particularly rambunctious at five thirty on a Wednesday afternoon, she may start crawling about at Olympic speed, inviting you to catch her, or show you a new activity she has learned, or just bounce and grab maniacally. Playing with an excited happy child can be almost as draining as dealing with a sullen or irritated one.

If you've been kept late at work or were stuck in traffic and your child's daytime guardians are pacing back and forth staring at the clock when you arrive, if you've got to shop for dinner, pay your bills, iron a suit, and do a laundry before you go to bed, you will have to scoop up your child and run. But if you have the time and can find the energy, it's a good idea to spend a few minutes focusing all your attention on just being with your child before you take her home or before the caregiver leaves and you start your evening chores. If your child's in a bad temper, let her fume or fight or whine a bit until the feelings start to ease up. If she's in high spirits, play with her awhile until she quiets down. If she's tired and clingy, cuddle with her a bit before bundling her off. If she wants to continue the game she was playing when you came in, let her go on for a few minutes and give her a three-minute warning before insisting it's time to stop. Expressing the emotions she feels when she sees you are part of her way of saying hello. The time she spends finishing a game or showing you something she's done during the day is time she needs to say good-bye to day care, just as you sometimes need to chat for ten minutes at the door before leaving a friend's house. Saying good-bye her way, like saying hello, gives her a little control over the events of her day. If after a few minutes your child still isn't ready to go, you can be firm about insisting it's time to leave.

Before you go, remember to say good-bye to the caregiver. Your child and the caregiver have just spent the day together; their relationship is important enough that saying good-bye is important to both of them. Bring your child with you when you say good-bye yourself. You'll find that the caregiver and your child will develop their own good-bye ritual. Once your child can speak, you can teach her to say a courteous standard good-bye as well.

Because the hellos and good-byes that surround day care are repeated predictably every day, they help both children and parents realize that separations are not desertions. They are part of the rhythm of life. Sometimes the daily separation may be welcome (there'll be mornings when you feel fine about escaping your domineering two and mornings she'll be eager to rush off to the park with her daytime guardian). Sometimes separating will be difficult. But even when she doesn't like to see you leave, your child, like you, will go on to enjoy the day's activities as best she can. Helping her say hello and good-bye will help her accept her feelings and give her the confidence she needs to explore new places, to step away from you into a life she will increasingly be making for herself.

Jennifer, Alex, and Katie are all accustomed to daily separations. This morning Carol is worried about leaving because Jen has been up crying most of the night. Alex, who is quite at home with Mrs. Weiss, says good-bye to Rita in a nonchalant fashion. Katie, in a foul mood, scarcely greets Sarah at all at the end of the day.

♦

JENNIFER
(Six Months)

Jen kicks, shifts her position on Carol's lap, and begins crying to herself again.

"Shhh," Carol says, rocking harder and stroking Jen's head. Jen looks up. Her eyes are red and puffy. Her round cheeks are streaked with mucus and tears. A bit of spit-up milk has formed a round, crusty spot on her pajama top.

"You don't look very adorable this morning, do you?" Carol says. She wipes some mucus from the end of Jen's nose and offers her a bottle of apple juice. "Do you want to try this again?" Jen sucks a few minutes, working her mouth but not really drinking. Then she arches and pushes the bottle away. She wails.

Jen began crying at 3:30 A.M. loud, hard, angrily. Carol changed her, offered a bottle, rocked her. Nothing helped. Jen didn't have a fever. She didn't seem to be in pain. But she wouldn't quiet down. She would whine awhile, then cry heartily, quiet down a few minutes, sniff, toss a little, seem to get drowsy—and start crying all over again. At first Carol had been worried she would wake Sam. After a while she began wondering what was wrong with Sam's hearing. How was it that Jen's slightest cry woke Carol while Sam could sleep through this?

Jen's timing, of course, was abominable. They had asked Mrs. Semple to come a half-hour early—she will be here soon, Carol realizes—because they both wanted to get an early start on a busy day. Sam had a breakfast meeting with two executives from out of town. Carol had been planning to get to the office by eight-thirty to review some background material before a nine-fifteen meeting with a new client—the first new case she had taken since Jen was born. Did Jen pick tonight to do this to punish her? Why should it be so damn hard just to get to work a half-hour early once in six months?

Jen's wail works its way down to a small, prickly whine. "I want to go to work," Carol thinks. "I want to get out of here. But what if something is really wrong?"

Carol gets up, holding a squirming Jen, and searches for the thermometer tape on the bureau to take Jen's temperature one more time. When Carol tries to hold the tape to her forehead, Jen pulls her head away, whining.

"Jen, you be still!" Carol snaps.

Jen, startled, stops twisting and stares at her mother. Carol seizes the opportunity to press the tape against Jen's forehead. Jen raises her hand to touch the tape and misses. She whimpers. Carol peels the tape off. Jen, a little calmer, twists her head to watch Carol. "Well, it's still normal." Jen reaches out and tries to grab the tape from Carol. She gets Carol's thumb instead. Carol looks at the perfect little fingers gripping her thumb. Her eyes tear.

"I'm sorry I yelled at you, sweetheart," she says softly. Jen kicks her legs and begins crying.

"What's the matter?" Sam appears at the door looking so alarmed that Carol stops being angry with him. Her head begins to hurt instead.

"I don't know. She began crying in the middle of the night. I haven't been able to get her to stop."

Jen looks at Sam through her tears. He walks over to her. "Hi." Jen whimpers. "Should we call the doctor?" Sam asks Carol.

"She doesn't have a fever. I don't think anything's really wrong. She just feels bad. I don't know . . ."

"I can't stay," Sam says apologetically.

"I didn't ask you to stay, did I?" Carol replies, enunciating the words with excessive care.

Sam looks at Jen. "Everything is going to be fine." He offers a reassuring smile. "Why don't you take your shower now?"

Carol hesitates a second. "All right." She gets up and hands Jen to Sam. Jen grabs her father's robe, pulls herself up to a sitting position, and watches Carol go to the door.

"I'll be right back," Carol says to Jen.

"There," Sam coos, "it's okay." The acrid, sour odor in his nostrils, he realizes, is Jen. He looks down at the swollen, crusty face. "Can't you give your old father a smile?"

Jen stares at him. "Ah!" she says, pushing the sound out with effort. A *bubble of saliva forms at the corner of her mouth, bursts, and trickles down in a thin stream.*

"She's disgusting," Sam thinks, feeling ashamed of himself. "But she is disgusting."

Jen turns her head to one side and begins kneading Sam's robe with both fists.

The doorbell rings a few minutes later. Jen turns her head to the sound. "I'll get it!" Sam calls to Carol. "You finish getting ready." Jen quiets down as Sam starts toward the door: her whole body seems to relax. Sam takes a giant step. Jen giggles.

Sam opens the door. "Good morning, Mrs. Semple."

Mrs. Semple stares at Sam's bathrobe. Usually he is dressed and heading out the door for work as she is coming in. "Good morning." She follows Sam into the kitchen and puts her bag on a chair.

"Good morning, Jennifer," Mrs. Semple says, taking her from Sam. She reaches into her pocket for a tissue. "What's this all over your face?" She starts to scrub.

Carol comes in just at this moment. "So what if Mrs. Semple thinks I'm a terrible mother," she tells herself. Jen sees Carol first and turns in Mrs. Semple's arms to reach for her. "Good morning, Mrs. Semple," Carol says. "Thank you for coming early."

"Good morning. Here, Jen, here's your mom."

Carol walks over and takes Jen. "Hello darling. I'm going to hold you a few minutes. Then I have to go to work."

"I'll be ready in five minutes," Sam tells her. "We can go down together."

Carol nods. She looks at her watch, then turns to Mrs. Semple. "We've had a hard morning, Mrs. Semple, as you can see. Jen"—Carol strokes Jen's head—"has had us up since three-thirty. She doesn't have a temperature. She seems all right now, but I'm still worried about her." Jen pulls at Carol's hair. "I'm going to the office," Carol continues, undoing Jen's fingers, "but I'll call you in two hours to see how she is. If she doesn't seem okay, I'll come back. And of course if she seems worse, don't wait for me to call. Call me—just tell the switchboard operator that you are Jennifer's baby-sitter and she'll put you right through."

Mrs. Semple touches Jen's forehead. "I don't think she has a fever."

Doesn't she believe me when I tell her Jen doesn't have a temperature? Carol thinks.

"Jen needs breakfast. There's some yogurt and peaches on the top shelf of the refrigerator."

"All set?" Sam comes in suited and briefcased with two trench coats over his arm. "I brought your coat."

"I think so." Carol looks at Mrs. Semple. "There's cold chicken for your lunch and, of course, you know my telephone number is right there over the phone."

"Yes," Mrs. Semple says, swallowing a sigh. The number is written on a large, can't-miss index card taped above the phone. Carol points it out every day. "Don't worry. It looks like she just had a bad night. But I promise to call you right away if there's any problem."

Carol looks down at Jen. Reflexively she straightens out Jen's pajama top, although it is filthy and will have to be changed right away. Jen reaches up and pulls at Carol's jacket, gurgling happily. "Mommy and Daddy are going to work now, sweetheart. We'll see you later."

Sam leans over, furtively looks for a spot without crud, finds one on Jen's forehead, and kisses it. "Bye, Jennifer." Carol presses Jen against her, holds her breath—please don't make a fuss, she thinks—and hands Jen over to Mrs. Semple. "There you go. Good-bye, darling. I love you. I'll see you later."

Jen reaches for Carol and begins to whimper. "She'll be all right," Sam says, gripping Carol's arm. Carol looks at him, then looks back at Jen. Sam opens the door and steers Carol out by her elbow.

"Good-bye," says Mrs. Semple. "Please don't worry. Really!" She looks fondly at the baby. "We're going to have a good day, aren't we, Jen?" Mrs. Semple smiles and closes the door behind Carol and Sam.

Jen, still whimpering, looks up at Mrs. Semple. Her face crumples. She begins crying seriously, huge sobs shaking her little torso. "It's okay," Mrs. Semple says, bouncing Jen in her arms. "We'll have a lovely day and your mommy and daddy will come home later. There, shhh . . ."

Jen is crying now in the ordinary desperate way she sometimes cries when she is overtired and Carol leaves. After her parents are gone, Mrs. Semple knows, Jen will settle down and cheer up. But Mrs. Semple wants Jen to stop now. With an intuition honed by her fifteen years as a nanny, she senses that Carol is listening in the hall.

Carol, her ear pressed against the door, feels like crying too. Sam paces impatiently. "Maybe I should stay," Carol says.

"Come on, Carol." Sam detaches his wife from the door. "We have to go now. Babies cry sometimes, that's all. Everything's going to be fine."

"All right," Carol says, looking backward while Sam steers her to the elevator.

———————————————◆———————————————

OBSERVATIONS

The World of Things

Though Jen was very unhappy, she still reached out to finger the thermometer tape and Sam's robe. Jen's curiosity about the world is so intense nothing can dampen it entirely.

The World of People

Sam and Carol were sincerely concerned about Jen but they didn't enjoy being with her this morning. Sam found his smelly, whiny daughter a bit repellent, and Carol felt drained. Carol was angry with Jen for waking her in the middle of the night, making her so anxious, and making it difficult for her to go to work, when nothing was really wrong. She lost her temper and snapped when Jen wouldn't sit still to have her temperature taken.

Most mornings, Jen watches her parents go without crying and fussing. This morning, however, she became very agitated when Carol handed her over to Mrs. Semple. She may have wanted Carol with her because she didn't feel well and having Carol close makes her feel safe. She may have started sobbing after her parents left simply because she had been up most of the night, her parents' departure was a change, and she was so tired she didn't want anything to change.

Jen loves Sam and is very attached to Mrs. Semple but right now the person with whom she feels most relaxed and secure is Carol. Carol is a little proud because she can often soothe Jen when others can't. But Jen's special feeling for her makes saying hello and good-bye more difficult for Carol. This morning Carol felt that Jen would have felt better if she had stayed home, so she wanted to stay. She also wanted to get away from her needy, exhausting daughter and begin her new case. Jen's desire to have her close by made Carol feel claustrophobic.

Jen's distress was exacerbating tensions in the relationship between Carol and Mrs. Semple. Mrs. Semple has cared for many children and she has helped Carol care for Jen most of Jen's life. She knew that Jen was just anxious because she had a hard night.

But she was concerned that Carol and Sam, who are new parents and a bit nervous, might think Jen's crying means she isn't doing a good job. She finds it easier to deal with Jen's fussiness than with Carol's. Mrs. Semple is annoyed, for example, when Carol repeats her instructions about the phone number every day, as though she wouldn't know to contact Carol in an emergency. This morning Mrs. Semple felt confident she and Jen would have a pleasant day, but she wanted Jen to stop crying before Carol left so that Carol wouldn't be calling home every half hour all day.

Carol likes and respects Mrs. Semple or she wouldn't have hired her. Mrs. Semple, Carol knows, has had a lot more experience with small children than she has. She wants Mrs. Semple to approve of her as a mother. She bridled when Mrs. Semple commented on Jen's dirty face and when she checked to make sure Carol was right about Jen not having a fever. And even though Carol respects Mrs. Semple's experience, she is still afraid Mrs. Semple will not take as good care of Jen as she would.

The relationships between the people around Jen, the considera-
tion they show each other and the tensions between them, are a very
important part of Jen's world. Jen doesn't understand or think about
these relationships yet, but she is already affecting them—and being
affected by them—in important ways.

Ideas and Words

Carol and Sam usually remember to say a kind of good-bye to Jen
even when they are only going into another room. For example,
Carol told Jen, "I'll be right back" when she left to take a shower. She
didn't use the word "good-bye," but she was warning Jen that they
were going to be separated and acknowledging Jen's concern.

By saying good-bye to her in various ways, Carol and Sam are
teaching Jen that people use language to let each other know about
their comings and goings. They are also teaching her that she can
trust them to warn her before they leave. And because they kiss Jen
and say good-bye the same way every morning before they go to work,
Jen is learning to associate the sounds "good-bye," putting on of coats
and going to the door with leaving.

Jen turned to look at Mrs. Semple when Mrs. Semple arrived. She
looked at Carol and reached for her when Carol came into the
kitchen. Turning, making eye contact, and reaching are Jen's way of
saying hello to her important adults.

Sense of Self

Jen is learning to distinguish different people in her life from each
other, and at the same time she is becoming more aware of herself.
Separations are starting to bother her now partly because she is learning more about her body and more about the way objects and people
exist in space and time. She seems to understand in a way she didn't
before that the people she loves can leave.

Jen's bad mood didn't seem triggered in any obvious way by a specific problem or event. Perhaps Jen had a bad night simply because

the processes that are making her grow threw off her internal balance in some way. Being alive and growing sometimes means feeling anxious and unhappy.

Carol and Sam were concerned that something was physically wrong with their daughter. They make a distinction between feeling unwell physically and feeling emotionally off-key. Jen probably can't make that distinction. When Jen feels out of sorts or anxious or restless or unhappy, she feels bad with her whole body. She cries and squirms and tosses. She probably didn't know why she felt bad tonight or what she wanted or when it would go away. Since Jen couldn't tell them what she was feeling, there was no way Sam and Carol could know what was wrong.

Jen doesn't yet have many resources to help her deal with feelings of distress. But simply getting through a troubled night and feeling better the next day will help her develop more confidence in herself. Jen and her parents are learning that they can't always make feelings like anxiety, discomfort, or resentment go away when they want—but that unpleasant feelings don't last forever either.

◆

ALEX
(Fifteen Months)

Robert joins his sons at the kitchen table. "Do you know where my blue work shirt is? The one with short sleeves?"

"In the laundry basket in our room." Rita takes the coffee from the bottom shelf of the refrigerator.

"Barney made a stinky poop in his box," Mike reports with relish, "a stinky, stinky poop."

"Pooh," says Alex.

"That's enough 'poop' talk, Mike," Robert warns.

Rita hears a thin skeep sound as she straightens up. "Damn, I just ran my panty hose and I think it's my last pair." She measures coffee and water into the percolator and plugs it in. "Will you pour some juice for the boys while I change?" she asks, heading toward the door.

"Sure." Robert gets up and takes the juice from the counter. "Here you go, Mike." He pours some juice into Mike's plastic cup, which has dinosaurs on it. "Be careful you don't spill it. Here, Alex." Robert holds a plastic cup with balloons on it up to Alex's lips. Alex looks at the toast scrunched up in his hand. He opens his fingers so the toast falls out. He reaches to take the cup himself, then looks up at Robert.

"Okay," says Robert. He takes a quick sip to lower the level in the cup. "Try to be careful."

"It's ten of eight," Rita says, coming back into the kitchen. "I don't have time to make breakfast. Can you give Mike some cereal and drop him off?"

Robert is absorbed in spotting for Alex as Alex lifts his cup. "Sure," he says.

"There's some leftover meat loaf in the aluminum foil if you need some protein." Rita turns to Alex. "Okay, big guy. Finish up your juice. I want to get you out of those pajamas and take you over to Mrs. Weiss's."

Robert notices Barney preparing to jump on the table. "Don't you dare," he growls.

Rita lifts Alex out of his chair. Holding him in her arms, she jogs down the hall to his bedroom. "Zoom," she says, hoping that the airplane game will keep him from struggling to get down.

"Zoooo," Alex says, laughing.

A few minutes later, Rita comes back in to say good-bye, a red canvas bag with Alex's things on one shoulder, her bag on the other, and Alex at her heels. "We're off," Rita says. "I'll pick you up after school, Mike. I didn't know you liked meat loaf for breakfast too. Let me give you a kiss." She leans over and kisses him.

"Mi," Alex says, his lips puckered.

"I don't want to kiss him," Mike says.

"Mike . . . ," Robert begins.

"All right," Mike reluctantly agrees. He leans down so Alex's lips brush his cheek. Alex smiles. Mike wipes his cheek off with the back of his hand.

Robert picks Alex up high in the air. "Have a good day, my man."

From his new vantage point, Alex spots a bag of fruit on the counter. "Pay," he says, pointing.

"Here." Robert puts Alex down and hands him a pear. "Good-bye."

"Good-bye," Rita says, herding Alex to the door.

Alex, looking back behind him, opens and closes his pear-free hand in a wave.

Alex and Rita walk down the block to Mrs. Weiss's building. "Do you want to knock for Mrs. Weiss?" Rita asks at the door. Alex, clutching the pear in one hand, knocks on the door with the other. He keeps knocking.

"Who's there?" Mrs. Weiss calls as she unlocks her door. Alex hides behind Rita's leg. "Hello, Rita," Mrs. Weiss says. She smiles. "Where's Alex?" she asks. "Did you bring him today?" Alex peeks his head out far enough that Mrs. Weiss is sure to see him.

"There you are," Mrs. Weiss says. "I'm glad you came with your mommy today." Alex steps out. "And what did you bring with you?"

Alex, not interested in social niceties, starts off into the living room. "Wait a minute, honey." Rita catches him. "Let me get that sweater off." Alex raises his arms to help, but tries to keep walking at the same time.

"Let me take your pear a second." Rita manages to hold him still long enough to get his sweater off. His growing belly has unsnapped the top snap on his pants. Rita gives him back the pear and he trots off.

"He's already outgrowing those pants," Mrs. Weiss observes.

"I know," Rita says. "He's going to be taller than Mike."

Alex plops down in the center of the living room, where Mrs. Weiss has placed his big red ball and his wheelbarrow.

"Would you like a cup of coffee?" Mrs. Weiss asks.

Rita looks at her watch. "A quick cup would be nice." She unbuttons her coat. "We were kind of rushed this morning."

Alex has put his pear in the wheelbarrow and is pushing it around the living room. Rita takes Alex's toys out of the canvas bag and puts them on the floor. Alex parks the wheelbarrow and begins filling it with toys.

Rita puts the canvas bag and her handbag on the table above Alex's reach. "I'm going in the kitchen for some coffee, Alex," she says.

"I don't think he ate much breakfast," she tells Mrs. Weiss as they walk into the kitchen. "He may be a little hungry."

A few minutes later Alex cries out. Rita slaps down her coffee cup and rushes into the living room. Alex is on his knees a few feet from the kitchen door.

"Did you fall down?" Rita picks him up and sits down with him on the sofa. He leans his head against her, crying a little. Rita touches a red mark on his knee. "You were coming to look for me and you went bump on the floor," Rita says. Alex turns his head to look at her. "You went bump," she says, reaching down and hitting the rug with her hand.

The last "bump" energizes Alex. "Baaaaaahp!" he says, hitting the couch. "Baaaaaahp, baaaahp!" His voice is escalating to a shriek.

Mrs. Weiss, watching from the doorway, winces. "Where's your wheelbarrow, Alex?" she asks.

Alex climbs down from Rita's lap, goes to the wheelbarrow, and pushes it over to Mrs. Weiss. "What have you got in there?" Alex takes out the pear and hands it to her.

"Alex," Rita says, picking up her handbag, "I am going to work now. I'll pick you up after you and Mrs. Weiss have lunch and you take your nap."

Alex begins a half-hearted whimper and steps toward Rita. "I'll see you later this afternoon," she says, kissing him on the head.

"Good-bye," Mrs. Weiss says, accompanying Rita and Alex to the door. She turns to Alex. "Why don't you say good-bye, Alex, and then we'll go into the kitchen and have something to eat."

Alex waves, opening and closing both hands. Before he is finished waving he has turned and is trotting toward the kitchen. He walks straight ahead, not looking down, stumbles on a toy, shifts his weight to keep his balance without bothering to see what tripped him, and continues on his slightly pigeon-toed way with a sort of dreamy doggedness.

Rita looks at him lovingly.

"Thank you, Mrs. Weiss. I'll be back by two. Have a good day."

OBSERVATIONS

The World of Things

Alex can help take care of himself now, in effective if often sloppy ways. For example, he fed himself toast and juice this morning. He likes taking care of himself: when Robert held the cup for him, Alex reached out his hand to indicate that he wanted to do it himself.

The World of People

Alex is learning the rituals of saying hello and good-bye and is trying to be part of them. He waves in his own special way by making a fist and then spreading open his fingers. When Rita said good-bye to Mike and Robert and when Mrs. Weiss told Alex to say good-bye to Rita, he opened and closed his hands this way. He wanted to kiss Mike good-bye the way Rita does.

Alex hasn't been finding it difficult to say good-bye to his parents lately. When he was younger he sometimes got upset when they left. In another month or two, he may go through a clingy period. But right now he is so interested in moving around and playing with objects, so eager to go from one new physical activity to another, so easily distracted that he is too busy to worry about separation for long. For example, even though Alex was very aware that Rita was leaving Mrs. Weiss's, he started toward the kitchen before she was gone. This doesn't mean he didn't care she is going or wouldn't miss her during the day. But hanging out by the door feeling bad isn't Alex's style: he wants action.

Alex and Mrs. Weiss get along well. Alex knows that Rita likes and approves of Mrs. Weiss because Rita makes a point of chatting a bit with Mrs. Weiss when she drops Alex off or picks him up.

Even though Alex likes Mrs. Weiss and sees her every day, he still sometimes acts shy in the mornings. He seems to need a little time to make the transition from being in his home to being in Mrs. Weiss's apartment. Mrs. Weiss knows this about Alex and respects his feelings. She is careful to follow his cues about saying hello. This morning, for example, she let him direct the peek-a-boo game. Instead of peering behind Rita and finding Alex, she waited until he felt ready to stick out his head and let himself be seen.

Ideas and Words

Alex enjoys repeating words the way he repeated "pooh" and "zoooo." It is difficult to tell when he is saying a word for the pleasure of repeating the sound and when he is saying it to communicate something.

Rita was able to comfort Alex after his fall by telling him the story of what happened to him, with some dramatic flourishes. Alex liked the rhythm of the story and the chewy sound of "bump." Rita's repetition of the act of hitting something and the sound "bump" helped him hold the idea of bumping in his mind. When he hit the couch and said, "Baaaaaahp!" he was getting bumping under his control.

Sense of Self

Rita initiated the bumping game. Alex himself initiates other games to actively shape his own experience. He uses peek-a-boo games, for example, to explore separations. When he hid behind Rita's legs until he was ready to greet Mrs. Weiss, he was taking charge of his comings and goings—something he can't really do in the course of his daily life.

Alex is also developing ways of reassuring himself. Taking and holding on to the pear may have been Alex's way of keeping a small piece of his home with him when he went to Mrs. Weiss's. Alex often drops an object he is carrying and forgets it when something more interesting comes along. But he kept track of the pear today. Keeping it near him and then giving it to Mrs. Weiss was a way of managing the transition from one place to another. Playing with the toys that Rita brings to Mrs. Weiss's each day gives Alex another way of making a connection between the apartment where he spends the mornings and his own home.

Though Alex's sense of himself as an independent person is growing stronger and stronger, he still doesn't like to be on his own for too long. He checks back with one of his adults regularly for emotional reinforcement; as soon as he does, he wants to go off by himself again. After playing alone in the living room today, he started toward the kitchen to find Rita. But five minutes later he left Rita at the door and was off to the kitchen to get on with his own business.

KATIE
(Twenty-eight Months)

Sarah looks at her watch again. It's four-thirty. "Do you think Lynn will find out if I leave now?" she asks Laura, who works at the other desk. "I'm ahead on the work."

Laura looks up. "No. She's at some big meeting. I don't think she'll be back at all today. What's the matter?"

"I'm worried about Katie. Joe called and said she'd made a scene when he left her this morning. I called the center and they said she was fine, but . . ." Sarah stops herself. She has noticed that Laura's eyes glaze over when she goes into the blow-by-blow details of her maternal life.

"Just go," Laura says. "It'll be all right."

We could make gingerbread, Sarah thinks, pulling into the day-care center parking lot twenty minutes later. Katie would like that. They hadn't baked together in a long time. For a second the sharp smell of ginger curls at the back of her nostrils.

The small day-care center, run by the education department of a local branch of the university, is in a one-story downtown storefront. It consists of four rooms, a kitchen and office in the back, a large front room filled with play things, and a little room to the side with cribs and cots. The yard in the back has been converted into a playground. Paul and Linda, two new education graduates, and Karen, a psychology student, take care of ten children ages nine months to three years.

Sarah stands by the door and skims the room for Katie. She's in the block corner. She and Allen, another two, are each absorbed in their own construction. Allen, bored, gets up and goes over to the jungle gym. Katie gives him a quick look, then turns back to her blocks. The room, Sarah notes, is unusually quiet. A redheaded toddler is trying to climb up the slide of a mini–jungle gym in the middle of the room and getting nowhere. Karen, holding a nine-month-old, is trying to persuade her to use the ladder instead. A boy wearing a yellow shirt is standing nearby, bent over at the waist, staring through his legs and making a low woo-woo-woo sound. A ten-month-old is scooting around the room on all fours. Linda, reading to three toddlers in the corner, catches sight of Sarah and smiles a welcome.

Sarah starts walking over to Katie. Paul, carrying thirteen-month-old Charlie into the bathroom, waves at her. "Hi."

"Hello, Paul." Sarah smiles. Katie looks up at the sound of Sarah's voice, then turns back to her blocks. Sarah continues over to her. "Hello, darling." She kneels down to kiss Katie.

Katie doesn't turn. She tenses her lips and puts another block next to the last one.

"I came early today," Sarah tells her, "so we'd have a little time to play before dinner."

Katie adds another block to the line.

Sarah reaches out her hand and touches Katie's shoulder. *Katie, please be glad to see me, she thinks. Please love me a little.*

Katie snarls and pulls away.

Sarah stands up to stretch her back. She thinks of herself and Katie in the kitchen, enveloped in the smell of baking gingerbread. It doesn't look likely.

There is a clanking noise. Linda has finished reading and the toddlers are loose. Paul, emerging from the bathroom with a freshly diapered Charlie, comes over. "How are you?"

"Pretty good," Sarah says.

"Katie, did you show your mommy the road you made with the blocks?"

Katie hesitates, but her hand reaches out to touch the line of blocks. She looks over her shoulder at Sarah and finally smiles, with obvious pride.

"That's a long road," Sarah says, "a long, straight road."

Katie stands up and leans against Sarah's legs. Sarah nods thanks to Paul. "You're getting to be a very good builder," she tells her daughter. "Daddy will be pleased."

Charlie starts squirming to get down. "There you go," Paul says, steadying Charlie as he gets his balance on the floor. "Katie said something about a hole in your bathroom?" Paul asks Sarah.

Charlie, a new walker, stumbles toward Katie. Sarah smiles, "The leak—"

"No!" Katie shouts. Charlie has walked straight into her road. Katie steps away from Sarah and hits Charlie hard on the chest, knocking him down. Charlie shrieks.

"Katie!" Sarah says, furious. She grabs her daughter's hand and pulls her away before she can stomp on Charlie. Paul picks up the sobbing baby and pats his back. "It's going to be okay."

Sarah has put her hands on Katie's shoulders to make Katie look at her. "Charlie is just a baby," she says. "He's smaller than you. You mustn't hit him." Sarah turns to Paul. "I'm sorry," Sarah apologizes for Katie.

Katie looks at her mother. Her hands tighten into fists and she breaks into tears too. Sarah picks her up. "I know, I know," she tells Katie. "It was a beautiful road and then I yelled at you."

Paul kicks a wooden crate away from the wall toward Sarah. "Here, sit down. Charlie and I are going to get some fruit. Would you like that, Charlie?" Charlie, sobbing, lifts his head to look around as Paul starts toward the kitchen.

Katie snuggles in Sarah's lap. She is still crying, but gently, almost as if she were singing to herself. Sarah rubs her back. "Here, Katie." Linda appears with Franklin, who has spent much of the day in the reading corner. Katie clutches him to her chest. She stops crying in order to suck on his ear.

"Feeling better?" Sarah asks.

Katie straightens up, leaning away from her mother. She puts Franklin down on her lap, wipes her nose with her shirt sleeve, and nods. She notices a piece of dust on Franklin's belly, picks it off, and examines it closely.

Sarah reaches into her shoulder bag and finds a crumpled tissue. She wipes away Katie's tears and, for what it's worth, gives her sleeve a quick wipe. "Katie, I know Charlie messed up your road, but he couldn't help it. He's a baby." Sarah kisses the top of Katie's head.

Katie looks at Sarah, her mouth tight again. She squirms out of Sarah's lap, letting Franklin fall to the wayside.

Sarah, still wearing her coat, is starting to feel warm and sleepy: it's the five o'clock slump. "Let's go home now," she says, "okay?" Katie turns away and goes over to the drawing table. She picks up a blue crayon and scribbles on a sheet of paper taped to the table.

Sarah gets Katie's coat and lunch box, puts the box on the crate by Franklin, and looks around for her daughter. Katie has dropped the crayon and is starting over to the other side of the room where Linda and Karen are singing "Itsy Bitsy Spider" with a group of children.

"Katie," Sarah says. Katie deigns a glance backward at her mother, who is holding up the coat like a matador trying to interest a bull. Katie continues toward the singers.

"Katie, don't ignore me!" Katie stops, looks at Sarah, then quickly looks down to study her toes. Sarah goes over to her. "It's time for us to go home."

OBSERVATIONS

The World of Things

Katie likes playing with blocks and uses them skillfully. She has had lots of practice playing with her father, who likes building things with blocks too. Block building for Katie is imbued with good feelings of time she spends with Joe.

The World of People

Sarah risked getting into trouble at work by leaving early to pick Katie up. She thought Katie, who had been unhappy about being left at day care in the morning, would be pleased to see her and to have some extra time at home. But when Sarah first arrived, Katie ignored her. When Sarah tried to touch her, Katie moved away. And Katie didn't seem eager to go home at all. She dawdled and would have joined in the "Itsy Bitsy Spider" song if Sarah hadn't insisted it was time to go. Katie's behavior made the reunion difficult for Sarah, not only because Sarah had been expecting a warmer greeting, but also because she had to deal with a confrontation of sorts at a time of day when she is especially low on energy. Sarah, who had been thinking of Katie all day and looking forward to seeing her again, ended up getting short with Katie.

Katie was acting as though she were angry with Sarah. She hadn't felt like going to day care that morning. Maybe she resented her parents for making her go anyway and was expressing the feeling by ignoring Sarah. Maybe she had forgotten about the morning and was upset because of something that happened to her during the day. Maybe she was just feeling grouchy and tired. Maybe she was trying to take charge of their leave-taking. Whatever the reason, Katie's chilly greeting was a hard-to-take indication of her trust for Sarah. Katie is clearly not afraid to be difficult with Sarah; she knows Sarah will love her no matter how she behaves.

Ideas and Words

Saying a word is a kind of action for Katie. Sometimes she can use a word to substitute for a physical action. But when she feels something very powerfully, she acts on the feeling both verbally and physically. When Charlie stepped on her road, for example, Katie yelled, "No!" and smacked him hard. The word, the action, and the feeling were all part of her immediate response: fury. She couldn't pause, identify her emotions, and separate different possible ways of expressing them in her mind.

When Katie had quieted down, Sarah explained that she shouldn't hit and that babies don't realize when they do bad things. She was thinking out loud for Katie. She wants Katie to learn to say the same kind of things to herself—before she hits an irritating baby. Katie will learn, with Sarah's help, but it will take some time.

Katie was able to arrange her blocks neatly in a line. The job required conceptual as well as manual skills: Katie had some idea of a line in her head, which helped her decide where to add each new block. Though she can't explain it, she understands that there is a way in which a road is a kind of line.

Sense of Self

Katie takes Franklin with her to the day-care center every morning. Though he spends much of the day sitting alone on a chair or resting in Katie's cubby, he is there when Katie needs him. Cuddling Franklin helps Katie comfort herself by herself. Even when Sarah is with her, as she was today, Katie still wants Franklin: he makes her feel more independent. He's a real resource.

Katie's confidence in herself has grown out of her ever-growing ability to do things and to make things like the road she made today. When Charlie walked into her road, he didn't just ruin a neat construction—he bumped into Katie's sense of self. She struck back in self-defense.

Since Katie can't really distinguish between feeling an emotion and expressing it, she may have felt Sarah was scolding her simply for being angry with Charlie. Sarah's scolding, Paul's attempts to comfort Charlie, and Charlie's continued crying seemed to upset and confuse her. Sarah realized this, dropped her scolding tone, and took Katie in her arms.

It seems unlikely that Katie was thinking of herself as a two-year-old hitting a baby when she hit Charlie. She didn't seem to be thinking at all. She just attacked. But she knows the word *baby*. She sees younger children in day care every day and probably understands, when she thinks about it, that she is more grown up than a baby and can do many things a baby can't do. Katie's awareness of the differences between herself and the other children she sees at day care will help her get a sense of herself as a child of a certain age.

14

OBSERVING CHILDREN AND CAREGIVERS

You are the person who matters most to your child. You are the base from which she moves out into the world. She is sensitive to your mood, your gestures, your tone of voice. Your enthusiasm encourages her curiosity. Your participation makes any activity important to her. Your praise and admonishments matter to her. She wants to please you. She works hard to be like you. She works hard to separate from you. She begins learning about herself, about other people, and about the world through her relationship with you, by sharing everyday life with you.

Your child will not love any caregiver as passionately as she loves you. A caregiver will not love your child as passionately as you do either. Your child's daytime caregiver is never going to replace you in your child's life. But the relationship between your child and her daytime guardian is not an inferior version of your parent-child relationship—it's a different kind of relationship altogether. Day care is an opportunity for your child to learn partly because it's an opportunity for her to have different kinds of guides and teachers. Your child needs you to help her benefit from these new opportunities. She needs you to watch over her and monitor the quality of care she receives. Evenwhen that care is excellent, she needs you to make it better. By looking and listening and developing your own relationship with her caregiver, you can make day care more enjoyable for your child.

To be involved in your child's daytime life, you need to have some sense of what it's like. Try to plan your schedule so that you can spend a few extra minutes with your child and her caregiver in the morning before you leave for work or when you pick your child up. If you can, you should also try to watch your child with her daytime guardian for longer periods once in a while. If your lunch break is long enough, use the time every now and then to drop in on the day-care center or house where your child spends the day, or to go back to your own apartment if you have private care. If your child stays at a center and your work schedule allows, you may want to arrange with the caregiver for you to come in for the whole morning. You might read a story to the children or bring ingredients for a snack. You'll get a better feel for the place if you participate in the activities, and the caregiver will appreciate your help.

A few minutes of observing each morning and evening and maybe a few longer visits each year isn't a lot of time. But observing your child with her caregiver, even if it's only for a few minutes here and there, will help you piece together a picture of your child's days to make sure they are happy and healthy.

You will have made sure before you leave your child in a center or in someone's home that the facilities are safe and the caregiver kind. Try not to forget about safety issues after your child is settled in. When it gets cold, for example, make certain that there is enough heat—and that your child isn't going to bump into a scalding radiator. If your child naps at day care, be sure her sheet is regularly washed, there or at home. Ask a family caregiver what she would do if there were a fire. Find out if a center has fire drills.

After safety and health, your child's relationship with the caregiver will be the most important aspect of day care for her. Small children learn within relationships, by sharing their daily lives with adults, and the caregiver is one of the adults who share her life. Watch to see how their relationship is unfolding.

Both your child and the caregiver will behave a little differently when you are with them, but if you observe them every day, even for five or ten minutes, you'll begin to get a sense of how they respond to each other. Do your child and the caregiver seem to like each other? Do they smile at each other? Does the caregiver alert your baby verbally before she picks her up? Does your baby help by lifting her arms? When you bring your child over to the neighbor who watches her, does she go off toward a toy or favorite space as if she feels at home? When you arrive at the center in the morning, does the caregiver greet you and talk with your child about the things she will be doing? Is the caregiver there to help you and your child say good-bye to each other? If you visit the day-care center at lunchtime, is the room lively, noisy, and messy, the way a room filled with children ought to be? When you come to pick up your baby at the end of the day, do you usually find her busy playing, or is she often sitting still, sucking her thumb and staring blankly? Does your toddler or two sometimes want to show you something she learned during the day—a new way of hopping, for example, or a drawing she made? Is one of the day-care staff aware of her new accomplishment and pleased about it too? If your child is cared for at home, does the housekeeper or nanny like to tell you stories at the end of the day about the things your child did?

You should feel welcome when you look and ask questions. If you don't, or if you're feeling uneasy about your day care arrangement, you, your spouse, or a friend should make a point of dropping in on your child and the caregiver when you aren't expected. If you go home at two in the afternoon and find the caregiver watching soap operas while the baby cries, something is wrong: you may have to find a new caregiver.

If you were able to find a day-care situation that felt right to you, chances are nothing will be wrong. But monitoring the caregiver and watching how her relationship with your child develops is not the only reason for observing your child in day care. Watching and talking with the caregiver for a little while each day will help the two of you get to know each other and develop your own relationship. You are partners in the very important job of caring for your child; both of you will do the job better if you share information.

Sharing information can help both you and the caregiver make practical decisions about your child's daily needs. For example, if you learn that your child didn't nap at day care, you might decide to put her to bed a little early before she gets overtired and cranky. If you explain that she didn't eat breakfast, the caregiver might want to offer her an extra mid-morning bottle. It will help you both, too, to know how your child is growing and changing. If you tell the caregiver that over the weekend your child started using a cup, the caregiver will know to offer her a cup at lunch. You might want to know that your child walked the whole distance to the park for the first time.

Ideally you and the caregiver should be able to help each other learn more about your child's emotional life too. You could tell the caregiver, for example, if you've taken a new job or if a relative has been ill and you've been going to the hospital every evening. The changes in your home routine may make your child uneasy; the caregiver will respond more sensitively if she knows what's going on in your child's life. If your child is cared for at a home or center where there are other children, you might ask the caregiver how your child gets along with her peers—something you may not have much time to observe directly yourself. This kind of discussion isn't always possible, however. If you're harried, or the caregiver is, or you're not the kind of people who can talk with each other easily, you'll probably restrict your conversation to more particular matters.

Even if you don't have detailed discussions about your child's development, if you and the caregiver exchange practical information and chat briefly each day, you'll be establishing some kind of relationship, which is important. Your child will feel more relaxed with the caregiver when she sees that the two of you listen to each other. Your concern and involvement will show the caregiver that you consider what she does important and also remind her that she is accountable to you. When you're in the habit of talking daily, it will also be easier for you to bring up any reservations or complaints you have about the care your child is receiving—and in the course of a year there's a good chance you won't like something the caregiver is or isn't doing.

No matter how much you like and respect the caregiver, it's unrealistic to expect her to have exactly the same ideas about child rearing as you do. (You probably don't always agree with your spouse about how to raise your child either.) You may find, for example, that the caregiver doesn't always praise behavior you would praise or stop behavior you would stop. You may not be happy about the way she handles arguments between children. Maybe she lets them have cookies at snack time and you wouldn't.

Making an issue of every disagreement you have with the caregiver isn't sensible. Your child can learn from spending time with different adults, each of whom will help her approach the world in a different way. For example, the caregiver might be less tolerant than you of your child's obnoxious habit of screeching, but more patient about food games. You may try to structure your child's play with matching toys to make it into a "learning" game, while her daytime caregiver lets her play with them on her own without supervision, or the other way around. Each of you is giving your child different kinds of learning opportunities.

On the other hand, you may think the caregiver or the center is doing something not just differently but wrong. Maybe you think the lunch isn't nutritious. Maybe the center lets your child play with toy guns and you don't approve. Maybe your child is scared of the dark and you think the caregiver is pushing her too hard to take her nap in a room with no light. When you are seriously concerned about some aspect of your child's care you certainly should make an issue of it. If there isn't time to discuss the problem when you drop your child off or pick her up, or if the discussion is likely to be intense and make your child uneasy, make an appointment to meet with the caregiver or her supervisor some other time. Often the caregiver or supervisor will be pleased you called her attention to a problem. But there may be times when she simply disagrees with you. You shouldn't tolerate any situation you think will compromise your child's welfare. But you should listen to the caregiver and at least see if it's possible to arrive at an arrangement that's agreeable to both of you.

When you talk out a problem with the caregiver, you are ensuring better, more consistent care for your child and also providing her with a model of adults working together.

Parents and caregivers sometimes have a hard time working together like reasonable adults. Because they have such intense feelings about their child, most parents have intense, not always rational feelings about her caregiver even when they think the caregiver is very loving and very competent. You may find yourself feeling jealous of smiles and hugs your child gives the caregiver, for example, or you may resent the caregiver for being the one who sees your child crawl for the first time. You may think the caregiver feels possessive about your child or distrusts you as a parent. You may distrust her. Your own experiences with parents and teachers as a child and your own confidence or doubts about yourself as a parent may influence your responses. You may find, for example, that you feel unduly humble around the caregiver and hesitate to question her when you have every right to do so, or you may feel suspicious of her on principle, because you distrust schools, institutions, professionals in general. Maybe you'll be dissatisfied with the caregiver simply for not being you. Maybe you won't have any of these feelings. Very few parents, however, can look at their child's caregiver with calm objectivity: their child is too important to them. Simply paying attention to your feelings can help you keep them from intruding inappropriately in your relationship with the person who cares for your child while you work.

The caregiver will probably have some strong feelings about you too. Your child will be happiest if she and the caregiver become close. But as she becomes more attached to your child, the caregiver may indeed feel possessive about her or disapprove of you as a parent in some way.

It may help to remind yourself that how the caregiver feels about you or even how you feel about her isn't as important as how the caregiver relates to your child. Your child is the reason you and the caregiver need to work together.

You can encourage a good working relationship with your child's caregiver by treating her with respect. You shouldn't treat a caregiver, even if she has a great deal of training, as an authority figure: you are the authority where your child is concerned and the caregiver is answerable to you. But you shouldn't treat any caregiver, even someone with very little education, as a servant. You are asking him or her to do an important job, a job you probably wondered if anyone besides yourself could really do and a job that requires, at the least, vital emotional and communicative skills. The person you hire to do this job deserves to be treated like a professional.

You should also treat her like a person. That sounds obvious, but parents sometimes act as if they think their caregiver never gets tired, is endlessly patient, and has no private life. Remind yourself every once in a while that caring for children is your caregiver's job—not something she does on the side for love—and that caring for a group of small children all day (or even one small child) is exhausting.

There are some very simple things you can do to show the caregiver you respect her work. For example, when you come to pick up your child at the end of the day, you might help the caregiver put up chairs or wipe the table. By helping her out this way, you'll be showing the caregiver that you don't look down on her work and that you appreciate how tiring it is. There are some things you should avoid too. Unless she makes it clear she's available and interested, it's generally not a good idea to ask a day-care worker to baby-sit. Many caregivers, especially those with professional training, find that insulting. Besides, after spending five days a week with small children, the last thing most caregivers want to do with their free time is take care of someone else's child, even a child of whom they are very fond.

Probably the single most important thing you can do to make the caregiver well disposed to you and your child is to pick up your child on time. This is not a trivial issue for a day-care worker. You may be aching to see your child again at the end of the day—but it doesn't follow that because you wish you could be with your child at six, that's where the caregiver wants to be. By five, she's aching to get back to her own child, or to get away from children altogether, or to be on time for a dinner date.

You can't help it, of course, if there's a traffic jam, or the subway stalls, or the boss asks you to stay late and it takes you a frantic half-hour on the phone to locate someone who can pick up your child. If you know you're going to be late, call in advance to explain what happened and apologize (the call will also reassure your child you are on your way; it's scary to be the last one picked up). If you're delayed en route, apologize when you arrive. Let the caregiver know that you realize he or she has a life outside of work and that you regret disrupting it. If because of your work situation or traveling conditions you find you are habitually late, arrange for another parent or a baby-sitter to pick up your child.

Another way you can show your respect for the caregiver is to learn from her. Because taking care of children is their job and they have had experience managing several children at once, caregivers have often figured out easy ways to deal with some of the practical problems of child rearing. You may have never thought of putting your whiny infant in her pack and carrying her around as you do chores, for example, until you see the person you've hired to stay with your child clearing the table with your baby on her back. You may see the two-year-old you've forbidden to use a knife happily spreading peanut butter on crackers at the day-care center using a Popsicle stick. The play dough recipe hanging on the wall may be well worth copying for use on a rainy Saturday afternoon at home with your toddler. You might arrive at your caregiver's apartment one afternoon and find your child busy using a vegetable brush and baking pan filled with water to scrub a carrot—something she could do at home too without destroying the kitchen.

Observing your child with the caregiver may also give you some perspective on any problems you are having controlling your child's behavior. Caregivers can often set limits on behavior more easily than parents because they are not so emotionally invested in the process. For example, you may find yourself worrying that if you don't insist your toddler clean up after herself, she will never learn self-discipline —or you may worry that if you insist she clean up all the time, you will stifle her spontaneity and make her overly neat. Your child's caregiver will be more likely to think of asking toddlers to clean up as part of the job of running a day-care program: the smoothest and happiest way to get space cleared for a new activity is to make cleaning up something for the children to do. And when the caregivers ask her to do something, your child may be more inclined to listen than when you ask. Precisely because her relationship with her caregiver is less intense than her relationship with you, your child will not feel the need to question, test, and demand attention as vigorously at day care as she does at home. If your child has been battling every rule you make lately, watching how she behaves with her daytime caregiver can reassure you she's not turning into a juvenile delinquent.

You're only going to be with your child and her caregiver a few minutes each day. Most days what you see and hear isn't going to tell you much about your child's daytime world. But if you pay attention during those few minutes you do spend with the caregiver, there will be days when some small incident does give you a real sense about how the other adult in your child's life responds to your child and how your child responds to him or her. Just look, listen—and trust your instincts.

The three families featured in this book are among the lucky ones: they each have found very good day care. Rita has always had a warm feeling about Mrs. Weiss; in fact she likes Mrs. Weiss to mother her. Today Rita finds that the older woman is not as concerned about Alex's new aptitude for pinching, biting, and grabbing as she is. Joe is surprised to learn that Katie's tastes change when she is away from home. Carol has a few moments of serious doubt about Mrs. Semple's character.

JENNIFER
(Six Months)

"Look, Jen. Look who is here." Sam is sitting on the couch bouncing Jen on his lap. Carol and Mrs. Semple have just walked in. Jen smiles, making her plump cheeks even plumper.

"Yes," Carol says, bending down so her face is close to Jen's. "Look who's here. Mrs. Semple came to help us even though it's Saturday." Carol wipes a bit of drool from Jen's chin. "She's going to play with you while Daddy and I cook."

Jen stares at her mother. She moves her face muscles as if she is chewing on something hard. "Aa, raah, cooomah," she says.

"We're having a dinner party. I bet you don't know what a dinner party is." Jen pats Carol's face.

Mrs. Semple puts her bag down on the floor by the couch and reaches out to take Jen from Sam. Jen squeals and buries her head in her father's arm. Then she peeks out at Mrs. Semple with a satisfied look.

"You are a tease, aren't you?" Sam says, looking at Jen. "Aren't you?" He tickles her tummy.

Jen giggles. Then she grows solemn and fingers a button on Sam's shirt. "That's Daddy's button," Sam explains. "See, here is another button." Jen stares at the floor, looking absentminded. Sam tickles her left foot. "Are you daydreaming?" Jen giggles and turns to look at Sam.

Mrs. Semple sits down on the couch. "Why don't you come sit with me?" she says, patting her lap. The patting catches Jen's attention. Mrs. Semple holds out her arms. Jen is ready to go to her this time.

"That's a good girl," Mrs. Semple says, settling Jen into her lap. She fishes into her bag for a tissue. Jen, sensing the tissue is coming, closes her eyes. Mrs. Semple wipes her face.

Carol cringes. The first thing Mrs. Semple always does when she takes Jen every morning is to pull out a tissue and scrub Jen's little face. Every morning, Carol cringes.

"Would you like some tea or coffee or something?" Carol asks.

"Yes, thanks," Mrs. Semple says, finishing with Jen's chin. "I'd love some tea."

Carol starts for the kitchen. Jen squirms and sits upright to watch Carol leave.

Sam bends down toward Jennifer. "Mrs. Semple is going to play with you while Daddy and Mommy wash the spinach," he explains. "If we don't wash that spinach, Mr. Lowry will take a bite and say 'yuck.'"

Jen stares at him.

"He'll say 'yuck, yuck, yuck,'" Sam says, squinching up his nose and sticking out his tongue.

Jen laughs. She reaches out and hits Sam's mouth.

"That's right. That's where the spinach is going to go." He stands up and takes a big step backward. "I'm going to the kitchen now. I'll be back soon." He waves and goes toward the kitchen.

Jen starts squirming, agitated.

Mrs. Semple waves one of her hands in front of Jen's face. "That's a wave, Jen," she explains. "Your daddy was waving at you." Sam glances back. Jen, giggling, is reaching for Mrs. Semple's nose.

A few minutes later Carol, holding a tray with a cup of tea and a plate of graham crackers, pauses at the entrance of the living room. Mrs. Semple is holding Jen tightly with one arm while she bends down and fishes in her bag with the other. Jen notices the bit of red scarf hanging from the edge of the bag. "Baaabaaah," she says, reaching and squirming toward the color.

"Careful," Mrs. Semple says, tightening her grip, "you'll fall."

She straightens up, some letters in her right hand. "We'll play with the scarf in a second. I just want to look at my mail. I got a letter from my daughter today." She brings her face in close to Jen's. "Did you know my daughter was once a little baby girl just like you?" Jen watches, then suddenly smiles broadly. She reaches for the mail. Mrs. Semple pulls the letters away. "No, Jen. Wait."

Jen whines. Carol waits too, curious to see what Mrs. Semple does next.

Holding the envelopes out of Jen's reach, Mrs. Semple glances at them quickly. "Let me just read her letter." Jen tries to grab it. Mrs. Semple opens the letter and hands Jen the empty envelope. While Mrs. Semple reads, Jen chews on a corner of the envelope. She makes a gurgling noise and a bubble of saliva appears on her lower lip.

"Yes," Mrs. Semple says without looking up.

Jen stares at her. She drops her envelope and reaches to get hold of Mrs. Semple's letter.

"Jen!" Mrs. Semple pulls the letter away. Jen squirms and whines. "I'll tell you what. You can play with the scarf for a few minutes." She places Jen carefully in a sitting position on the floor. "See?" She pushes the tote toward Jen and turns back to her letter.

Jen gurgles. She reaches for the little piece of red, which has come into view again. It's too far away. She falls forward on her extended arms, then stretches out on her tummy. She still can't reach the scarf.

Why doesn't she pay more attention to Jen? Carol wonders, reminding herself that she herself has occasionally tried to read something with Jen around.

Jen whines.

Mrs. Semple absentmindedly pushes the bag a few more inches toward Jen and pulls the scarf out until it is touching the floor. She turns to the next page of her letter.

Jen stretches her arms out. The scarf is still out of reach.

Why don't you just give it to her? Carol thinks.

Jen makes angry little eh eh eh sounds and kicks her legs.

Mrs. Semple sighs and puts down the letter. "You know, Jen," she says, "you're a lazybones." She nudges the bag a little closer with her foot. "I know you can reach this."

How dare she! Carol thinks. Teasing Jen and calling her names. Carol's stomach tightens. She steps forward, prepared to leap in and rescue Jen. Then she stops still again.

Jen has raised herself up on her hands and knees in a crawling position, something she has only done a few times.

"There you go," Mrs. Semple says.

Jen rocks back and forth.

Mrs. Semple taps the floor in front of the bag. "Just a little farther."

Jen rocks back, almost sitting on her haunches, then pushes her way forward onto her arms, rocks back again and pauses. She doesn't seem to have figured out what to do next. She pushes once again and succeeds in moving a few inches—but backward.

"You can do it, Jen," Mrs. Semple says, pushing the bag a few inches closer.

Jen looks up at her and stares for a second. Then she slides forward onto her stomach, grunting softly. She bends her legs and pulls them up close to her rear like a frog and suddenly pushes them out again, propelling herself forward.

"Well, that's another way," Mrs. Semple says. Jen repeats the motion again, and then for a third time. She reaches out and grabs hold of the scarf.

Mrs. Semple claps. "Good girl!" she says.

Clutching the scarf, Jen rolls onto her back. She sucks on a corner of the scarf, kicking her legs rhythmically.

Carol blinks back a tear. "Here's your tea," she says, stepping forward.

◆

OBSERVATIONS

The World of Things

Jen applied an impressive repertoire of movements to get hold of the appealing scarf. She stretched and reached. She got up on her hands and knees in a crawling position and managed to push herself a few inches in the wrong direction. Finally she managed to get the scarf by creeping forward, pushing against the ground with her feet.

Because they are with her every day, Sam and Carol don't always notice how much Jen is learning. Adopting the role of outside observer, Carol was struck by how much and how quickly Jen has changed.

The World of People

Jen communicates with adults best when they are physically close to her. The patterns of faces and small movements they make fascinate her. Her responsiveness has taught Carol, Sam, and Mrs. Semple to hold their faces close to hers when they talk to her. For example, Carol brought her face right opposite Jen's when she talked about Mrs. Semple and dinner parties. Jen watched and listened to her mother closely and babbled as if she wanted to talk too.

Jen knows and likes Mrs. Semple. But she still needed a few minutes before she was ready to go to her. When Mrs. Semple first came into the room with Carol, Jen ignored her. When Mrs. Semple first held out her arms to take her, Jen hid her eyes for a few seconds. Sam continued to play with her for a while. Jen must have been using the time to get used to Mrs. Semple's presence. A few minutes later, when Mrs. Semple sat down and patted her lap, Jen turned to her.

If Carol had been sitting with Jen today, she probably would have given her the scarf. Even watching from a distance, Carol had trouble doing nothing when Jen became frustrated. Mrs. Semple was less disturbed by Jen's fretfulness. She encouraged Jen to keep trying to reach the scarf herself. She didn't seem tempted to move in and take over.

Jen is able to benefit from being cared for by three different adults partly because her three adults treat each other respectfully. Sam, Carol, and Mrs. Semple's relationships are not untroubled, of course. Carol sometimes finds herself feeling suspicious of Mrs. Semple, as she was today. She also finds that some of Mrs. Semple's mannerisms irritate her more than they should. Carol knows that Mrs. Semple's habit of greeting Jen by wiping her face is not important, but it gets on her nerves.

Carol made an effort to look at Mrs. Semple's behavior objectively. When she saw her keeping the scarf just beyond Jen's reach, Carol was afraid Mrs. Semple was teasing Jen. She was also disturbed when Mrs. Semple called Jen "lazybones." But she continued to watch Jen and Mrs. Semple long enough to understand what was really happening. After a few minutes she realized Mrs. Semple was only trying to encourage Jen to extend herself.

Jen was not aware of Carol's doubts about Mrs. Semple. If Carol and Mrs. Semple had argued, Jen would have been very aware of it indeed.

Ideas and Words

Jen's relationships with adults interest her more than anything else. A great deal of what she is learning, she is learning through interactions with adults. Their involvement makes an activity exciting to her. For example, though the envelope Mrs. Semple gave her only interested Jen a little while, she persisted in trying to get at the letter Mrs. Semple was reading for quite some time. Mrs. Semple's interest in her letter made it interesting and important to Jen.

Jen was able to focus her attention on the job of getting the scarf for a full two or three minutes because Mrs. Semple became involved in the task too. She kept calling attention to the scarf by pushing it toward Jen. When Jen was getting frustrated, Mrs. Semple assured her, "You can do it." As Jen got nearer her goal, Mrs. Semple cheered her on. Their interchange probably absorbed Jen as much as the scarf itself. By concentrating on Jen's exertions, Mrs. Semple helped Jen concentrate on them too.

Sense of Self

Jen doesn't always like being fussed over, but when she wants attention from an adult, she wants it badly and will work to get it. She definitely didn't like it today when Mrs. Semple, preoccupied with the letter, stopped paying attention to her. She continued to pester Mrs. Semple until Mrs. Semple put the letter down and played with her.

Mrs. Semple was expressing her faith in Jen when she insisted Jen get the scarf herself. Her involvement in the task communicated her confidence in Jen and made Jen more confident in herself.

Jen is becoming a different person, a person who can move by herself. In order to get the scarf she had to push herself out of the small area bounded by the reach of her arms and legs. She is creeping toward greater independence.

◆

ALEX
(Fifteen Months)

"Enough mushy stuff, huh?" Rita releases a squirming Alex from her hello hug and adjusts his overall strap, which is hanging down over his shoulder. She pats his stomach and stands up. "Who's your new friend?" she asks, looking at the boy about Alex's age sitting on Mrs. Weiss's lap.

"This is Bobby." Mrs. Weiss smiles at the boy in her arms. "My grandson. My daughter's in town for the week and I'm looking after Bobby this afternoon."

"It's nice to meet you, Bobby," Rita says. Bobby pulls closer to Mrs. Weiss.

Alex fingers Rita's skirt and looks down at the floor.

"Are you getting shy all of a sudden?" Mrs. Weiss pats him on the head. She turns to Rita. "Come on in."

Rita and Mrs. Weiss step into the living room. Alex takes Rita's hand and walks with her. Bobby is kicking Mrs. Weiss's ample middle with his feet. She lowers him to the floor. "There you go."

Bobby lowers himself down on his hands and knees and crawls rapidly across the floor. Alex drops Rita's hand and follows him. They race around on all fours circling the furniture.

"Are you in a hurry or would you like a cup of coffee?"

Rita is watching Alex and Bobby, who have started climbing on the couch. "I'd love some, or maybe some tea."

"I'll bring it in here."

Rita takes her coat off and sits in an armchair opposite the couch. Alex and Bobby are climbing up the back of the couch and then sliding down onto the throw pillows.

"Here, dear." Mrs. Weiss hands Rita a cup of tea and sits down.

"Thanks."

"They're adorable together, aren't they?"

"They sure are. Bobby's a cutie pie."

Alex has just plopped down on the pillows. "Rah, rah, rah," he repeats, bouncing up and down on his bottom.

Bobby plops down next to him, laughing, then scrambles up on his feet. "Rah, rah, rah," Bobby says, starting to jump. Alex, imitating him, works his way to a standing position too. Bobby's foot slips into the crack between the cushions. He falls down, crashing into Alex and landing on top of him.

"Ahh," Alex grunts, struggling to get from under Bobby's body.

Bobby screams.

"Alex!" Rita leaps up. Bobby, still on top of Alex, is crying. Alex is scratching and hitting him. Rita lifts Bobby away, pulls Alex out from under, deposits him rather roughly on the side of the couch, and turns back to Bobby, who is crying and clutching his arm. "Let me see." Rita unpries his little fingers. There's a pinch mark underneath. Mrs. Weiss has come over and bends down over Bobby. "The Claw struck again," Rita explains. Alex, very quiet, has crept back and is pulling at Rita's blouse.

"Alex pinched you?" Mrs. Weiss says to Bobby. "There." She rubs the hurt spot lightly. Rita watches. Alex, still holding on to her shirt, watches too.

"That'll be all better," Mrs. Weiss says. She lifts Bobby onto her lap.

"Did he do that before?" Rita asks.

Mrs. Weiss nods.

"It's something new," Rita says.

Alex climbs down to the floor and starts playing with his white mouse pop-up toy.

Rita tucks in her blouse and kneels down next to him. "Alex."

He looks at her, smiling.

"You mustn't pinch people, Alex!"

He stares blankly at her.

"It's all right," Mrs. Weiss says, rocking Bobby, who has stopped crying.

"Bobby fell on top of him. Alex had to do something."

Rita sighs. It wasn't all right as far as she was concerned, but she has obviously missed her chance to scold Alex. He seems to have forgotten about the pinch. She sits down again.

"He started pinching and scratching a few days ago," Rita explains to Mrs. Weiss. "Grabbing things too. I would have warned you if I knew Bobby was coming."

"Okay, Bobby," Mrs. Weiss says. "I'm going to talk to Rita now." She puts him down on the ground.

"I'm sorry," Rita apologizes again. "I hope Alex isn't turning into a bully."

"Really, it's all right."

"Getting pinched is all right?" Rita takes a sip of tea.

"No, but having Alex here has been good for Bobby. He doesn't have much of a chance to play with kids his own age. It was nice seeing him and Alex together. I figure the rough stuff comes with the territory."

"I guess Alex doesn't really have many friends his own age either," Rita says. "There are some kids we see in the park all the time, but mostly he plays with Mike and his friends if they let him. The big kids are really rough; maybe that's where he's getting it from."

Bobby, who seems to be completely recovered, pulls a large cushion off the couch and drags it around the room. Alex is playing with his white pop-up toy. He hits the button and the mouse jumps out.

Bobby drops his pillow, comes over, and gently touches the box. Alex pulls the box away and pushes the mouse back down.

Bobby didn't even grab, Rita thinks, he just touched it. She resists her impulse to get up and make Alex share his toy. Mrs. Weiss is the authority in this house.

Very tentatively, Bobby touches the corner of the box again. Alex pushes his arm away.

"Bobby," Mrs. Weiss says, "that's Alex's toy." He looks at her. "He doesn't want you to touch it. Why don't you play with Sammy Bear?" Mrs. Weiss gets up and hands Bobby his teddy bear.

"I would have told Alex to let Bobby play with the toy," Rita says.

"This has been going on all morning," Mrs. Weiss tells her. Alex picks up the pop-up toy, stands up, and looks dreamily at something far away. "Sometimes I told them to share. But I think it's good for a kid to know how to keep something for himself when he wants to."

Alex starts circling the room, going around behind the armchairs.

"I don't know. . . ." Rita says.

Bobby has forgotten the pop-up toy. He puts Sammy down next to the cushion on the floor. Then he takes a small accent pillow from the sofa and adds it to the pile.

Alex, whose perambulations have brought him back to the couch, squats down, drops his pop-up toy, picks up the accent pillow, raises his arms over his head, and flings the pillow down again. Then he picks up Sammy.

Bobby stares at the bear in Alex's arms and shrieks, "No!"

Mrs. Weiss sighs. She gets up yet again, goes over, and kneels beside Bobby. "Bobby, let's tell Alex you really want your bear." Alex crawls backward, holding the bear tightly.

Mrs. Weiss holds out her hand. "Alex, Sammy is Bobby's special bear. Please give it back to him." Alex looks at her without responding.

"Alex," Rita says, "you give Bobby back his bear this minute."

Alex looks at Rita. He drops the bear on the floor. Bobby, sobbing, plops on his bottom and reaches for it. Alex pokes him.

◆

OBSERVATIONS

The World of Things

Alex is interested in investigating all levels of his environment and in learning to move his body in as many different ways as he can. Though he is a good walker, he still enjoys crawling. When Bobby decided to crawl, Alex decided to join him. He is very fast and secure on his hands and knees. He is also a dedicated climber and is getting good at that too.

He and Bobby crawled, then climbed up on the couch. Then they bounced. Pillows are of course ideal for bouncing since unlike floors they respond when you jump on them. Bouncing side by side, each boy could feel the rhythm of the other's movements. Alex tried to stand up on the couch like Bobby to see if he could bounce on his feet. Before he had a chance to try, Bobby fell on him.

Alex is learning to use his body aggressively. When he was younger he would sometimes hit at someone to express frustration or anger, but his movements were not very controlled. Now he has figured out things he can do with his body to hurt other people—like pinching and scratching. Rita isn't pleased with this development, but it is unquestionably development. It takes quite a bit of physical control to fight effectively.

The World of People

Alex and Bobby were clearly playing with each other, though it would be difficult to tell at any given moment whether they were responding to each other the way older children do or just enjoying playing side by side. They didn't make eye contact much, but most of the time Alex seemed to be aware of what Bobby was doing and wanted to do whatever it was too. When Bobby started off across the floor on his hands and knees, Alex joined him. When Bobby stood up on the couch, Alex did too. Other times, however, Alex's awareness of Bobby faded out. He watched for a while while Rita and Mrs. Weiss comforted the other boy, then went off to play with his pop-up toy.

Alex and Bobby were interested in each other's toys the same way they were interested in each other's activities. Bobby first noticed the white mouse pop-up toy when Alex began playing with it. When Bobby tried to touch it, it became very important to Alex to keep it to himself. Bobby's strong reaction when Alex picked up Sammy probably made Alex more interested in the bear too. He didn't want to relinquish it.

It's unlikely Alex understood that Sammy was a special toy for Bobby. Alex may be aware, however, that being able to hold on to things and dispose of them is a kind of social power. He seemed to be doing his best to establish himself as the toddler in control of the most desirable objects. He succeeded. Alex, who is used to playing with an older brother bigger, stronger, and more capable than he, got to be the stronger child today. He could play with Bobby at his own pace, instead of working to keep up.

Ideas and Words

Alex is not used to having another child his age around: Bobby's presence probably excited him. When Rita arrived, Alex may have sensed that she and Mrs. Weiss were talking about him and watching him and Bobby play. Bobby had no doubt been attracting Mrs. Weiss's attention and affection all day. While it's unlikely Alex was consciously trying to establish himself as the toddler in charge, he may have spontaneously tried to keep the bear and the pop-up toy to himself to counter a general feeling of being encroached upon. On the other hand, maybe he just wanted to have the toys and that was it.

What is clear is that Alex doesn't distinguish between aggression and assertion, even though adults do. He isn't deliberately manipulative yet either—he doesn't have enough understanding of other people's needs and desires or of social situations in general to manipulate them.

Alex does understand that Rita doesn't like some kinds of behavior, and he sometimes seems to test her by doing things he knows she doesn't like. But he certainly doesn't and can't make moral judgments. It's unlikely he would realize when he was doing something wrong if Rita didn't remind him—or that he could stop himself from acting on a strong impulse if he tried.

Since Alex can't make decisions about how to act based on ideas about right or wrong and can't control his own behavior very well, for the time being his adults have to direct his behavior for him. All Rita and Mrs. Weiss can do is what they did today: stop him when—or better yet, before—he behaves badly and let him know as clearly as they can what it is they want him to do.

Deciding what they want their toddler to do, however, can be difficult for parents and caregivers. Rita and Mrs. Weiss didn't agree about how Alex should be directed today. Since they didn't know why Alex was behaving the way he was, or how much he understood about what his behavior meant, the two women's own concerns about aggression and submission influenced the way they responded to him.

When Alex pinched Bobby, refused to share his toy, and held on to Sammy, Rita thought Alex was being mean. She wanted him to be gentle and sharing. Alex doesn't understand the idea of sharing yet, but he is learning. He sees people in his family share with each other, and he sometimes offers toys or food or interesting objects to his brother and parents spontaneously. Mrs. Weiss, who believes a certain amount of physical fighting is natural for toddlers, thought Alex was showing an admirable ability to defend himself and hang on to the things that were important to him. Mrs. Weiss defended both boys' property rights. She tried to explain to Bobby that the pop-up toy belonged to Alex, and she tried to explain to Alex that Sammy belonged to Bobby.

Rita discussed her feelings with Mrs. Weiss: she explained that she would have urged Alex to share more. Because of this conversation, Rita may become a little more tolerant of Alex's grabbing and fighting in the future. Mrs. Weiss may encourage Alex to be more generous.

A child as young as Alex might be confused if his parents and the person who cares for him during the day valued very different kinds of behavior. But that isn't really the case here. Both women want Alex to be giving, and they both want him to be able to fight in the right way for the right things. For example, even though Mrs. Weiss didn't scold Alex for not sharing the pop-up toy as Rita would have, she did intervene to negotiate between the boys before there was another fight. She explained Alex's behavior to Bobby and suggested he play with his bear. Rita, for her part, showed her respect for Mrs. Weiss's opinions and competence. She did not criticize or contradict the older woman in front of Alex. When Alex was holding Sammy, she resisted the impulse to intervene and instead let Mrs. Weiss handle the situation; she didn't want to undermine Mrs. Weiss's authority.

Alex will probably benefit from spending time with a caregiver who responds to his behavior in slightly different ways than his mother. For now, it's useful for Alex to learn to recognize the feelings that go with fighting and those that go with sharing. Understanding values and using them to decide when and how to respond will come later.

Sense of Self

Alex may have known what he was doing on some level when he tried to monopolize the toys, but when Bobby fell on him and he couldn't move, Alex just reacted. He began struggling every way he knew how to get free. Alex didn't think, "I'm going to pinch this kid." He just did it.

Alex is evidently just beginning to develop a sense of possession—a rather egocentric one. He seems to think that every object that interests him belongs to him. Once again, there's no way to know exactly how a toddler thinks, but Alex doesn't seem interested in accumulating objects for their own sake (and unlike Bobby and Katie, he doesn't have one special toy that he associates with himself). What Alex seems to like is the experience of holding on to something and controlling it: having power over objects helps him define himself.

Alex got to be top toddler today instead of the tag-along baby—a new role for him, and no doubt a pleasant change. Rita, who usually scolds Mike for bullying Alex, scolded Alex for bullying Bobby. As Alex has more opportunities to play many social roles, he will begin to develop a sense of who he is independent of his position in any particular situation.

◆

KATIE
(Twenty-eight Months)

"Daddy!" Katie runs over to the door and gives Joe a hard hug.

"I came to have lunch with you. Remember I told you I was coming this morning?" He puts Katie down. "I'm boiling." Katie giggles. "Let me get rid of this coat."

Linda, the head caregiver, sees Joe and comes over. "How are you? We're glad you could come."

"I wish I could get here more often."

"Daddy!" Katie grabs Joe's hand and starts pulling him into the room. "My blocks."

"Excuse me," Joe says to Linda. "Katie, let me take off my coat."

With Katie pulling at his hand, Joe walks through an obstacle course of toys, dress-up clothes, and pillows to get to the closet. "Okay. Now show me what you've been building."

Katie grins and trots to the block corner. Joe follows. Katie points and then looks up to watch Joe's reaction. She has stacked two layers of big blocks on top of each other. "House," Katie says.

"That's beautiful, Katie," Joe tells her with real admiration.

Katie stares at her work, filled with admiration herself. She sits down and carefully adds a block to the top story of the house.

Linda comes by a few minutes later. "Katie, it's time for lunch. Why don't you and your daddy put the blocks away?" Katie looks up at her. She hesitates.

"You can show Joe how to match the shapes on the shelf," Linda suggests. Katie considers. She picks up three blocks.

Joe is watching with mild amazement. At home, he and Sarah practically have to get on their knees and beg Katie to put away her blocks. Joe picks up some stray blocks himself—leaving the house intact for the moment—and follows Katie to a shelf on the wall. Linda and Paul have pasted paper outlines of the blocks on the bottom of the shelf. Katie puts her three blocks on the floor, picks one up, places it on the shelf, and positions it neatly over one of the cutouts. She turns to Joe and smiles. "Good girl," Joe says.

They walk back to the block corner to get the rest. Katie looks pensively at her house. Then she kicks it. She giggles as the edifice falls. She kicks the blocks again, though they are all on the floor. Joe reaches down and starts collecting blocks to put away.

"We could help Karen and the other kids put the dress-up clothes away," Joe suggests when they are done.

Katie nods. They start toward the clothes. Paul, one of the caregivers, and Allen, another two-year-old, pass in front of them. Paul is carrying three big pillows and Allen is carrying one. The pillow covers half of Allen's face, so he has trouble seeing where he is going. Katie can see but she isn't looking. Joe takes her hand and pulls her back, preventing a collision.

"Excuse us," Paul says.

"Scuses," Allen repeats into the pillow.

"Okeydokey," Katie says.

"Okeydokey," Allen says.

Joe grins at Paul. "So that's where she got it. She's been saying 'okeydokey' instead of 'yes' for two days now."

"It's sort of become their password for the week," Paul explains.

Katie has apparently forgotten about the dress-up clothes. She watches Paul and Allen deposit the pillows in their corner. "My jump," Katie says, grabbing Joe's hand and dragging him to the pillows.

"Katie," Paul says, "it's time for lunch now." Katie pauses, her knees bent to begin jumping. She looks up at Paul. "Why don't you show Joe how you can wash your hands? Everyone else has already washed theirs."

"Come on, Katie." Joe holds out his hand.

"Okeydokey." Katie grins and takes her father's hand.

The small bathroom has one regular sink, two toddler-high sinks, a toilet, and a changing table. Katie, very businesslike, turns on both faucets in one of the sinks. She turns them on all the way. Drops of water bounce off the basin onto the floor. "Easy," Joe says. He adjusts the water. Katie takes the soap from a dish on the side of the basin, works up fistfuls of lather, and pushes the soap back in the dish. It slides onto the floor. Joe rescues it. Katie rinses her hands, walks to the roll of paper towels on the wall, and unrolls her own height in towels. She pats her hands and smiles at Joe. "Good girl," he says, "but you don't need quite that many towels." Katie bunches the towels, drops the bundle into the trash can, and struts toward the door.

The other children are sitting down by the time Joe and Katie leave the bathroom. Linda is helping eleven-month-old Sabrina find a seat near Karen, who is transferring the contents of each child's lunch bag to a paper plate. Paul's patience is being tried by three children sitting in high chairs who are busy smearing their applesauce everywhere.

Katie runs over and sits down next to Allen. Linda smiles at Joe. "We've got a special visitor today," she tells the children. "Katie's father is eating lunch with us." The children all stare at Joe, who smiles a little self-consciously. Allen turns away, reaches into his lunch bag, and takes out a container of yogurt.

"Sorry about the accommodations," Karen says, bringing over a rickety but adult-sized chair for Joe to sit on. Joe pulls the chair up next to Katie.

"Chicken," Katie says when Linda brings over her plate.

"That's the chicken you and I made for dinner last night. You helped me shake the bread crumbs on it. Remember?" Katie nods.

Allen has turned his container of strawberry yogurt upside down to see if it's easier to open that way. "Can I help you with that?" Joe asks.

"I do," Allen says, not looking up. And he does indeed pry the top off the upside-down container. A blob of yogurt falls on the table with a gentle splat. Allen, his mouth open, watches with obvious pleasure.

Katie watches too. "Uh oh," she says.

Joe reaches across Katie to reverse the container in Allen's hand. "It's better with the open part on top," he explains.

Katie picks up her spoon and reaches under Joe's arm, aiming for the yogurt. "Katie," says Joe, licking yogurt off his fingers, "you should eat your chicken. Karen will help Allen wipe up his spill."

Katie looks at Joe. He looks back. A silent moment of decision making passes. Katie grins. "Okeydokey." She turns to the drumstick.

Karen arrives with two sponges. Katie, eating her chicken, watches Karen and Allen wipe. Karen puts the remaining yogurt in a dish, takes the rest of Allen's lunch out of the bag, and arranges it on his plate.

Allen takes a bite of cheese.

"My want cheese," Katie says.

Joe is surprised. Katie doesn't like cheese. She actually hates cheese. The last time they offered her a piece of cheese she threw it on the floor.

Allen looks at Katie and keeps chewing.

"My want cheese," Katie repeats, looking at Joe. She reaches for his leg, but he slides it out of the way. He doesn't want chicken grease on his pants.

"Ask Allen, Katie," Joe says. "It's his cheese. And say please."

"My want cheese, please," Katie says to Allen. She smiles and repeats the rhyme, "Cheese, please."

Allen deposits a fistful of cheese on the table next to Katie's plate. She picks it up, looks at it with interest, and takes a big bite.

OBSERVATIONS

The World of Things

Katie is learning to match shapes. She was able to align the blocks to make a house. She was able to match blocks to the outlines the day-care staff has pasted on the block shelf.

Katie may have turned the faucets on all the way not because she lacked the manual dexterity needed to adjust them, but because the sound and feel of gushing water pleased her. She is definitely capable of pulling out only one or two sheets of towel, but she finds pulling out six or seven more satisfying. Being able to do things in a big way makes her feel strong. For the same reason, she enjoys knocking things down as much as building them up. She likes to watch the way things crash and change shape, and she is fond of loud noises. Far from being reluctant to destroy her house, Katie happily gave it a hefty kick.

The World of People

Katie knows the day-care staff is there for all the kids, but Joe is her adult. She was eager to show Joe her world of day care. Because he came at lunch, she could share more of her daytime activities with him than she can at the end of the day when the main activity is getting ready to go.

Katie and Allen are the oldest children at the center. They have a different kind of relationship with each other than with the other children. They are curious about each other. They relate to each other through language, which the younger children don't do yet: saying "okeydokey" is a game only Katie and Allen share.

Katie was very interested in Allen's lunch. When he made the yogurt splat, she wanted to play with it. His cheese looked good to her. She made a verbal announcement, "My want cheese," and at Joe's suggestion asked Allen to give her some. (A year ago, she would have just grabbed it off his plate.)

When he told Katie, "Ask Allen," Joe was presenting her with two fairly complicated social ideas. First, he was telling her that the cheese belonged to Allen and that even though Joe is an adult, the cheese was still Allen's and only he could give it away. Second, Joe indicated he was unwilling to be a mediator and persuade Allen to share with Katie. He wanted Katie to deal directly with Allen, using words. Katie followed Joe's suggestion. She didn't reach or grab for the cheese. Joe guided her, but Katie actively approached Allen on her own, in a grown-up way.

Katie seemed very accommodating today. In fact, her good behavior surprised Joe. She put the blocks away and left the pillows to wash her hands when she was asked. When Joe told her to stop reaching for the yogurt, she did. And not only was Katie a more obliging girl at day care today than she usually is at home, she was a girl with different tastes, a girl who likes cheese.

As we suggested in the introduction, many children, like Katie, seem better behaved and more flexible at day care. Katie can't explain herself, so we can only speculate about why she is less stubborn at day care.

It's unlikely that Katie is a difficult, cheese-hating child at home and a cheese-loving child who does what she is asked at day care because the day-care staff are more skilled caregivers than Joe or Sarah. Katie probably expresses and asserts herself more with her parents than with the day-care staff because her relationship with her parents is so much stronger and more complicated. Katie may sometimes refuse to do what her parents ask and get stubborn or angry because she wants to establish herself as someone with her own strong desires and with power of her own. She needs to struggle against Joe and Sarah to establish her independence. And Joe and Sarah are the people Katie trusts the most. Katie doesn't have to win their love, so she can afford to be contrary with them.

Katie's feelings about Paul, Linda, and Karen are not so intense. Since she isn't tied to them as strongly as she is tied to her parents, she probably doesn't feel the same need to challenge them. Day care is a good place for her to practice social skills like cooperation.

Ideas and Words

Katie was playing with the word "okeydokey" today. The rhyme and up-down rhythm appealed to her. She seemed to like the way the sound made her lips move. She and Allen treated it as another kind of toy, a social toy to roll back and forth or bounce up and down. Later she noticed with pleasure that "Cheese, please" rhymes. Katie is learning language can be a source of delight—a fine motivation for learning to use it well.

When Katie greeted Joe, Joe reminded her that he had said he'd be coming. When she looked at her chicken, Joe asked her if she remembered making chicken together the night before. Joe's questions helped Katie make her own connections between past and present, cause and effect.

Sense of Self

If Katie at day care and Katie at home were two radically different personalities, Joe might have some cause for concern. But it's clear that though Katie seems less willful at the center, even there she is not a compliant child. Linda didn't just ask Katie to clean up—she tried to put the chore in a positive and attractive light by reminding Katie about matching the blocks to the outlines. To get Katie to stop jumping, Paul suggested she show Joe how she washes her hands. And on both occasions, Katie hesitated in a way that suggested the caregivers' appeals don't always win such a quick response. In short, Katie's comparatively good behavior in day care shouldn't be interpreted as a sign that Joe and Sarah are overindulgent or the day-care staff too strict or that Katie is a confused girl with a weak sense of self. Katie is simply adapting her behavior to get what she needs from different situations, which, within limits, is a healthy thing to do.

15

INTRODUCING YOUR CHILD TO BABY-SITTERS

Public discussions about the "child care crisis" usually refer to the shortage of good day-care facilities for working parents. Finding good, affordable nine-to-five day care is indeed the major problem of working parents, but nine-to-five day care is only part of the support parents need—and parents who don't work need child care support too. Small children can never be left alone, which means that if you live with an insouciant toddler, having to go to the bathroom can create a child care problem.

Spending time with baby-sitters is part of the daily or weekly routine of many children. Maybe the parents have to be at work at eight and the day-care center opens at nine, so a neighbor watches the child for an hour in the morning and takes her to day care. Maybe the parents and another couple agree to share pick-up and drop-off duties. Maybe grandparents have volunteered to stay with the child every Friday night. Adults who serve as baby-sitters on a regular basis become a steady presence in a child's life. But children also spend time with baby-sitters they don't know, or don't know well, when they don't expect to—an experience which is not a familiar part of their ordinary day or week, except that one of the ordinary characteristics of everyday life is a tendency for ends to unravel, happy exceptions to arise, and traffic to jam.

If you're like most parents, you'll find yourself constantly devising child care arrangements not just to manage an occasional night out, but also to patch up the inevitable holes in your daily system. You'll need a baby-sitter if the day-care center closes at five thirty and you have a vital errand that must be done right after work, if your job involves travel and the plane is delayed, if the day-care center closes for Presidents' Day and the Friday after Thanksgiving and the store where you work doesn't, if your child is sick and you have no sick days left, if the day camp your six-year-old attends is on one side of town and the apartment where a neighbor watches your two-year-old is on the other. Even if you had the option of staying home with your kids and took it, you'll sometimes need help—for example, if your five-year-old needs to be picked up at school and taken to Cub Scouts when the baby has a high fever. If you're a single parent, you'll have an even greater need for stopgap support—and less money to spend on it.

While your child is still a small baby, try to find two or three baby-sitters you both like. When you can, always use these same people to watch your child. She will be most comfortable with sitters she already knows. You can try asking a relative, a neighbor, or a neighbor's teenage son or daughter to sit for you. You may be able to work out an arrangement where you sometimes leave your child with another couple and they sometimes leave their child with you. If you don't know anyone to baby-sit, you can ask a friend for a recommendation.

Sometimes you may have to find someone to watch your child at the last minute, no one you know will be available, and you won't have the time to shop around for a baby-sitter with as much care as you would like. Obviously there's nothing you can do about emergencies. It may reassure you to remember that a baby-sitter isn't going to be as involved with your child as a caregiver and doesn't need as many qualifications. His or her basic job is simply to protect your child from physical harm and see that her most basic needs are met. He doesn't have to be knowledgeable about child development but should be gentle and above all, responsible. When you are thinking of hiring someone neither you nor a friend knows personally, make sure he or she is trustworthy by asking for references and checking them.

Children under three sometimes have a hard time relaxing with a baby-sitter, especially if the sitter is someone they've just met or if they're at a stage when they want to keep their mother in sight at all times.

During their first months of life many babies seem to regard everyone with bemused tolerance, but around seven months most children begin crying or pushing away or seem to freeze if a stranger picks them up. They definitely prefer that their parents stay nearby and pay proper attention. They like predictability too: the repetition of familiar routines sustains their confidence in themselves and their sense of an order to the world. When her baby-sitter does things differently, your baby may become uneasy or protest. She doesn't understand what is happening, why she has been left with a stranger and for how long.

A toddler's buoyant curiosity may help her overcome her initial shyness with a baby-sitter. At the moment you actually say good-bye at the door, your toddler may take your departure with good spirits. She knows you sometimes go away and come back. But later, she may get confused or upset and go looking for you, not quite grasping that you aren't there.

Many two-year-olds are old enough to understand when their parents explain that they are going away and will come back, but they may not be able to hold on to the idea and their sense of time is shaky. Your two understands time in terms of recurrent sequences of familiar events. She knows, for example, that you come to pick her up at day care after she wakes up from her nap, has a snack, and plays in the yard for a while. But when your two stays with a baby-sitter, the usual order of her day is disturbed. She has no way to measure the time until you return and she may grow worried. She may, for example, feel it is dangerous to go to sleep before you get back.

Staying with a baby-sitter, in short, can make children anxious. There will be many times in the course of your child's first three years when you have to leave her with a baby-sitter, and some of those times she may be nervous or uncomfortable. She will still be learning. Where the repetition of routines gives your child opportunities to anticipate and participate in the vital activities of daily life, and to form relationships with people outside her home, the special events and disruptions in her life give her opportunities to learn to adjust to, and sometimes enjoy, unexpected situations. When she stays with a baby-sitter and feels anxious, she's learning that she can be upset when you leave, feel better after a while when she gets used to the baby-sitter and something catches her attention, start missing you again, feel better when she gets absorbed in a new activity, miss you again—and nothing terrible happens to her. She is managing without you, even if she doesn't feel cheerful all the time, and eventually you do come back. And she'll have some interesting experiences.

When she's with a baby-sitter your child has a chance to use her own social resources to begin a one-to-one relationship with a new adult. Staying with a baby-sitter, for example, might give your baby an opportunity to study the differences between people: the baby-sitter may be a teenager or her grandfather or an older woman, all of whom touch and sound and play differently from you. An older child can discover that a new adult, like her parents, will smile back when she smiles, knows how to play peek-a-boo, and tells her stories. Two-year-olds are old enough to learn something about how the world works from staying with baby-sitters. If she stays at the home of friends with a child her own age, your two will notice how things are done in a different household. And when you tell her why she is staying with someone else, you are helping her to understand how the adult world works—that men and women who love each other sometimes like to do things alone together, for example, or that adults can't stay home from work whenever they'd like. You are also telling her, of course, that you are not the only adults who can protect and help her.

There are a few things you can do to make your child more comfortable with a sitter. First, you can prepare her. Adjusting to a sitter will be easier for your child if you tell her ahead of time that you'll be leaving and someone else will be coming to take care of her. She'll trust you more too, if she knows you won't suddenly confront her with an unexpected change in routine. It may not be helpful to tell a child under three about your plans the day before. If she lacks a clear sense of when tomorrow is, she might just feel vaguely worried about the future. But do let her know where you're going and who will be staying with her before the sitter actually arrives—a few hours or a few minutes before, depending on her capacity to remember and anticipate. Warn her even if she's too young to understand the words: she may sense from your tone that something unusual is going to happen.

Once the sitter arrives, you can help your child get to know her. Your child will feel more secure with a new sitter if you give the two of them the chance to get acquainted while you are still there. Ask the baby-sitter to come early. Introduce her to your child; stay with the two of them until your child begins to feel comfortable with the stranger. Then leave them alone while you are still nearby. Even when your child and the sitter know each other well, it's a good idea to give them a few minutes to get reacquainted in your presence.

You can also help the baby-sitter get to know your child and your family. Your child will feel more at ease if the sitter follows the routines and plays the games she is used to. Tell the sitter about your family's mealtime and bedtime rituals. Describe some of your child's favorite activities; for example, make sure the sitter knows if you and your daughter always play with the hand puppet together just before you get her ready for bed. If you are leaving your child with the sitter in the sitter's home, be sure to bring a few of your child's favorite objects so she has something from home with her. Tell the sitter about each of the items and how your child uses them. Introducing the sitter to your child's habits serves another function: when she watches you showing the sitter around the house or explaining her favorite toys and games, your child will sense that this new person is someone you approve. (And before you leave, don't forget to leave numbers where you or a friend or relative and your pediatrician can be reached.)

Asking a sitter to come early or hiring someone already familiar to your child isn't always possible. When you discover your child is sick at eight in the morning or the sitter who was supposed to watch your child while you take your parents out for a thirtieth-anniversary dinner calls an hour before you are to leave and says she's suddenly become sick, you'll have to get on the phone and call all the potential sitters you can think of until you find someone, who will probably arrive just as you're stepping out the door. Your child will be okay. The worst that will happen is that she'll feel anxious for a few hours, and feeling anxious won't damage her. It would be gratifying if you could protect your child from all sorrow and fear and make her world pure joy, but you can't. Your child can and will develop her own resources and strategies to deal with unwelcome events. Children are not emotionally helpless. They have the resiliency and inventiveness of new life.

Katie is trying hard to understand why even though her parents are going to work as usual, she is not going to day care. Jen will be spending the day with her enthusiastic half brother. Alex is getting acquainted with a shy teenage baby-sitter.

JENNIFER
(Six Months)

Carol wakes up ten minutes before the alarm, decides to get out of bed anyway, and goes to the kitchen to get the bottle. In a few minutes, she knows, Jen will get bored playing alone and will cry for her. Suddenly Jen does cry out, but not her usual "come play with me" call, a real alarm. Bottle in hand, Carol rushes to her daughter's room.

James, Sam's twenty-year-old son from his first marriage, is holding Jen, who is crying and struggling. "Jen," James is cooing, "what's the matter, don't you remember me?"

"Good morning, Jennifer," Carol says, coming in. Jen reaches out des-

perately, trying to get to Carol. Carol takes her and holds her upright against her chest, stroking her back. Jen grabs Carol's robe and presses her cheek against her mother's bare skin, whimpering with relief.

"I don't know what I did," James says apologetically. "We were getting on fine last night, but when I came in to say hello she started to scream as if I were the werewolf or something."

"She was probably just startled. She's used to seeing Sam or me first thing in the morning." Jen reaches for the bottle greedily. She grabs the nipple and pulls it toward her open mouth. "I usually feed her awhile before changing her. Then I give her the rest of the bottle afterward, if she's still hungry." Toes curling and uncurling, Jen sucks busily.

"Victoria's still sleeping?" Carol asks.

"Yeah," James says, "she's really been into sleep this vacation."

Jen, still sucking, opens her eyes and peers up at James for a moment, then lets her lids fall half shut again to concentrate better on the milk.

"She'll get used to you in a little while," Carol says. "But I'm afraid it's not going to be the easiest day. I told Sam to warn you but he probably said—"

"Everything will be fine," James fills in, imitating his father's voice. Sam's optimistic habit of belittling problems has obviously irked James at some time or other too. Carol grins, enjoying a rare second of feeling really at home with James.

It's Good Friday. Mrs. Semple has the day off, but Carol and Sam do not. James and his girlfriend Victoria, who are on spring break from school, offered to come down to the city and look after Jen.

"Everything won't be exactly fine," Carol says. "Jen can have a lot of ups and downs in ten hours."

James is watching Jen, who doesn't look nervous anymore. She is sucking with total dedication. "Let me try feeding her," he suggests. "Maybe that will win her over." He smiles. "It works with dogs."

James is only making a joke, Carol thinks, and what's happened to her sense of humor anyway? She looks at James watching Jen: his expression is drowsy and tender. "Would you like that, Jen? Would you like your big brother to feed you?" Jen opens her eyes and looks at her mother's face. "I'm going to give you to James now, okay?"

She puts Jen in James's outstretched arms. Jen is fine for a second, then suddenly realizing she is in strange arms, she twists her head, looking for Carol. She puts her hands on James's chest and pushes away.

"Okay, okay, I'm here." Carol takes Jen back and offers her the bottle again. Jen arches her head back and crinkles her nose. She doesn't want any more for the moment. Carol puts the bottle down.

"We'll change her," Carol says. "She should be a little more agreeable after that. We're going to change you, okay, Jen?" Carol places Jen on the changing table. "I think I showed you where everything is last night." Carol starts unzipping Jen's pajamas. Jen babbles merrily to herself. "But I put a list on the bureau in case you can't find something. Try to remember to use the cream. She had a rash last week that's just clearing up."

As soon as Carol frees Jen from the stretchy, Jen starts kicking. She catches hold of a foot and sucks a toe. James runs a finger down her soft leg. "You should try out for our gymnastics team," he says.

"It's a good trick," Carol acknowledges. "But it makes changing her diaper difficult. Jen, you've got to let go of your foot so I can get your diaper off."

James notices a tiny bell mobile over Jen's head. He gives it a whack. The bells start spinning around each other, clanging harmonies. Jen lets go of her foot and shrieks with pleasure as she twists to look at the toy.

"She hasn't noticed that in days," Carol says. "We don't usually give it such a good push." She has pulled off the old diaper and is wiping Jen's bottom.

"Yes," James is saying, running a finger along Jen's nose, "you and I are going to spend all day goofing off together."

"This is the cream." Carol feels a little uncomfortable holding Jen's genitals exposed, but, of course, James is scarcely a strange man and Jen isn't what you'd call a hot number. "Do you want to put the diaper on?"

"Sure." Jen kicks her feet and makes a silly face at James. James sticks out his tongue. Jen laughs, coos, and puts her hand on her crotch. James, to Carol's relief, doesn't seem to notice. He takes a diaper out of the box. "Let's see if I got it down," James says. He slips the diaper underneath Jen and starts to adjust it between her legs.

"Move it down just a bit," Carol suggests. James shifts it slightly and tapes the sides.

"Okay, cutie. There you go. Now." He puts his hands under Jen's arm-pits and lifts her high in the air.

Carol waits for a scream. Jen laughs instead. James lowers her down and starts to swing her. Jen lets out a warning cry—this is definitely too much. "Okay, okay," James says, holding her in a sitting position against his chest and patting her back. "I'm sorry." Jen whimpers.

"Remember this kid has two tired middle-aged parents," Carol says. She smiles at James. "But I bet she'll like having a big brother to wrestle with in a few months."

Jen pulls at James's robe. "Yes, Jen, a robe," James tells her.

"Can you take her to the kitchen and get her started on a banana while I get dressed?"

James nods.

"I showed you where the kitchen stuff is?"

James smiles. "And you stuck a list on the refrigerator, remember?"

"I'm a bit compulsive," Carol apologizes.

As she steps out of the room, Carol hears Jen's cry of distress behind her and a cooing male voice.

Carol, dressed, comes into the kitchen a few minutes later. Jen, who is sitting in the high chair, gives a happy cry and starts bouncing in the chair. "How are you doing?" Carol asks.

"One piece of banana eaten, one on the floor, one squished in her hand."

Carol pours herself a cup of coffee and puts in toast for her and Sam. Jen rubs banana mush on her cheek.

"It's going to be a long day for you, I'm afraid," Carol tells James. "If you want to do something besides the park, you can try taking her to a museum in the backpack. Sometimes she sits very quietly and enjoys looking around." Carol grins. "But then sometimes she doesn't."

"Everything okay?" Sam walks in and heads toward the coffeepot. "Victoria still sleeping?" Carol nods.

Jen starts hitting the tray of her chair. "You used to do that when you were little," Sam says to James.

Jen keeps banging. "Enough," Carol says, handing her daughter a piece of toast and sitting down.

"So what were Victoria's parents like?" Sam asks. Jen babbles loudly.

After breakfast, James walks Carol and Sam to the door. Jen is in

Carol's arms, holding tightly to her coat. "She's going to make a fuss," Carol warns James. "But everyone says she calms down after about half an hour. I'll call around noon to see how she's doing. If you're going out, call me first or I'll get hysterical and destroy my career."

"Everything will be fine," Sam says.

Carol and James catch each other's eye.

◆

OBSERVATIONS

The World of Things

Jen sees her mobile every time she gets a diaper change. Sometimes Carol and Sam blow on it or give it a tap. Sometimes Jen bats at it, but she doesn't pay as much attention to it as she did when it was new. When James hit the mobile, however, she reacted with great excitement. James hit it harder than her parents do, so the bells moved faster and clanked to a faster rhythm. James made the mobile behave differently, so he made it new again for Jen.

The World of People

Even though Jen met James at Christmas and played with him last night, he's still unfamiliar to her. When he first came in to her room, she was frightened. After Carol joined them and she had a few minutes to be with James and her mother together, Jen began to enjoy her big half brother.

James is more physically energetic than Sam, Carol, and Mrs. Semple, the people Jen spends most of her time with. He gave the mobile a bat instead of a tap. He lifted her legs and slipped the diaper under her rear with more vigorous motions than her parents use. Jen found James's way of touching and moving quite exciting. She was delighted by the way he made the mobile bells clang and liked being lifted up in the air—but being swung by the armpits, she made quite clear, was more stimulation than she cared to have.

Carol was a little concerned about James's roughness. She might have preferred that someone more like herself care for Jen, but she did appreciate having a family member willing to help out in an emergency. She realized that having a grown-up half brother will be fun for Jen as she gets older.

Jen seemed to enjoy sitting at the breakfast table with all the adults around her. When Sam asked James about Victoria's parents, Jen started to babble as though she wanted to be part of the conversation too.

Ideas and Words

The harder the mobile is hit, the faster the bells move and the louder they tinkle. Jen can't make the intellectual connection between the speed of the motions she sees and the rhythm and volume of the music she hears, but her experiences with the mobile are helping her begin to understand physical changes in a sensual way.

Jen's cries are clearly communicative now. When James started to swing her, she let out a shriek that both James and Carol took to mean "Stop this."

Jen has seen James a few times before, but not often enough to remember and recognize him. He is still a stranger to her. She does not yet understand, of course, that she and James are related or what being related is. She is learning about what it means to be a member of a family in an inner emotional sense through her daily life with Carol and Sam, but it will be a long time before she will understand that James is Sam's child too.

Sense of Self

Three months ago Jen might have cried if the mobile suddenly started spinning and tinkling very fast. Being lifted high in the air would have inspired terrified cries. She is becoming better able not only to tolerate but to enjoy noise, excitement, motion, and change, partly as a result of the natural processes of maturing, partly because Carol and Sam and Mrs. Semple have helped her negotiate new situations every day by reassuring her, encouraging her, and interpreting events for her. Their support has made her bolder about drawing on her own growing resources. But Jen has not been magically transformed. Ten hours is a long time for a six-month-old to be with someone like James, who is both new to her and very energetic. Carol and Sam will probably come home to an exhausted and fretful baby—and two rather harried college students.

♦

ALEX
(Fifteen Months)

Rita, wearing a bathrobe, a towel over her wet hair, is leaning over the bathroom sink putting on makeup. She hears the surprisingly heavy clunk of Alex's feet in the hall. The doorknob turns. Alex pushes on the door. Nothing happens. Alex hasn't yet figured out he has to hold the knob to the side while he pushes the door—and, in any case, this door doesn't push in, it opens out. Maybe he'll give up and go do something else, Rita thinks optimistically. The door rumbles: Alex, forgetting about the doorknob altogether, is trying to force the door open by pushing with both hands. "Ma!" he says.

"Okay," Rita tells him, hurrying to finish putting shadow on her right

eye. She does it too quickly and smears it. She opens the door. "Come in."
Noticing Alex eyeing the toilet she hurriedly puts the top down. Alex starts
to open it. "Why don't you sit there and watch Mommy get ready?" Rita
says, picking him up and putting him on the toilet seat.

"Mamam froooophphph," Alex says.

"Yes," Rita says. "Mommy and Daddy are going out to dinner." She
turns back to the mirror and carefully removes the messed-up shadow with a
cotton swab. Alex watches. She starts on the other eye. Alex clambers
down off the toilet. He nearly falls but rights himself and takes a lipstick
from the edge of the sink. Rita grabs his wrist and retrieves it. "No, honey."

The doorbell rings. Alex turns his head in the direction of the front door.
"Robert, can you get that?" Rita calls.

"Yeah," Robert shouts back.

"That's Helen, Mrs. Weiss's grand-niece. Why don't you go to say
hello?" Alex is on his way.

"Let me take your coat," Robert is saying.

Alex, who has stopped about eight feet away to watch, cautiously comes
up close and takes hold of Robert's leg, standing behind him.

Robert picks Alex up. "This is Alex, my younger son."

"Hello, Alex," Helen says, smiling.

"Alex, this is Helen. She's going to watch you tonight while Mommy and
I go out." Alex buries his head in Robert's sleeve. Helen looks as if she
wants to hide her head too.

"I guess he's a little shy," Robert says. "Come on. I'll introduce you to
Mike."

"Mi," Alex says, struggling to get down. Robert puts him on the floor.
He trots ahead to the boys' room. "They've had colds," Robert says. "Did
Rita tell you?"

"Alex, you nerd!" a voice screams.

Robert glances at Helen, who looks uneasy. They hurry toward the bedroom. There are no visible boys. Between Mike's bed and Alex's crib is a
card table covered with a blue sheet held in place with Scotch tape. Alex
suddenly emerges from the folds of the sheet, pushed by Mike's hands. He
falls forward, lands on his stomach, whimpers, pulls himself up to his hands
and knees, and starts to crawl forward. His foot gets caught in the edge of

the sheet. He continues crawling, pulling the sheet after him. "Alex!" Mike yells. He pushes Alex again. Alex falls and begins to cry.

"Mike!" Robert says above the sobs.

"What?" Mike answers from inside the tent.

"Mike, get out of there."

Mike crawls out. "He knocked my cars down."

"I don't care what he did. You can't push him."

Robert lifts Alex to his feet and pats his shoulder. "You're okay," he says. Alex, looking very unhappy, holds on to his pants leg. Mike has noticed Helen standing near the door.

"Hello, Mike," she says.

Mike looks at the floor.

"Mike, this is Helen. She's baby-sitting tonight." Mike studies the corner of the room. "Can you say hello?"

"Hello," Mike says and immediately looks away.

"I like your tent," Helen tells him.

"Hello." Rita comes in, still in her bathrobe, but with her wet hair towelless, all made up and feeling pretty. "You're Helen. Pleased to meet you." Rita puts out her hand. Helen takes it. "Your aunt is one of my favorite people. She's just great with Alex."

Mike pulls at Rita's robe. Rita puts her arm around him.

"Ma," Alex toddles over. Rita puts her other arm around him. Alex peers out at Helen from behind Rita's legs.

"Maybe you should get ready now?" Rita says to Robert. "I'll show Helen around."

"Is she going to give us dinner?" Mike asks.

"Yes. You and Helen are having spaghetti," Rita says.

Robert rubs Mike's head on his way out. "Don't give Helen a hard time tonight." Mike grins and climbs back into the tent.

Alex lets go of Rita's hand and goes exploring.

"After dinner, the boys take a bath," Rita explains. "They can bathe together. But they can skip their baths tonight. Then Alex goes to bed. I usually read to him. We try to get him to bed by seven-thirty. Mike can stay up until eight-thirty in the living room. I always read to Mike. He just got a new book he's excited about. He'll show you."

"Ta, ta," Alex says, coming up to Rita and holding out a roll of Scotch tape.

Rita tears off a piece and sticks it on his finger. "Here you go."

Alex holds his finger up and studies it closely. "Ta," he repeats with wonder in his voice.

"It's your favorite thing lately, isn't it?" Rita says.

"Ta." Alex tries to stick the tape to the wall, but, since he is pressing the smooth side to it, nothing happens.

"The pajamas are over there," Rita is saying.

"Where are the diapers?" Helen asks.

"In the bathroom. I'll show you when Robert gets out."

After pressing his taped finger on the wall several times with no results, Alex rolls the piece of tape into a little ball. He presses it against the wall, Mike's desk, the dresser. Finally, it sticks to one of Mike's books. He babbles to himself, smiling.

"Maybe you can give Alex another piece of tape while I get dressed," Rita says. "I'll show you the kitchen stuff later too."

"Okay," Helen says.

"Mike," Rita calls.

From under the card table: "What?"

"It's time to put the tent away."

"Aw, Mom. . . ."

"Come on out."

Mike crawls out of the tent reluctantly. "When are you coming back?"

"After you're asleep. I'll come in and give you a goodnight kiss. Will you show Helen where the card table goes?"

Mike looks at Helen, sizing her up. "Okay," he says finally. He turns back to the tent-table and notices Alex on the other side of the room about to rip the pages of a book. "Alex, no," Mike says fairly gently this time. He takes hold of the book. "No, Alex, you can't play with that. You'll hurt it and it's my book." Alex doesn't let go. Mike starts pulling.

"Alex," Helen says. "Let's put the book away and take down the tent." She holds out her hand.

Mike lets go of the book. "Give it to her, Alex." Alex looks at Mike, then extends his hand with the book.

"Thank you." Alex gives her a big flirty smile.

"I'm going to get dressed," Rita says.

"Can we have ice cream for dessert?" Rita hears Mike ask sweetly as she steps into the hall.

Robert is straightening his tie. Rita looks at his back: a solid, chunky back of which she is very fond. This is going to be their first dinner alone in— God—months. "I hope she'll be able to handle them," Robert says, with a touch of pride. "She's kind of quiet."

"Yes," Rita agrees, going to the closet. "Mike was gearing up for ice cream." She takes a red dress out, looks at it quizzically and puts it back. "Well, the worst that can happen is Mike will get her to let him finish the carton and then they'll stay up until we get home."

"Alex!" They hear Helen's voice pleading from the hall. "Alex, your parents are getting dressed. Why don't you stay here with Mike and me?"

Rita smiles.

◆

OBSERVATIONS

The World of Things

Though Alex has examined everything in the bathroom thousands of times, he still wants to examine everything in the bathroom again. Rita knows he likes splashing in the toilet water, which is why she put the lid down as soon as he came in. When he tried to lift the lid, she sat him down on top of it.

When Alex saw his mother putting on makeup, he got down and picked up a lipstick. He wanted to do what she was doing.

Alex was delighted today when he found the tape. Tape has become one of his favorite playthings. Maybe he enjoys trying to manipulate something so small (which he can't do too well yet). Maybe he likes using it because Mike, Rita, and Robert use it. Maybe he likes the feel of the stickiness on his finger and the way he can get the tape to hang on to something else. But though he knows tape is sticky, he doesn't really understand what it's for or how it works. Today he just kept playing with the tape until it happened, by accident, to stick to the book.

Alex's explorations often involve destroying things. He would have torn Mike's book apart if he had had the chance. For him, taking things apart is just another way of using things. He doesn't realize, for example, that a book is something to read and that once he tears it up he won't be able to look at the pictures anymore. When he is playing with the book, he is not thinking of the pictures or words it holds. He is absorbed in doing all the neat things he can do with paper, like crumpling it, chewing it, and ripping it.

The World of People

Alex was being a bit of a pest today, as toddlers often are. He followed Rita into the bathroom when she wanted some time for herself to get ready. He knocked over Mike's cars and almost destroyed his book.

Rita and Robert had Helen come early to show her the house and explain the routines and to give the boys time to get used to her while they were still at home. They trusted Helen because Mrs. Weiss recommended her, but they were a little concerned that she might be too timid to control the boys. The boys were a bit shy with her too, at first, but soon began to warm up.

Alex was able to overcome his initial shyness with Helen so quickly partly because he seems to be a naturally social little boy, but also because he didn't have to be alone with her: another member of his family was always there as backup.

Alex and Mike often argue, but Alex trusts Mike. Even when he and Mike were fighting, Alex looked to his older brother for approval before handing the book to Helen. Mike's presence will probably continue to reassure Alex through the evening: someone he knows will be with him all the time. (Alex's presence may make Mike more comfortable too.)

Ideas and Words

Alex doesn't have much of a feel for cause and effect, which makes him clumsy. When his foot got caught in the tent sheet, he just kept on crawling. He didn't realize that the pulling sensation on his foot meant it was tangled in the sheet and that if he kept going he would pull the tent down.

Rita and Robert told the boys that they were going out and Helen was coming to stay with them. Mike understood everything they said. Alex probably understood enough to know that something unusual was going to happen. He may also have sensed that something special was going on when he watched Rita putting on her makeup.

Sense of Self

Alex is learning he can trust his parents to let him know what is going to happen to him. Knowing what is going to happen makes him feel more secure in a world that is largely out of his control.

Alex is unshakably determined to do what he wants to do. He persisted in trying to get into the bathroom even though he couldn't open the door and Rita wouldn't respond at first. He kept bothering Mike until Mike finally pushed him out of the tent.

Though Alex felt shy when he was first introduced to Helen, he adjusted very quickly to her presence. His parents didn't press him to play with her, but their approval, and later Mike's, made Helen acceptable in his eyes. When he was ready, he took the initiative and started a relationship himself, smiling at Helen after he gave her the book.

KATIE
(Twenty-eight Months)

"More juice," Katie says. She holds up her plastic cup.

"Coming right up!" Joe lowers the light under the eggs he is scrambling and quickly fills Katie's glass.

Sarah is packing Katie's lunch. "I'm putting in some extra peaches for you and Allen," she says to Katie. "You are going to Allen's house to play today, with Jessica. Remember?"

Katie stares at Sarah. "No," she says. She looks down and starts to tear little pieces off her napkin.

Katie's day-care center is closed for Easter vacation. Sarah and Allen's mother have asked Jessica, one of their regular baby-sitters and a high school student also on vacation, to watch the two kids Monday, Wednesday, and Friday. They will leave the children with Allen's grandparents on Tuesday and Thursday.

"You're sure you don't want eggs?" Joe says to Sarah.

"No, I'm really nauseous."

Joe spoons eggs onto two plates, puts one in front of Katie, and sits down with the other. Sarah sits down too, taking the chair opposite Katie.

"Remember last night, when I told you that your school was on vacation?" Sarah says. "You know you go to school during the week. Then there's the weekend. On the weekend, we don't go to work and you don't go to school. Well, during the year, people take longer times off to do something different. That's called a vacation."

Sarah looks apologetically at Joe. She always finds herself in the middle of explanations she knows Katie can't understand, with no way out but to keep going forward. "Your day-care center is closed this week so you and the other children and Linda and Paul and Karen can have a vacation. Mommy and Daddy don't have a vacation this week, only children and teachers do."

Katie stares blankly at Sarah. "My go school."

"School is closed today, Katie," Sarah says. "No one is there. You're going to play with Allen at his house today."

"My feed gerbils." Katie pushes her eggs away.

"Eat your eggs, Nutmeg," Joe says, pushing the plate back. "I'm going to take you to Allen's house after breakfast. Jessica—you remember Jessica—is going to take care of you."

"No," Katie says. She starts climbing down from her chair. Her elbow hits her cup of juice. Juice flows across the table and down onto the floor. Katie begins to cry. Joe hurriedly rights the cup and starts wiping up the juice.

Katie sobs, rubbing her eyes. Sarah picks her up. "It's okay," Sarah says. "It was just an accident." When Katie finally stops crying, Sarah offers her the plate of eggs. "Do you want to eat your eggs before Daddy takes you to Allen's?"

Katie bends her head down to peer at the plate and pushes a bit of the egg apart with her finger. "Dirt," she says.

"Where?" Sarah asks. "That's not dirt, that's a little speck of pepper."

"Okay," Joe says, finishing the last mouthful of his own eggs. "We better get going."

"Katie, why don't you go with Daddy and get your jacket? I've got your bag all packed." Sarah starts to lift Katie down from her lap. But Katie burrows her head in her mother's shoulder. "No go," she says.

"No, you're going to Allen's and there's no time to cuddle," Sarah tells her, cuddling a little anyway.

Katie is uncharacteristically quiet during the ride to Allen's. She stares out the window sucking her hand for a while, then examines Franklin very carefully.

"We're here," says Joe, trying to sound enthusiastic. He can't tell if Katie is angry, upset, or just confused. They walk to the door. Joe knocks. Jessica opens the door.

"Hello," she says. "You just missed Ruth and Bob." She looks at Katie, who is standing very close to Joe, hugging Franklin. "Hi, Katie." Allen, who has come up behind Jessica, sees Katie, starts jumping up and down, and darts back into the living room.

"I think Katie's a little confused," Joe tells Jessica. Katie watches his face carefully. "She wanted to feed the gerbils with Linda today. We told her the day-care center is closed for vacation, but I'm not sure she understood."

Jessica smiles at her. Katie looks at the ground. "Hello, Franklin," Jessica says, trying to strike up a conversation.

Katie tightens her grip on Franklin and steps behind Joe. Jessica gives up for the moment. "Come on in," she says. Katie stares at her.

Allen is in the living room pushing a small car. He freezes when he sees Katie. The two children look at each other. Allen turns and runs, arms swinging, down the hall to his room. Katie steps a few inches away from Joe to peer down the hall after him.

"Let's go see where Allen went," Joe suggests.

"Ball!" Katie cries with delight at the doorway of Allen's room. Next to Allen's bed is a giant blue beach ball. Katie drops Franklin and holds her arms straight out in front of her, the position she assumes when she plays catch with Sarah.

"That's a big ball you have there, Allen," Joe says. Allen gives the ball a kick.

Katie squeals with delight and runs into the room. The ball bounces wildly, knocking a container of baby powder off the bureau in its progress and finally landing next to Allen's bookshelf. Katie runs toward it.

"Come on," Jessica says. "Let's take that outside before we break everything." She picks up the ball.

"Yard," says Allen.

Katie looks up at Joe. "Go on, Katie," he urges. "I'll stay with you for a little while before I go to work."

They walk to the yard, Allen leading the way. Jessica tosses the ball up in the air. Katie and Allen run after it. While they play, Joe gives Jessica his and Sarah's work numbers. When he looks up, Katie has stopped playing with the ball. She has squatted down and is digging in dirt by the fence, using a large, flat stone as her shovel.

"Katie," Joe says. She doesn't seem to hear. "Katie, I'm going to work now. Mommy will pick you up after work."

Katie stands up, the stone in one hand. Allen passes by pulling a wagon, the blue ball sitting precariously on top of it. Katie's head turns to watch the wagon.

"Good-bye, Katie," Joe says.

Katie looks at him. "Bye," she says, waving her hand and running to the wagon. Joe seizes the moment and makes a quick escape.

◆

OBSERVATIONS

The World of Things

The size and bright color of Allen's ball caught Katie's attention immediately. As soon as she saw it, she threw her arms out to catch it. She is learning to catch and throw by playing with her parents.

Katie made a tool. When she was digging up the soil by the fence, she picked up a flat stone and began using it as a shovel.

Katie thought the specks in her eggs were dirt. Though Katie loves digging in mud and sand, she has developed a sense of "dirtiness" and feels squeamish about things which are "dirty" and not right.

The World of People

Katie wanted to go to school—and she didn't want to go to a strange place. She tried several tactics to get her way. She repeated over and over that she was going to school, as if she could make it happen by insisting. When it came time to actually leave, she tried a more emotional appeal: she clung to her mother. She certainly succeeded in communicating her desire, but her parents still told her she couldn't go to school.

Jessica and Katie have met before. Jessica said "Hi" to Katie right away. When Katie didn't respond, Jessica tried to reestablish their relationship by greeting Franklin. Perhaps because she was confused,

Katie just stepped behind Joe. A few seconds later, however, she began staring at Jessica, a small but real approach.

Katie doesn't yet have a sense that other people each have worlds of their own. She may have been surprised to find Allen in his living room, for example, because she has only seen him at the day-care center. Perhaps in her mind he belongs with the center. (This is not as childish as it seems: adults sometimes experience a small shock when they see an acquaintance from the office on the street or in a restaurant.) Allen didn't seem to know what to make of Katie either. He ran away when he saw her. It was Katie's excitement at seeing the beach ball which finally drew the two children into play. She used the ball as a kind of social bridge.

Ideas and Words

Words, actions, things, and ideas are closely interrelated for Katie. When she saw the ball, for example, she automatically put out her arms in a catch position as though her mind couldn't make the association between ball and game without her body helping out. She said, "My go school," and repeated, "No go," as though saying the words could make them true.

Both the night before and this morning, Sarah and Joe told Katie that the day-care center was closed and she would be going to Allen's house. Katie knew the words in Sarah and Joe's explanations, but she didn't understand what they were saying. For Katie, daily routines define time. When the alarm clock rings in the morning, one of her parents dresses her and they all meet quickly for breakfast. Then Katie knows she is supposed to go to school. She couldn't understand why the pattern wasn't being followed today. To understand the idea of vacation, she needs to be able to think about time more abstractly.

Joe and Sarah felt frustrated because they couldn't make Katie understand why she couldn't go to day care. By repeating their explanations, however, they probably did help Katie make a little more sense of what was happening.

When Joe repeated the story of the morning to Jessica, for example, Katie listened very carefully. She heard her name and the same explanations she had heard earlier. Joe's summary may have helped Katie to at least understand that she would be spending the day at this strange house instead of day care.

Sense of Self

Katie was confused this morning and she knew it. She seemed to realize she didn't know what was going on.

She became very upset when she knocked over the juice. Katie is old enough to know that the "right," grown-up thing to do with juice is to drink it, and she is self-conscious enough now to feel ashamed or worried when she does something wrong. Spilling the juice probably added to her feeling of being bewildered and out of control.

Though Katie was upset, she didn't make a scene or become furiously angry with her parents. She made a valiant effort to get her parents to take her to school. When that failed, she set to work trying to understand what was going on and to deal with it. She was very quiet in the car, presumably waiting to see what was going to happen. Later she latched on to Joe's story about the morning to help herself grasp the situation. After a few minutes at Allen's, Katie's intense interest in the things around her helped her overcome her anxiety. She used the blue ball to help herself step away from her father and into the day. A few minutes later, she was so absorbed in digging in dirt that she didn't pay attention the first time Joe called. She said good-bye easily and turned right away to investigate Allen's wagon. (This doesn't mean that Katie has decided she's perfectly happy spending the day at Allen's; later, when there is a lull in the play, she may miss her parents again.)

Though Katie may not have understood that school was closed, Joe and Sarah's many explanations probably helped her understand that she wasn't being sent to Allen's on a whim: there was a reason. Joe and Sarah were also letting Katie know that they wanted her to understand what was happening and that they have confidence in her ability to understand things. Later Joe showed his respect for Katie's feelings by staying with her for a little while to help her make the transition to a new place and then by alerting her that he was leaving. Her parents' confidence in her and their respect will help Katie trust herself and her ability to learn.

Conclusion

◆

THE WONDER OF THE ORDINARY

Much of the sweetness and spice of life, for everyone of every age, is in the ordinary pleasures of ordinary days: in the renaissance of sunlight every morning, in the warmth of a dinner shared with close companions, in the touch of a loved hand, in the comfort of newly washed sheets, a hot bath, a soft cotton shirt. Most adults regret that someone has to wash the sheets and the shirt, clean the bathtub, shop for and cook the dinner. Adults don't generally enjoy the endless, routine round of chores that keeps ordinary life going. Routines weave our lives together—but they aren't interesting to us. We use the time we are shopping or filing our nails or cleaning up to think of other things.

As we've tried to show in this book, children under three don't distinguish routine chores from play or work or adventure the way adults do. For them, every event is as sensually rich and as important as the next. But ordinary routines quickly become special to children because they are ordinary: they are repeated over and over. Children recognize them. They come to rely on them to give rhythm and order to their lives. They become familiar with the sequence of activities that make up each different chore. They begin to join in whatever way they can. Through their participation in everyday activities, they begin to develop the ideas about past and future, beginning, middle, and end, space and time, cause and effect, pattern and meaning, self and other, friends and strangers that will help them sort out their experiences the way adults do.

Perhaps a vacation in a foreign country gives adults a taste of how life feels for a small child. In an unfamiliar place, obligations and appointment books left behind, the world seems fresher. We notice the angle of sunlight, the sound of a strange word, the color of a bus, the variety of faces. In a foreign country, taking a walk or going shopping becomes an adventure again. The delightful self-satisfaction a traveler feels when he first learns to count a new currency, speak a few key phrases in another tongue, or recognize the native foods on a menu must be something like the pleasure children feel as they master the ordinary.

By the time she is five or so, a child will have mastered a great deal of the amazingly complex activities we call ordinary. She can talk, listen, imagine, think. She can dress herself, feed herself, bathe herself, straighten up her room, buy herself an ice-cream cone. Her mastery of routines and the reliable way they structure her day will give her confidence when she goes to school and begins a life of her own apart from her parents. The routines themselves will continue to provide her with new opportunities for learning at each stage of her life.

For a six-year-old, a trip to the supermarket is a chance to sound out the words she sees on signs and boxes and to discover that she can reach the crackers on a high shelf. The nine-year-old sent to the supermarket by herself to pick up a carton of milk is practicing responsibility. The thirteen-year-old who goes to the supermarket with the family shopping list and comes back with junk food, a lipstick, and no change is using the assignment to pick a fight with her parents. When a twenty-two-year-old moves into her first apartment, goes to the supermarket to stock her refrigerator, and assembles all her favorite foods, she is connecting herself with her old home and reaffirming her new independence at the same time.

We've suggested in this book that observing your child will help you understand how she is learning from everyday activities and how you can make your daily life together richer. Observation is certainly a vital resource. Unfortunately, observing your child won't be as easy as observing the imaginary children in this book. Ideas about child rearing presented in books somehow never quite apply to many of the real problems real parents with real children face. There isn't always an answer to the question: what would be best for my child? But the really extraordinary thing about ordinary, everyday activities is that just by doing them with your child—just by chatting with her while you make dinner, taking her with you when you stop at the drugstore on the way home, reminding her to brush her teeth—you are helping her to grow in important ways. You are sharing your experiences with her, welcoming her into adult life, and there is no greater gift a parent can give a child.

INDEX

◆

basket. Then, handing more pins to Katie, he pulls down the sweatshirt and pants. "Okay," Joe says. "We're done."

Katie goes over to the laundry basket and tries to pick it up. "Too heavy," she says.

"You take the clothespins." Joe leans down to pick up the basket.

"No," Katie says insistently. "My do." She leans over and tries to pick up the basket again.

Joe picks up the clothespin tin with his left hand and, without saying anything, takes hold of one of the handles of the basket. Katie holds the other handle. Since she is less than half her father's height, the basket tips danger-ously toward her side. They walk a few steps, then Katie suddenly drops her end, giggles and begins running toward the house. Joe picks up the shirt that has rolled out of the basket and carries the laundry basket to the back porch.

Katie is hiding behind one of the chairs. Though Joe can see the top of her head, he plays along. He puts down the clothespins. "Where's Katie?" he asks, slowly turning around as though he were looking for her.

When his back is to her, Katie leaps out. "Katie here!" she shouts.

"Hello, Katie," Joe says. Katie hugs him. Joe shifts the weight of the laundry to one arm and pats her on the back.

"It's getting late, Nutmeg. Let's stop at the bathroom and get your mother's bras and stockings, and then we'll put this basket in Mommy and Daddy's room."

Joe pulls the stockings down from the shower curtain. Katie climbs into the tub to get a brassiere hanging on the rack in the back. "Katie in tub," she says, pointing to her sneakers. "Shoes on."

"Yes," Joe says. "Your sneakers are on your feet. Are you going to wear your shoes in the tub when you take a bath?"

"Nooo," says Katie, giggling.

Joe helps her out. "Well, why don't you take them off while I take this stuff to Mommy and Daddy's room."

"No," Katie says.

"You have to take a bath," Joe says, "and then go to bed."

Katie hits him.

"Don't hit me," Joe says. "You have to take a bath and go to bed."

"No," Katie shrieks.

"If you don't take a bath and get ready for bed," Joe says, "I won't read you your new book. Your choice."

Katie is stumped.

Joe sticks the laundry basket in the hall, figuring he'll take it to the bedroom later. Katie steps out with him, unsure of what to do.

Joe bends down and starts to undo her shoelaces. "Come on," he says, "it's bedtime."

◆

OBSERVATIONS

The World of Things

Katie can carry things, shake clothes, and even do some folding. She has enough skills now to really help Joe take down the laundry.

Katie, like Alex, isn't good at comparing her size with the size of things in her environment. She didn't realize her pants were too high for her to reach. Joe had to point out that she could reach Sarah's robe.

When Katie looks at things she often tends to focus on the small details that interest her. She picked out the dog in the badminton photograph without paying too much attention to the people because she is fascinated by dogs. She is interested in colors and so a tiny speck of red paint on the tin can, so small Joe didn't notice it, caught her eye immediately.